355.115 Willenz, June A.
WIL   Women veterans

Women Veterans

WOMEN VETERANS

America's Forgotten Heroines

JUNE A. WILLENZ

CONTINUUM · NEW YORK

1983
The Continuum Publishing Company
370 Lexington Avenue
New York, New York 10017

Library of Congress Cataloging in Publication Data
Willenz, June A.
Women veterans.
Includes bibliographical references.
1. Women veterans—United States. I. Title.
UB357.W54   1983   355.1'15'088042   83–7850
ISBN 0–8264–0241–0

To
Two women who gave me
the support and confidence
to write this book—
Sara Friedenberg, my late mother
and
Gertrude V. Cotts

Contents

Foreword

by Alan Cranston
United States Senator

Despite the great contributions that women have made in their long history of service in the United States armed forces, women veterans have often been ignored. As was noted in a 1982 report from the General Accounting Office, "Although women have served in the military since at least World War I, they have not always received recognition as veterans and VA benefits equal to those given to male veterans."

During my over fourteen years in the Senate, I have been deeply involved with veterans' issues, and I am very gratified that more attention is finally being paid to women veterans. Significant strides are now being made in recognizing the contributions they made and in improving the availability of benefits and services for them. It is vitally important that these advances be sustained, particularly as more women seek benefits due them as veterans.

Women Veterans will play an important role in stimulating this long-overdue progress by helping to educate and sensitize individuals working in the veterans area to the rich history of the participation of women in our armed forces, the neglect that they have faced after their service, and their present legitimate needs based on their service and status as veterans.

I can think of no one better able to tell the story of women veterans than June Willenz. June is a tireless advocate on behalf of veterans and, as the Executive Director of the American Veterans Committee, she has made and continues to make a major contribution to shaping veterans' benefits and programs.

Women Veterans offers a realistic, and often unpretty picture of a less-than-stellar chapter in America's treatment of its service personnel. It should be read by all concerned with veterans' and women's issues.

Preface

After spending more than twenty years in the veterans' field, I began to wonder where the women veterans were and why they were not visible. There were women veterans; the American Veterans Committee (AVC) had some within its own ranks, but somehow, in all the reports, statistics, writings, and in all the diversity of papers that crossed my desk as the Executive Director of a veterans organization, they were missing.

I began to look for them and found that there were many more of them than I would have imagined. As of April 1982 the official count was 1,218,000. The Ford Foundation, several years ago, helped AVC do an exploratory investigation of government agencies' response to women veterans. This investigation revealed just how much they had been left out. This led to my curiosity about who they were, how they joined the service, and what happened to them afterward. The more I found out about them, the more astonished I was that they had been overlooked.

Not only wasn't there any academic research on this group, nor any government statistics available on them, but library research using the computer showed nothing. Here were over a million women who never got listed as a subdivision of either veterans or women. Not only were they forgotten: they were invisible. In books on veterans *women* are not mentioned.

As I began to find them (they found me, to some extent through columns I had written in *Stars and Stripes*), I was amazed at their accomplishment and the corollary lack of recognition by either the public or the government. Their dedication and their willingness to give themselves to their country for defense as volunteers was scarcely noted by anyone. And like the work of many other women in the pages of American history, their participation was unchronicled. Above all, they were shortchanged because the veterans' benefits system apparently had not worked for them. We will never know for sure because the Veterans Administration did not keep any data on them. Even though their veterans' benefits entitlement by law was the same as for men, they were either unaware of or indifferent to their rights. Why?

These were some of the questions I was seeking answers for when I embarked upon the work for this book. What I have found is more rewarding than I ever dreamed. Here is a page in American history of achievement that women can be proud. It will be followed by other pages as women continue to participate in the military in ever greater numbers. Indeed, the entire nation can salute the women veterans who served in the defense of the country—they have always been "true volunteers."

This then is a beginning to the chapter in history that women veterans deserve. Let us hope that public policy will respond to this forgotten population. Recent events point in that direction. With vigilance and continuing oversight, women veterans can begin to assume their proper places in the veterans' world and also to use their benefits, particularly the VA health care and hospital system. It is time they turned up on the computers, in both libraries and government statistics.

* * *

To all the women veterans who cooperated so generously in the discussions and processes of this book, my deepest appreciation. To Gus Tyler, Chairman at the American Veterans Committee, and the leaders of the AVC, who encouraged and supported me in this endeavor, I am grateful.

There are others who helped make this work possible. My daughters, Nicole and Pamela, were a continuing source of inspiration and support. This book would not have been possible without the encouragement and editorial assistance of George Czuczka. Elaine Handley's help and editorial suggestions were invaluable for the progress of this work. Colonel Bette Morden was a gracious guide to Army historical records. Bill Brew of the Senate Veterans Affairs Committee minority staff provided me with important information at crucial stages, for which I am grateful. To Leona Levine, who typed a good part of the manuscript, I am indebted. There were others who were cooperative and helpful along the way. Thanks.

If this book helps lift the veil on the story of American women's part in the military, past and present, it will have accomplished its purpose. These pages are for them.

The substance and insights for this book are derived from the correspondence, calls and visits with the many women veterans I have been in contact with. The names used in the profiles are fictitious, unless otherwise indicated.

J. A. W.

·PART I·

WHAT THEY DID

Women and War

In American society there are 1,218,000 women veterans, the Bureau of Census told us in 1980. There are thousands more women who served overseas in connection with one of America's wars, sharing dangers and deprivations, but they were not in military uniform and are not recognized as veterans.

These women have been unsung heroines in our society, content to have done their part and oblivious to their lack of recognition by their country. While they were not consciously trailblazers, they helped open up opportunities for women in a redoubtable male world—the military. In many ways their courage and dedication contributed to the women's movement two decades later.

This book describes them, reviews their history, examines their accomplishments, and places them *as veterans* in our society. Long ignored by government agencies and the academic community, they have been unrecorded and unstudied. Women veterans on the whole have not been activists in the veterans community and have not developed strong identities as veterans.

A cross section of American women, they have come from all parts of the country and from every background. They returned to their homes and communities after military service with stretched horizons and deepened self-esteem. Recognition of their accomplishments and impact upon our country is long overdue. This book places women veterans historically and in today's world.

* * *

Women have always suffered the agonies and turmoil of war in one way or another. As mothers, wives, daughters, and sisters of fighting men killed or maimed by war—as women taken prisoner, hurt, raped, or killed by opposing armies, as survivors and dependents, or as actual combatants, women know war firsthand.

To a significant degree the full impact of war upon women has not been totally recognized or documented, perhaps because history has concentrated on the consequences of war from a male perspective. At a time of an awakening consciousness among women of their roles in history, an exploration of what war and its aftermath has meant for them, is long overdue.

While widows and orphans have been recognized as victims of war, other victims are the women whose husbands or sons have come home wounded or disabled. There are other women in our society who have not been identified as war victims: the sweethearts and fiancées of men who lost their lives—women who never marry. They have been deprived of wifehood and motherhood; their bereavement is lifelong.

Each war seems to bring on new suffering and illnesses. Perhaps these troubles only *seem* new because history has not identified or recorded them earlier. We have become more aware of the fact that use of toxic defoliants has momentous implication for the health of not only the veterans but the veterans' children. We have also learned that emotional and mental health problems, such as the post-Vietnam syndrome (PVS), can develop from special circumstances, including societal attitudes toward a particular war.

The women related to the men taken prisoner who often have suffered deterioration of health because of their imprisonment must cope with those health problems. Women associated with veterans suffering from PVS have experienced frustration and bewilderment because this condition was not recognized or treated as a genuine health problem. Women whose husbands were exposed to toxic defoliants have been faced with the possible health problems not only of their husbands but also of their children.

There is a long list of the victims of war, including civilian populations who suffered bombings and bombardment and the consequences of invasion and devastation. Women and children are a large part, perhaps even the majority, of this population. There are the women who have participated in resistance movements and wars of liberation. The dangers, wounds, and losses that they suffered were similar to those suffered by the men at whose side they stood.

The presence of women in military forces today is not solely an American phenomenon. A review of women's presence in the NATO nations, for example, reveals a wide range of women's participation, including access to combat roles in some of them. Other countries around the world also have women in their military forces, mostly on a voluntary basis.

Despite the growing number of women in military forces and, consequently, the emergence of women veterans as a population group, little attention has been paid to them within their own countries or in international forums. For example, during the International Women's Year in 1975, and the International Decade of the Woman, United Nations documents did not refer either to the military or to veteran women's groups. Nor do they refer specifically to women survivors or dependents.

Since war is a convulsion that occurs when political processes fail to settle disputes among or within nations, the aftermath of war includes an upheaval of the status quo. These alterations create the momentum for social change and political equality that continue to have profound implications for women and for society in general. Women develop new perceptions of themselves, and society gains new perceptions of them.

Despite the fact that today millions of women around the world have the vote (although millions still do not), there continue to be wars, and the threats to peace have become increasingly menacing. Perhaps women have not used their political power as well as they might. But, one must not forget that they have no collective memory of political power to draw upon. However, if they are short on experience, they are strong in their determination to turn their vote into an instrument of political effectiveness. ·

In a complex multinational world threatened by nuclear annihilation, women are finding out that paths to peace are linked with national security considerations and that arms limitation agreements require the foundation of sound confidence-building measures. In the past women generally have avoided dealing with the hard facts of modern-day military and security issues sometimes because they involved language and technology women were not familiar with. Perhaps women's failure to acquire detailed knowledge about military matters and national security was due to their socialization, and that women, as children, never identified with "war games."

Whatever the reasons, there is now a trend in the other direction. Women are awakened to some new facts of political life. They recognize that ignorance is not bliss but remains ignorance that keeps those without knowledge outside the sphere in which policy is made.

Historically, men usually have made the decisions that led to war. Because women too have suffered with men from the consequences of war and because the distinction between warrior and noncombatant disappears totally under the shadow of possible nuclear oblivion, women have an equal stake in peace. Today the major challenge for man- and womankind is to establish a peaceful framework in which nations can coexist. Women must work together with men to eliminate the possibility of another war in which no nation can be the victor and in which all peoples run the risk of total obliteration.

* * *

Wars do not take place without women's assistance. This may have been true in earlier ages, but the direct involvement of women with the processes and supportive services for war making is a more modern phenomenon. This may explain some of the ambivalence that men have demonstrated in regard to the role of women in war. On the one hand, men have assumed the role of protector of the weaker sex; on the other hand, they have had to call upon women to assist them in their war making.

In many of America's wars, male policymakers seem to have attempted often to keep women in a quasimilitary status rather than a full one. In that way they did not have to admit that women play an important part in the war-making process. It also means that no special place or recognition needs to be given for women's services. It denies the contradiction between men's protective role toward the "weaker sex" and their need for women's assistance. By putting women in an ambiguous position vis-à-vis the military, men have sought to avoid direct responsibility. The history of women's participation in the military is marked with hassle and contradiction, both of which confused women's perception of their status and obfuscated society's view of it.

While the push by women for equality in the services began in the sixties—coincident with the women's movement and general thrust for political, social, and economic parity with men—it was not until the late sixties and seventies that women began to experience equal opportunity and treatment in the military. Again, this paralleled what was going on in the civilian sector when in a very few years, through legislative and executive action, women gained momentum for political changes affecting their status.

With the emergence of the All-Volunteer Force after the end of the Vietnam War and the end of the draft in 1975, there has been a shift to an occupational model for the military. The participation of women was considered essential for the success of the new system. For women, as for men, this change in the nature of military service altered their motivation and attitude toward it. It also somewhat reduced the inequalities between men and women.

What the future holds for women's participation in the military is unknown. Because of the demographic fact that a drop in the available labor pool is anticipated in the late eighties, women's roles in the military may be seen in a light different from the one in which the early eighties views them. The unpopularity of the draft persists, a legacy of the Vietnam War. It is unlikely that politicians will want to take on a negatively perceived modus operandi to produce needed personnel for defense purposes.

The alternative to the draft is to turn to the other source of "manpower": womanpower. It is quite possible that, as the economy turns around and productivity and employment swing upward, the shortfall of young males will be felt even before the demographic facts of life create a shortage. Able young women then will become once more an attractive resource for the armed forces.

Young women who see military service in employment and career terms will not be satisfied to be outside the mainstream of promotion and prestige within their chosen profession. The question of what occupational specialities will be closed to them as a result of a recent broad interpretation of combat restrictions is likely to be a burning issue in the years to come.

With the strong possibility that more and more women will indeed find their way into military service, the implications for the VA system are many. Women veterans will be an increasingly young population, one younger than the male veteran population. The needs of young women coming out of military service will be different from those who served during World War II and in Korea. On the other hand, the World War II generation of women veterans, like the male veterans of that era, need long term, gerontological services that the VA at present is only beginning to provide. Women veterans will be expecting the same benefits and treatment as their male colleagues. They too served, and they too have rights and entitlements. Women veterans will no longer be content to sit on the sidelines and forgo using the programs set up for all veterans.

Historical Background

Early Wars

Women become veterans just the way men do—they serve honorably on active duty in a military service for a minimum of 181 days.[1] The U.S. Code, with one exception,[2] does not make a distinction between male and female veterans. Today in the United States 1,218,00 women have veterans' status.

The women veterans' population is likely to get larger because more women are serving in the military today than ever before. Total strengths are Army, 73,374; Navy, 44,834; Marines, 8,632; Air Force, 62,944; and Coast Guard, 1,876. A current debate on future strengths raises questions about women's roles but does not question women's solid position within the military services.

The fact that women are serving is not new; what is new is that they are serving in peacetime in such numbers. Officially they have participated as members of the services since the formation of the Army Nurse Corps in 1901 and the Navy Nurse Corps in 1908. But women have had roles *with* the military services, if not *in* the services, since our country was founded.

> No official record has been found in the War Department showing specifically that any woman was ever enlisted in the military service of the United States as a member of any organization of the Regular or Volunteer Army. It is possible, however, that there may have been a few instances of women having served as soldiers for a short time without their sex having been detected but no record of such cases is known to

exist in the official files. Women were often employed as laundresses and as nurses, but they were merely civilians while so engaged and were in no sense in the military service of the United States.[3]

Histories of the Revolutionary War give little credit to women for participating in that war. Recent scholarship, however, indicates that women did contribute directly to the day-to-day work of the Continental Army and at times to the combat operations.

Since few records were kept of the functioning of the patriots' military effort, both in the Army and in the militia units and committees of public safety, it is difficult to get a true picture of what women's involvement was in the Revolutionary War. Many women, wives, widows, common-law wives—with their children—followed the Army and earned their rations in return for domestic skills that the Army needed.[4]

These "Women of the Army" did washing, cooking, and mending and were under Army orders as to what they could or could not do. Women often rode in the baggage wagons, much to General Washington's consternation.

> Washington's frustration affords an indirect glimpse of these hundreds of women who would not be separated from their husbands or from their ad hoc work in the camps, thus making it impossible to keep them off the wagons or from drawing their own subsistence rations. Like it or not, Washington was stuck with what even he had to refer to as the "Women of the Army."[5]

Women served as nurses during the Revolutionary War. Medicine in the eighteenth century was a far cry from what it is today. Nurses were on the bottom of the scale in the medical heirarchy in terms of skill and pay. Surgeons provided the major medical treatment while most nursing tasks were performed by male surgeons' mates. The nurses served as "orderlies," keeping the patients clean and fed, and on occasion, administering medicines. The desired ratio of nurses to patients was one to ten or fifteen, but hospitals during the war were always tremendously short-staffed. General Washington had tried to have the hospital system regularized and sought decent pay for the nurses, but hospitals remained chaotic and inefficient.

There are records indicating that women took part in the militia units which played important roles on behalf of the patriots. Lists of citizens were drawn up of those between the ages of fifteen and fifty who were capable of bearing arms, and these often contained the names of women. Oral testimony reported the presence of women in militia units: "A British raid into Connecticut was expected to encounter only rebellious women and formidable hosts of boys and girls."[6]

In a frontier society in which skirmishes with hostile Indians were common occurrences, women had been trained to assist in the defense of a fort or stockade. Sometimes they had to defend themselves and their homes. There are numerous accounts of women not only loading guns but killing and maiming their opponents when they were faced with life-or-death situations. Women had also served as scouts and messengers, performing dangerous missions for the early settlers. One Ann Bailey was nicknamed "Mad Ann Bailey" by the Indians in admiration for her daring and courage.

There were also the legendary heroines who donned men's clothing and fought with the troops. One of the best known is Deborah Sampson who fought under the name of "Robert Shurtleff" until she was wounded and hospitalized. Another woman, Sally St. Clair, was killed at the Battle of Savannah. Yet another famed heroine was Molly Pitcher. "Molly Pitcher" was not a single person, but represented a group of women, much like "GI Joe" connoted male American soldiers in World War II. Many women served as water carriers for artillery units; they were essential because after a cannon was fired, it had to be swabbed with water before it was reloaded.[7]

The support services and sometimes direct roles of American women in the Army and militia units of the Revolutionary War are often overlooked when the history of that period is recounted. But there is evidence that the services of women in a largely guerrilla war were much sought after.

> The influence women exerted on the war effort is difficult to evaluate. . . . But the shrill tone of public instructions to

women—Washington ineffectively trying to keep them in line, economic planners anxiously seeking their cooperation—suggests both that women had significant services to render if they would and that their cooperation could not be taken for granted.[8]

If they were not formal members of the armed forces, women certainly undertook crucial service roles. Individuals who perform those tasks in modern armies generally wear their country's uniform and are regular members of the service.

I have don as much to carrey on the warr as maney that sett now at the healm of government.[9]

Despite their contributions, women were not included as citizens in the new democracy.

The legend of Lucy Brewer, who was supposed to have disguised herself as a man and served on the *U.S.S. Constitution* during the War of 1812, became part of the folklore of the nineteenth century. Her book, *The Female Marine*, had wide circulation and credibility. However, its authenticity has since been discounted.

There is rich tradition in American balladry of women disguising themselves as soldiers or sailors in order to follow their men into battle. "Jackaroe" offers an excellent example of this tradition and may well have been a song known to the author of "The Female Marine." . . . However, Lucy's ingenious escape and subsequent career—her male disguise, enlistment as a Marine, and duty aboard "Old Ironsides"— are unique in our literature, for [in] no extended work of American fiction prior to 1815 was the theme of the female warrior exploited. For this reason alone, "The Female Marine" is an important, though overlooked contribution, to the history of American literature.[10]

It was during the Civil War that women were acknowledged to have participated actively on both sides. Not only did they serve in a fighting capacity, disguised as men, but they acted as scouts, spies, and saboteurs.

During this period nursing came into its own. Seven thousand women served as nurses for both the Union and the Confederate forces. In the North, America's first woman doctor, Elizabeth Blackwell, organized the Women's Central Relief Association, which trained battlefield nurses. There were thousands of women involved in this and other volunteer relief organizations. The Sanitary Commission, mandated by President Lincoln, became the center for northern women to organize effective health care for wounded soldiers and to standardize sanitation measures.[11]

Women served on converted transport ships to minister to the wounded, performing their nursing duties under the most primitive conditions. Another group of heroines were members of a nursing sisterhood who cared for the wounded men aboard the floating naval hospital ship *Red Rover*. When the war ended, the nurses were dismissed and men soldiers took over their duties.[12]

Clara Barton devoted her enormous energies to supplying the Union troops with supplies, medicines, and equipment. A few years later, in 1881, she was to found the American Red Cross. Another American heroine to emerge from the carnage of the Civil War was Dr. Mary Walker, who first served as a nurse and then was finally commissioned as a lieutenant in the Medical Corps, becoming the first woman doctor in the Army. Dr. Walker was taken prisoner and later received the Congressional Medal of Honor.

To try to deal with the acute shortage of nurses, the Secretary of War appointed Dorothey Lynde Fix on April 12, 1861, to serve as Superintendent of Women Nurses for the Union army. Her duties were vague and her authority limited, but she headed a group of six thousand women who performed nursing duties for the Union army.[13]

Women's contribution as nurses were sought after and appreciated during the Civil War. Before that, they were at the bottom of the scale in recognition and pay. Their contributions to the health and well-being of the fighting men of both sides were welcomed and acknowledged.

The Spanish-American War also found women involved in a medical capacity. Because an epidemic of typhoid fever broke out in army camps early in the war, there was a desperate need for nurses. Disease caused five thousand deaths while combat casualties were less than one thousand. The Surgeon General requested permission to hire and pay civilian nurses. Dr. Anita Newcomb McGee, the vice-president of the National Society of the Daughters of the American Revolution (DAR), was named director of the new civilian nurse corps, and over fifteen hundred women nurses served the Army as "contract nurses" under her direction.

The contract nurses, who were recruited by Dr. McGee from nursing sisterhoods, the Red Cross, and from civilian life, had to meet high standards. More than a dozen nurses died of typhoid fever from their efforts in the war. After the war ended, the contract nurses continued to serve; they were assigned to Cuba, Puerto Rico, the Philippine Islands, Hawaii, China, Japan, and on the hospital ship *Relief*.[14]

The performance of women nurses during the Spanish-American War convinced the Surgeon General that the nurses were a valuable addition to the medical capability of the Army. The record of the nurses during that war left an impression on the country:

> American women may well feel proud of the record made by these nurses in 1898–99 for every medical officer with whom they served has testified to their intelligence and skill, their earnestness, devotion and self sacrifice.[15]

A Nurse Corps, to be administered as an auxiliary unit under the Medical Department of the Army, came into being when Congress passed the Army Reorganization Act of 1901. While some doctors were concerned that the nurses would coddle their patients too much and be a distracting influence, the testimony of those who had served with them in the war proved otherwise. However, nowhere in the hearings was anything said about the courage, the physical stamina, the nurses showed during their service under dangerous and difficult conditions.[16]

Shortly thereafter, in 1908, the Navy Nurse Corps was created. The first twenty women who reported for Navy duty became known as "the sacred twenty." Neither Army nor Navy nurses were commissioned; they were appointed. They had an ambiguous quasimilitary status and were neither enlisted nor commissioned officers. Creation of both Nurse Corps proved to be the beginning of women's formal roles in the military forces.

World War I

It was during World War I that women nurses in both services worked under combat conditions on a daily basis. During this period approximately 22,000 Army nurses and 1,400 Navy nurses served in the United States and abroad. The nurses assigned to units that went to Europe were subject to shelling, gassing, disease, filthy living conditios, and all the horrors of war that the troops suffered, except direct combat. One hundred and fifty nurses cared for the 9,000 wounded. Close to 300 nurses died from diseases, others were wounded; some were taken prisoners by the Germans and were incarcerated. Their ambiguous quasimilitary status meant they received no pay for the period they were imprisoned.[17]

After the war a campaign was mounted, mostly by civilian nursing leaders, to obtain commissioned officer status for the military nurses who had performed so admirably. They argued that rank was needed if nurses were to be able to order orderlies and aides. As might be expected, there was resistance to giving them rank as commissioned officers. However, most of the surgeons who served with the nurses supported the granting of rank; moreover, General John Pershing threw his weight behind their cause.

Finally, recognition was given to the nurses' outstanding contributions to the war effort with passage of the Army Reorganization Act of 1920 which authorized "relative rank" for the nurses. While the Act allowed the Army nurses to wear the insignia of relative rank, the nurses did not have the pay, rights, and privileges that went with the rank. It wasn't until 1947 that Congress gave nurses permanent commissioned officer status in the Corps, with passage of Public Law 36.[18]

* * *

World War I was the first war in which women were officially recruited into the military services, other than the Nurses Corps. Wanting to free men for sea duty and fearful that the Civil Service would not be able to meet their needs, Secretary of the Navy Josephus Daniels took advantage of the law specifying that "persons" could be recruited into the Navy and issued a call for women to join up.[19]

Over twelve thousand women rallied to the colors and became members of the Naval Reserve Yeoman (F) (affectionately called "Yeomanettes"). Some served overseas with Navy hospital units in France and in Puerto Rico. Mostly, the Yeomen (F) filled clerical and administrative positions, allowing the "freed" men to serve on ships. The women also became draftsmen, recruiters, camouflage designers, and translators. The Coast Guard recruited a few hundred women who were also known as Yeomanettes.

The Marine Commandant also decided to enroll women in the Marine Corps Reserve for clerical duty and sought approval from the Secretary of the Navy. When it was granted, the Marine Corps issued a call for women. The response was overwhelming, so the Corps could have its pick. The Corps was determined to get the very best and applied the most rigid criteria. The competition was tough, and it was an honor to be chosen.

The women were told that they had to live up to the tradition of the Marine Corps, subject to the same rules and regulations that governed the male members. Failure to do so would mean their "disenrollment." The women were officially called Marine Reserve (F), but they were nicknamed the "Marinettes."

Besides performing clerical and administrative duties, women Marines served as messengers and as recruiters' aides. Their tour of duty was brief because the women were recruited in August and the Armistice was signed on November 11, 1918. In all, 305 women served in the Marine Corps during World War I. Commenting on the performance of the women Marines, the Commandant stated:

> It is a pleasure but not by any means an unexpected one, to be able to state that the service rendered by the reservists (female) has been uniformly excellent. It has, in fact, been exactly what the intelligence and goodness of our country-women would lead one to believe.[20]

As true veterans of the war, the women Marines received the same benefits as the men: right to government insurance, World War I compensation, a $60 bonus, medical treatment and hospitalization for service-connected disability, military burial rights in Arlington National Cemetery.

* * *

The Army found itself in a different position. The War Department, despite the acute shortage of personnel, did not want women in the Army, not even in civilian employment. Why the War Department was so suspicious of women is not clear, although the attitude of Secretary of War Newton Baker may provide the answer. Furthermore, the law governing Army personnel specifically referred to "male persons," so the question of enlisting women didn't even come up. The Army did not follow the Navy's example and recruit women.

However, General John Pershing needed French-speaking telephone operators and urgently wired Washington to send him a hundred. His request could not be refused, and the War Department hired two hundred French-speaking American women to go to France to work under General Pershing's command. These women staffed communications near the front lines, and their dedication and heroism under combat conditions became well known. They were civilians despite the fact that they were under military orders and military discipline. It wasn't until 1977, more than a half century later with the passage of Public Law 95–202, that the Signal Corps women achieved veteran's status.

Besides the telephone operators, the American Expeditionary Force (AEF) had requested hundreds of women with clerical skills in order to permit men to be sent to the front lines. General Pershing and the other commanders in Europe had seen the remarkable contributions British women were making in the Auxilliary Corps. The Quartermaster Corps, Ordinance, the Medical Corps all wanted skilled women, and the Surgeon General wanted women doctors. There were already five thousand American women volunteers overseas doing all kinds of volunteer welfare work for "the boys."

But the needs and desires of the Army field commanders did not meet a receptive climate of opinion in the highest echelons of the War Department. There was strong resistance to formation of a women's corps even though legislation had been introduced in Congress. The War Department had commented negatively on the proposed bill and effectively killed it. It has been conjectured that if the war had lasted longer, legislation to recruit Army nurses might have prevailed.

General Pershing and other AEF commanders had to be satisfied with the few hundred American civilian women sent by Washington. Finally, they called upon the British to lend them the skilled women needed to make up personnel shortages. The war ended soon after that, so did the need for a women's corps.

In 1920, to counter a trend among women toward pacifism, the Secretary of War appointed Anita Phipps as Director of Women's Relations for the department. Phipps was caught in an ambiguous position, not knowing whether her job was that of a supervisor of the Army's thirty–odd hostesses, or whether it would be expanded into the post of planner-in-chief for a women's army corps.[21]

In 1930, after years of frustration and aggravation, Phipps resigned, leaving a plan to form a women's corps in the Army. The response to her proposal was negative. There were strong reservations about setting up an organization of women headed by a woman and a group of influential civilian advisers, which would become a powerful machine within the War Department. In the end nothing was done about the Phipps plan.

Another effort was made in 1925 with the appointment of Major Martin Hughes to study questions relating to the formation of a women's corps in another possible emergency. Keeping in mind the case of the Signal Corps operators who had no protection and benefits because they were civilians, Major Hughes recommended in his plan that women, if needed, should be integrated directly into the Army. But the Hughes plan, like the Phipps plan, got nowhere and was buried in the files. It was then resurrected six months after the WAAC was set up in 1942. All the mistakes that Major Hughes had hoped to avoid with the suggestions entailed in his plan were made by those who worked out the blueprints for the WAAC.

World War II

It took from May 28, 1941, to May 14, 1942 to get the bill introduced by Congresswoman Edith Nourse Rogers establishing the Women's Army Auxiliary Corps (WAAC) passed by Congress. According to chief lobbyist General Hilldring of the War Department, the WAAC bill was "more difficult than the rest of the hundred combined."[22] Finally, the bill passed, and President Franklin Roosevelt signed Public Law 554, establishing the WAAC. It was to be an auxiliary *with* the Army, not *in* the Army. This ambiguous status was to hamper its effectiveness and to haunt its veterans in the years to come.

Planners at the War Department, together with WAAC Director Mrs. Oveta Culp Hobby, had been working for months on the many aspects and details of the Corps. They were concerned about the leadership of the new Corps and were determined to get the most qualified women to serve as officers because they had learned from the British experience that the entire future course of a women's corps might be determined by these choices.

The 360 women chosen for the first-officer candidate school of the WAAC to be trained at Fort Des Moines, Iowa, a former calvary base, were required to enlist without guarantees. They were an elite group—mostly college graduates, many with graduate degrees; 99 percent had been successfully employed in civilian life. Some were mothers of servicemen, although none had small children.

The facilities at Fort Des Moines, mostly stables, had to be modified and renovated to accommodate the women. Ill-fitting uniforms, by designers who did not seem to have women in mind when they put them together, were distributed. Director Hobby addressed the future WAAC officers:

> May 14 is a date already written into the history books of tomorrow. . . . Long-established precedents of military tradition have been given way to pressing need. Total war is by definition, endlessly expansive. . . . You are the first women to serve. . . . Never forget it.[23]

In the early months the WAAC continued to be plagued with clothing and supply difficulties, a situation rapidly turning into a comedy of errors. In the winter the women froze. World War I overcoats had to be issued to cover the summer uniforms the WAACs were wearing. Their cumbersome or inadequate clothing made it impossible for them to do the kinds of tasks assigned to them. Often, there was not enough of one item or too much of another. The picture the public got of the WAAC operation was one of a big snafu.

Just when the WAAC needed to expand, the public image of the Corps was at its lowest. Some undesirable recruits got in through recruitment loopholes and further damaged its image. With industry crying for women to enter high-paying defense jobs in the factories, the WAAC began to have a difficult time recruiting qualified women.

Enrollment dropped off, standards were lowered, and personnel problems increased. It was a difficult period for Director Hobby and the supporters of the Corps. Furthermore, the Director's authority had never been totally clarified. The Army General staff wanted tight control over the WAAC and intervened often to override the Director. There were misunderstandings and bottlenecks in the chain of command, which presented numerous operational problems for the Director and made the WAAC efforts even more chaotic.

A "slander campaign," whose source was unknown, took fire on the East Coast and slowed recruitment. Records showed that sexual morality in the WAAC was closer to the conventional ideal than the civilian average. The pregnancy rate among unmarried women in the WAAC was one-fifth that of civilian women. Venereal disease among the WAACs was practically nonexistent.

Particularly damaging, and totally untrue, was the rumor that prophylactics had been issued to WAACs. This hurt the morale of the Corps and their families. Since the rumors were doing so much damage, it was decided to respond to them. President Franklin Roosevelt, Mrs. Roosevelt, the Secretary of War, and others publicly disavowed the rumor as false.

Other problems that developed as a result of the ambiguous status of the WAACs were judged to be too annoying and difficult to cope with. The War Department decided that the WAAC should be placed on a firm military footing. Legislation was introduced in 1943 that terminated the WAAC and set up the WAC (Women's Auxiliary Corps) as a regular part of the Army. On July 1, 1943, with passage of Public Law 110, the legislation was enacted. The WAACs were discharged and invited to enlist in the new Corps. Most of them did. Those who chose to return to civilian life found that they were not entitled to veterans' benefits because they were not officially veterans. Many years later this injustice was corrected, and the WAACs who did not become WACs were declared eligible for some veterans' benefits. (See Chapter 5, "Veterans' Benefits.")

The changeover to the WAC did not turn out to be simple. Women had to be discharged from the WAAC and given the option of joining the WAC. The Army's Judge Advocate General ruled that the Army could not transfer women from the WAAC to the WAC without their consent because they would be brought under court-martial proceedings, and only a selective service law could do that.

Information on how the WAACs were to become WACs never got out to the field. Some stations let their WAACs go home; some WAAC officers swore in their enlisted women. In order to bring order out of the chaos, Director Hobby's officers visited every WAAC company to inform them of the proper procedures.

There were new problems for the director with the newly formed WAC. How far should equal treatment of the sexes go? Were the same standards of sexual morality to be applied to the women as to the men? If they were, then some offenders who were lowering the morale would not be punished or discharged.

Whether or not the standards of conduct of twentieth century American women were overstrict or illogical, the fact was that they existed and could not be converted to those of men by an Army Regulation.[24]

Director Hobby tried to have the discharge boards make a distinction between men's and women's conduct, but she did not succeed. Throughout the WACs existence, Director Hobby was frustrated by its second-class status and her lack of authority. The WAC was not high priority for the Army. That the WACs did as well as they did is a tribute to the patience and fortitude of Director Hobby and her assistants.

WACs participated in a variety of military occupational specialties. Regulations permitted WACs in "any suitable noncombatant positions," or even in combat units provided that the job was noncombatant and located in a fixed installation. Men had to be replaced one for one, and duties for women had to be within their strength and endurance. Commanders were enjoined to provide working conditions and environment suitable for women.

WACs served in technical and professional areas: motor vehicle, supply and stock, foods, mechanics and trade, communications, radio, and electrical. More than half served in administrative and clerical functions. Near the end of the war more women moved toward the technical and professional skills, but their participation in those fields did not reach more than 18 percent.

Other women assisted in the aviation missions of the fighting forces. Over forty thousand women served as "Air WACs," and were assigned to air bases all over the world. The Army Air Force, being of newer vintage, was less stratified and was more open to having women in nontraditional specialties. All Army Air Force schools were open to women except combat and aviation schools. Morale among Air WACs was high. The women felt they were needed and that they were contributing directly to the war effort.

WACs served in all overseas theaters of war—in Europe, North Africa, the Mediterranean, China, India, Burma, the Middle East, Southwest Pacific, and Southeast Asia. They also went to Alaska. Their presence expanded greatly the capability of American fighting forces in those areas. Commanders did not seem to get enough WAC units and were continuously asking for more.

Often women were underutilized by the Army, but so were the men. WACs resented promotions going to men even though they were actually doing the work. There were also abuses in the use of personnel, particularly WAC officers. Fourteen percent of WAC officers served as personal assistants and aides to commanders. There was a strong warning from Washington to cease and desist from such improper use of WAC officers.

Many WACs wanted to go overseas; seventeen thousand did. Late in the war four thousand WAVES (Women Accepted for Voluntary Emergency Service [in the Navy]), one thousand women Marines, and two hundred SPARs were sent to Hawaii, and two hundred SPARs to Alaska. Women shared the dangers, the shelling, and the deprivations. Their performance was lauded all over the world. There were some injuries and a few casualties, particularly in the Nurse Corps.

* * *

During World War II the two-front ocean war stretched the Navy's resources to the hilt. Its experience in using women during World War I made it eager to use women again. For some reason the Navy had a history of being receptive to using women. As early as 1811 a naval surgeon recommended that nurses be used in naval hospitals.[25]

When the Navy requested Congress to authorize having women in its Reserve, it received quick approval. The WAAC had already been formed and was having growing pains. By bringing its women directly into the Reserves, the Navy saved itself and its women enlistees a good deal of trouble. Public Law 629 set up the WAVES, the acronym given women in the Reserves.

Most members of WAVES performed clerical, administrative, storekeeping, and medical duties. They could not go overseas, nor could they be on combat ships, but a few served for a short time on hospital and transport ships. They became control tower operators, link trainers, and radar communicators; one in four served in naval aviation. A small number taught aircraft gunnery, celestial navigation, and aerial photography. Some occasionally served on crews in a noncombatant basis.

WAVES staffed the communications network of the Chief of Naval Operations and other stations which were highly secretive. Other WAVES personnel spent long tedious hours sending and receiving coded radio messages; some handled homing pigeons used on blimps. One group learned Japanese and monitored Japanese radio broadcasts. Thirteen thousand served in the Hospital Corps.

Mathematicians and technicians were taught the design, manufacture, and use of naval guns, torpedoes, and bombs. Some women became gunnery instructors; others wrote abstracts of battle reports. At the Potomac River Naval Command women assisted in the testing of airplanes in the wind tunnels at the Washington Navy Yard and at David Taylor Model Basin. Women engineers helped test and evaluate equipment. Others routed ships in harbors, attended convoy conferences, and checked vessels before they sailed. WAVES members also served as control tower operators, pilots, instrument trainers, parachute riggers, and aviation mechanics.

By the end of the war women Naval Reservists were in thirty-eight of the sixty-two enlisted ratings. At peak strength there were 86,000 officers and WAVES enlistees serving at over nine hundred shore stations in the United States and in overseas territories.[26]

The women chosen to be officers usually had plush berths compared to the other services. Officers were trained under very pleasant conditions at Smith College and Mount Holyoke College. The first boot camp training for enlisted WAVES took place at Hunter College in New York City and later at twenty other colleges and universities. Starting out in a college atmosphere rather than a military installation gave the women a different experience from the WAACs.

WAVES recruited from a narrower segment of society than did the Army. Middle-class, white, Protestant women were likely to enlist in WAVES. The attractive Mainbocher uniform added to the "elite" image of this corps.

* * *

The smallest group to serve in World War II were the women pilots who ferried planes for the Army Air Force. These were the WASPs (Women's Air Force Service Pilots), numbering eleven hundred, who ironically did not become veterans because they were not militarized. The WASPs battled for over thirty years before achieving veterans' status.

Possibly no other women's service group in World War II was as glamorous as the WASPs, with their Santiago blue uniforms, silver wings, and their unique mission. Their daring exploits received belated recognition years later. During the war, when these crack pilots were clocking sixty million miles for the Army Air Force ferrying all kinds of planes under all conditions, their feats in flying were largely unknown.[27] The War Department considered their work an experiment and kept their activities quiet.

Women had been in aviation for years. They had broken records and competed in air races; they had their own heroines. Jacqueline Cochran was one of them—a dynamic doer who had established herself as a leader in aviation circles. Even before the

United States entered World War II, she had suggested the establishment of a women pilots unit for the Army. President Roosevelt asked her to research a plan to organize women pilots to serve with the Army Air Force.[28] At the same time another outstanding pilot, Nancy Love, had also come up with a plan for women to fly planes to free the men for action overseas.

The stories of these women and their parallel efforts to utilize the skills of women flyers are fascinating, ones replete with drama and conflict. Love's proposal was to have women pilots in the WAAC to ferry planes. Cochran wanted a separate unit under its own commander. Originally two separate units were created, one headed by Love and the other by Cochran. The Love group consisted of a small number of professional, highly trained pilots each with over eleven hundred flying hours behind them; they were known as the WAFS—the Women's Auxiliary Ferrying Squadron. Cochran's group would train those with less expertise and flying experience; they formed the WFTD (Women's Flying Training Detachment). Eventually the two groups would merge to form the WASP.

WASPs were sent to Avenger Field, the Army Air Force's training base in Sweetwater, Texas, where they were drilled and trained by Army Air Force pilots. Later on they became trainers and instructors themselves. There were some casualties, but their safety record was as good as that of the male pilots. The women were under military discipline and considered themselves part of the Army Air Force. Throughout their years as WASPs, the women expected to be legally militarized.

WASPs often ran into a lack of acceptance from some male pilots. No matter how many planes they ferried, no matter what obstacles they overcame, what flying feats they performed, they had to cope with jealousy and a second-class status.[29] The Army Air Force itself had doubts about their roles and never committed itself fully to the operation.

Still the WASPs flew the newest and untried planes, ones that male pilots wouldn't touch. They tested planes that were often judged to be faulty or had poor performance records. The WASPs did everything that was asked of them, like the good soldiers they thought they were. One of their most dangerous assignments was to fly target planes—planes with a target in tow for student fighter pilots and their gunners to practice against. Two WASPs were killed in this dangerous exercise.

The record of the WASPs in ferrying planes from factories to air bases was outstanding. In the summer of 1944, they delivered thirteen hundred aircrafts. By the fall of 1944, half of the ferrying division's fighter pilots were women, and three-quarters of all domestic deliveries of fast fighters were made by WASPs. A few of them even got to fly big bombers after specialized training.

In 1944 everything was in the works for the commissioning of the WASPs. Legislation had been presented by the Army Air Force to Congress that would militarize the WASPs. However, the air war had simmered down, and there were many recently trained male pilots who had no assignments. There was an announcement that 36,000 male fliers in the War Service Training program would be assigned to go into the infantry.

At the same time that Secretary of War Stimson had endorsed the proposed legislation that would commission the WASPs to continue their domestic flying assignments in the Air Training Command and the Ferry Command, the male pilots were being put out of business. There was an intense campaign by the pilots' associations and the pilots to block the legislation that would keep the WASPs flying.[30]

Congress was annoyed that the Army had never made a request for an appropriation for the WASPs and that no Army budget ever mentioned them. Furthermore, the House Committee on Civil Service had examined the costs of the program and determined that the cost of expanding the WASPs was not justified. The Army did not want to be in an adversary position with Congress on this issue, so it did not make a big effort on behalf of the legislation. General Hap Arnold testified for the Army Air Force in favor of the legislation. This combination of events and circumstances led to the defeat of the legislation.

When the Congress decided not to militarize the WASPs, Director Cochran agreed for it to be disbanded. She was concerned that her pilots as civilians didn't have enough protection. For reasons never clarified, she had opposed the WASPs becoming part of the WAC. In December 1944 the WASPs officially ended, and the women were demobilized, much to their surprise and chagrin. This was the end of women pilots flying during World War II. To counter a negative report that the Army Air Force had put out on the WASPs, Cochran stayed on to write a second report which refuted that official negative image.

* * *

Over twenty thousand women served in the Marine Corps Women's Reserve during World War II. The Marine Corps was the last of the services to organize a women's corps—on November 7, 1942—even though women Marines had served during World War I. There was pressure for a corps within the high ranks, but the commandant initially resisted this idea. The Women's Reserve of the Marine Corps was the only women's service that shared the name of the service. It was not an auxiliary but a regular part of the Marine Corps. Even the women's uniforms were modeled on the men's.[31]

It is easy to see how the Women Marines identified as Marines under these circumstances. Women Marines were eligible for 225 different jobs, such as aviation gunner, mechanic, plumber, M.P., radar repairman, aerial gunnery instructor, baker, motion picture technician, automotive mechanic, cryptographer, and post exchange manager.

The WAVES allowed Marine women to use their facilities for training. Over thirty specialist schools were open to them; nine thousand women attended these schools. Marine Corps noncoms and enlisted men took training with the women Marines. Half of the women Marines were assigned to office jobs; the rest were in nontraditional positions.

One advantage women Marines had was that they were privy to field demonstrations where the weaponry and combat tactics were used by the male Marines. Women served in aviation posts as line trainer instructors and control tower operators.

There were many sensitive matters of authority and command that the Marine Corps had to deal with in relation to the Women's Reserve. For instance, the director, though a major, had influence in developing policies but could never take any independent action. The Corps was plagued by the question of what kind of authority women officers were to have. They were not supposed to have any authority over the enlisted male personnel, even if the latter were under their command. It became clear that curtailing women's authority in many situations would diminish their effectiveness and performance as well as hamper the mission. To correct this, a recommendation was issued that gave authority to the women indirectly by saying her commands were really coming from her commanding officer.

Originally, neither Navy nor Marine women were supposed to go overseas. However, there was a push to relieve more men for combat duty, so Congress passed a law which permitted female Navy personnel to serve anywhere in the Western hemisphere, including Hawaii and Alaska. Two detachments of women Marines were sent to Hawaii. The Corps, with a big supply of volunteers, was highly selective in choosing the one thousand women Marines for Hawaii.

*   *   *

SPAR (*Semper Paratus*—Always Ready) of the Coast Guard was the smallest among the women's corps during World War II. In November 1942 Congress enacted legislation—signed into law on November 23 as Public Law 773—which established the Women's Reserve of the Coast Guard. During World War II it was under the Treasury Department; it eventually became part of the Navy. The first director of the Coast Guard, Dorothy Stratton, was a lieutenant in the Women's Naval Reserve. It was she who came up with the acronym SPAR for the women in the Coast Guard.

The Coast Guard also got its first personnel from the Navy. They were trained at naval facilities until the Coast Guard developed its own. Among the ratings Coast Guard women had were yeoman, storekeeper, parachute rigger, link trainer, radio operator, radar operator, coxswain, air control tower operator, gunner's mate, and others.

Officers were trained and commissioned at the U.S. Coast Guard Academy at New London, Connecticut, thus becoming the only servicewomen to be indoctrinated at one of the nation's military academies. Approximately one-fifth of the officers came out of enlisted ranks.

By the end of World War II there were one thousand officers and ten thousand enlisted women in the Women's Reserve of the Coast Guard.[32] In July 1947 Congress revoked the authority for women to serve as reservists in the Coast Guard. It took another act of Congress in 1949 to reestablish the Coast Guard Reserves since it had not been included in the Integration Act of 1948.

Post–World War II Period

The participation of thousands of women in the military services during World War II was a major experiment for the nation, with long-range consequences for the civilian as well as military sectors of our society. The impact of this is still reverberating and has not been fully understood. Not only did women make a clear contribution toward the war, but they had crossed over in large numbers into a strictly male world. Furthermore, World War II had radically altered social roles and created new conditions for men and women in the labor force and in the family. Women's expectations were changed. It would be difficult to exclude them from any future military involvement.

> Experience in World War II proved that women play a vital role in the military effectiveness of any nation. And American Women's Army Corps showed that, contrary to dogmatic opinion, the previously untapped potentiality of womanpower could be directed into the channel of personnel power with positive results. The record shows that their contribution erased any doubt as to the ability, adaptability, and stability of American women in time of national crisis.[33]

While no formal evaluation and analysis of the roles of the women's service corps were made, the Army and WAC officers reviewed how things might have been done better. There was agreement that, in the event of another emergency, women needed protection from ruthless male officers, that the command needed to set a tone discouraging any scurrilous or negative comments or attitudes, and that more attention needed to be paid to their environment and their personal needs. Morale was judged to depend a great deal on the work the women did and whether they felt it was significant. Proper assignment of talents and skills was also considered important to the women's mental health. It was suggested that more jobs be opened to women, not fewer.

Though most of the postwar commentary and references to women's military roles were positive, there were still many hurdles ahead in regard to a permanent female role in the military. From the Hoover Commission came a warning that the utilization of women for war has dangerous implications.

> The whole subject of the use of women for war must be studied against the background of the American philosophy. The proper utilization of women in the Armed Services and elsewhere for war purposes can undoubtedly aid military efficiency and the national effort. The factor of increased efficiency must be weighed against a break with the philosophy of the past and the possible dangers of too great a growth of militarism. . . . The utilization of women for war has certain dangerous implications for our way of life. The subject deserves the most careful and cautious study.[34]

It is not clear why the utilization of women would foster militarism, but the Commission may be suggesting that women could become the tools of ambitious officers because they were weaker and less able to resist strong coercive forces. On the other hand, the WACs were in a higher educational and mental percentile than their male counterparts. Notwithstanding their vulnerability, they might be the ones to question any improper use of office or call attention to any abuse of power.

Despite the Hoover Commission's reservations about future utilization of women in the military, there were others who thought differently. General Dwight Eisenhower, whose mission had benefited considerably from the WAC detachments under his command in the immediate post–World War II years, expressed support for a permanent women's component in the Army.

The law had required complete demobilization of the women who served within six months after the end of the war. But there was enough pressure in 1946 and 1947 from high levels for the Eightieth Congress to pass the Women's Armed Services Integration Act of 1948 (Public Law 625). This Act was to establish a permanent place for women in the Army, the Navy, the Air Force, and the Marine Corps. Only the Coast Guard was omitted. "The act was many things to many people: to feminists, a leap forward for women's rights; to most women veterans, recognition of their contribution and vindication of their service: and to the military women who worked for its passage, sweet victory."[35]

The act that brought women into the peacetime military force placed a ceiling on their participation: no more than two percent of the regular service was to be female. The WAC maintained its own identity within the Army; the other services integrated women with the male personnel.

Integration without a separate corps created a whole set of new problems to be dealt with. Who was to supervise women's sleeping quarters? How were women's dependents to be treated? What kinds of arrangements—housing, allowances, etc.—should be made for a servicewoman if she were married to a serviceman? How should promotions be handled? These and many more questions were dealt with differently by each of the services.

Despite integration, equal treatment for women was only partially on the horizon. If a woman had to assume responsibility for minor children, she was automatically discharged. Pregnancy was immediate cause for dismissal. The law gave wide discretion to the Secretaries, without formal administrative proceedings, to terminate the tours of enlisted women and women officers. Women in the same rating, however, did receive the same pay as men.[36]

While the Integration Act permitted women to serve in peacetime in the regular services, they did not serve on an equal basis with men:

> Thus P.L. 625 was never intended to plow new ground or to give women greater status in the peacetime forces than they had "enjoyed" during the war, but rather to consolidate the ground gained during the war and to prepare for the mobilization of the nation's womanpower in the event of another.[37]

* * *

The Air Force was created by Congress in 1947 as part of the Armed Forces Unification Act. As the newest branch of service, the Air Force (developed from the Army Air Force) had an open field in which to develop its own sense of purpose and identity. Initially, to avoid the many pitfalls of the separate corps of World War II, the aim was to fully integrate women into the Air Force. The Air Force found that it is one thing to have an idea, another to implement it. The new director of the WAF appointed on June

16, 1948, Geraldine P. May, found she had little authority beyond her own small staff.

Determined to have the women's component as a model, the Air Force integrated women into its Officer Candidate School. This was the first time that enlisted women and men who were thought capable of command trained together. While a number of women became officers in this way, it was still not a strong enough source to supply the women officers needed. Women who had served honorably in any of the women's services during World War II were invited to join the WAF. The largest group of WAF officers were to come from this group.

Good intentions and the willingness to experiment did not make the policy of integration smooth in the Air Force. Among other things, the entrenched attitudes of older officers, both male and female, who felt uncomfortable with the new integration and nostalgically harked back to the "safeness" of a separate women's unit, were obstacles to change. The problems of trying to place and administer women who were not really on an equal status with men in a predominantly male environment turned out to be more difficult and burdensome than anticipated.

At one point Jacqueline Cochran, called in by Chief of Staff General Hoyt S. Vandenberg to review the flagging WAF program, suggested that there be a separate women's unit with a female head. This did not appeal to Air Force generals who did not want to share decision making with a woman. They also drew back from a commitment to total integration. As a middle ground, they strengthened the director of the WAF office so that women's problems and concerns would get immediate and direct attention, and agreed to reorient the women's program more as a separate personnel component.

* * *

In 1949 the Women's Reserve of the Coast Guard was reestablished. At the outbreak of the Korean War a number of former SPARS returned to active duty. After Korea the number in the women's reserve dwindled so that there were only a handful of enlisted women and officers left in 1971. This prompted the Coast Guard to examine how to utilize women, which led to many changes and increased numbers of females.

Korean War

When the United States entered the Korean conflict in 1950, nurses were needed immediately. Contingents of Navy and Army nurses who were sent to Korea made their mark tending the wounded, not only of the United States but of other U.N. forces as well. Surprisingly, despite the records that servicewomen had compiled in World Wars I and II, the services refused to assign nonmedical women to Korea.

Although field commanders did request women, the Pentagon continued to refuse to permit them to go to combat areas. One of the arguments was that there was a fluid fighting line, which made it impractical to provide for women's stay and safety. Finally, the services did permit women to be deployed in commands near Korea, i.e., Okinawa, Iwo Jima, the Philippines, and Japan.

The ranks of military women had thinned out considerably in the post–World War II era. There were only fifteen thousand women in all the services (exclusive of the Nurse Corps) at the time of the Korean War. Women reservists were called up and given direct commissions, just like the men. There was a strong recruitment campaign which doubled the numbers by June 1951 but which still fell short of the services' expectations.

Why women didn't respond to the services' call has not been thoroughly understood, although probably several reasons contributed to the phenomenon. There was no consensus and little enthusiasm from the public about U.S. involvement in Korea. It was a distant war which many felt we had gotten into by accident or mistake. Neither pride nor patriotism were stimulated among the citizenry so the incentive to volunteer was absent. It has been suggested that, if the Korean conflict had lasted longer, there would have been the kind of public reaction and revulsion that took place a decade later with our involvement in Vietnam. Furthermore, there were many new career opportunities for young women in an upturn economy. There were also fewer women because of the low post–depression birthrate. The baby boom of the World War II era would not expand the potential personnel pool until a decade later.

An attempt to overcome the low enlistment rate of women led to the formation of the Defense Advisory Committee on the

Armed Services (DACOWITS) whose primary original purpose was to help in the recruitment drives for women. Then Secretary of Defense George Marshall issued in 1951 a directive authorizing a civilian group of advisors chaired by Mrs. Oswald Lord to help interpret the role of military women to the American public and to stimulate interest in military service among young women. DACOWITS continued to play an important role in the Department of Defense, providing the Secretary with information and counsel on the problems and concerns of military women. Today DACOWITS has representatives of women in the services as military representatives in their meetings.

Vietnam War

The situation for military women during the Vietnam War was similar to that during the Korean War. The women in the services were ready and anxious to go overseas with the fighting forces, but the services were reluctant to send them. About 7,500 military women actually did serve overseas in Vietnam, but they were mostly from the Nurse Corps. One report stated that "hundreds of military women served in Vietnam, Thailand and the Philippines."[38] Another 600 to 700 women in the Air Force served in Southeast Asia.

Arguments that were raised against sending women to Southeast Asia included the theory that it was too dangerous and therefore improper to send them into the kinds of combat zones that characterized the Vietnam War. Furthermore, during the post–Korean period women had not been trained or conditioned to live or work in a combat area like Vietnam. The guerrilla nature of the war also argued against women being there. As a result of the exclusion of females from Southeast Asia and the Pentagon's one-year rotation system for service in Vietnam, women's career and promotion possibilities were hurt or stymied. However, a small number did serve in Vietnam.

However, in 1967 women's opportunities in the military were enhanced by passage of Public Law 90–130, which repealed the two percent ceiling on women's representation in the armed forces. This law also expanded the number of jobs women could hold in the service and allowed them to be promoted to flag rank.

The largest group of women to serve in Vietnam, approximately six thousand nurses, constitute another chapter in women's heroism during wartime. Exposed to many of the combat conditions of the fighting forces, the nurses in Vietnam serviced eighteen hospitals, nine dispensaries, and naval hospital ships. While most of them were in areas that were strongly defended, there were units close behind fighting troops, which had casualties brought in by medics and helicopters: "At CuChi, fighting is never far away. Mass casualties can hit the 12th EVAC without a word of warning."[39]

Even the relative security of medical positons in Vietnam did not keep all nurses from physical danger. In 1964 four nurses were awarded Purple Hearts for injuries sustained during a Viet Cong bombing of Saigon. Even though they were wounded themselves, they provided first aid and assistance for others who were more seriously injured. Etched in the granite walls of the Vietnam War Memorial in Washington are the names of seven women among the thousands of names.

It has been suggested that the performances of nurses in Vietnam, as well as in Korea and World War II, demonstrated the physical and emotional endurance of women under the most trying and dangerous circumstances: "Women with little or no indoctrination into military thinking have shown their ability not only to accept military discipline but also to create their own corps with comparable standards of military demeanor."[40]

While nurses were suffering and dying under combat conditions, the media image of wartime nurses created highly romanticized and sanitized realities. One result of this unrealistic picture of wartime nurses has been a lack of public appreciation of what nurses have had to endure during modern war situations such as Vietnam.

Military authorities never seem to have questioned the necessity of having nurses close to the combat lines, which meant they had to endure innumerable physical and emotional hardships. Whether nurses have been prepared for the kinds of situations they find themselves in during modern wars remains in doubt. Nurses are expected to take their chances and put up with whatever they encounter.

Typical of the somewhat superhuman emotional and physical feats expected of nurses was the expectation that they would not suffer from any of the physical and emotional disorders that the male veterans of the Vietnam era complained about. It took years before the Veterans Administration recognized that the women who served, the nurses, would have Post Traumatic Stress Disorder (PTSD) symptoms. Even the Readjustment Counseling Program enacted in 1979 specifically to address these problems ignored the women veterans who had served in Vietnam.

With the establishment of a Women's Working Group under the Readjustment Counseling Program in 1982, attention was finally paid to the special forms of stress and disturbance that their wartime experiences had on the women who have been in Vietnam. Women counselors are being appointed to outreach centers, and sensitivity training is being given to the other staff so that the centers can respond to the emotional problems and needs of the Vietnam women veterans.

Post–Vietnam Era

With the end of the draft in June 1973 and the change to the All-Volunteer Force, the services turned to women to help supply the needed volunteers. At the same time the Army initiated a major expansion of the WAC, which increased from a strength of 12,000 in 1972 to 53,000 in 1978.

A new personnel management system for officers was also inaugurated by the Army in July 1974, which meant that WAC officers had to be assigned to the branch of their career specialty, i.e. ordnance, intelligence, quartermaster, etc. The WAC branch, which consisted of WAC officers, essentially ceased to exist from that time. It took a few years, but by October 1978 under Public Law 95–485, the WAC was officially eliminated as a Corps.

In April the office of the Director of the WAC was eliminated. Between 1972 and 1975 other services had eliminated their women directors. Women were on the road to integration with men in the services.

Between 1972 and 1978 there were many changes in the training and in opportunities for women in the Army. In 1975 the separate promotion lists for women officers were eliminated; now women had to compete with men. In 1976 the Army created new sources of women officers. They now graduated from West Point, the

Army ROTC, and the integrated Officers Candidate School at Fort Benning. On December 30, 1976, the Army deactivated the officers' school at Fort McClellan where WAC officers had been trained since World War II.

Weapons training for women was reactivated in 1975. Before then for over ten years there had been no weapons training, even if women wanted it. After July 1, 1975, women had no choice but to take the weapons training. Then in 1977 they had to undergo the same basic training as men, although the training took place in separate camps.

A year later, in October 1978, women were integrated with men in basic training. While the women and men had their own separate platoons, companies consisting of several platoons became coed. There were also coed commanders of the companies. The Army had achieved a higher degree of integration of the sexes than ever before.

Other changes took place. With the influx of women beginning in 1972 existing barracks could not accommodate the increased numbers. On the other hand, the enlistment of men had so fallen off that some barracks were half-empty. It made sense to give the unoccupied quarters to the enlisted women rather than to build new barracks. After a while it became standard procedure for women and men to have separate quarters but to share a building. In this way the Army saved itself a lot of new construction.

Integrated basic training continued until 1982 when the Army announced it was ending this practice. Women had found the integrated training challenging and generally supported it. There was therefore considerable resentment at what seemed to be an arbitrary policy decision. But the Army, after four years of a seemingly successful venture, decided that women were slowing men down and returned to segregated training. It did not offer any evidence but cited the dissatisfaction of field commanders with the troops' performances. The implication was that the women's were slowing the men down. Women in the Army, who had been proud of their integrated training, felt that something was taken away from them. This new policy seems to be symptomatic of the Reagan administration's reduction of women's roles and opportunities in the Army.

·PART II·

WHO THEY ARE

Profiles:
World War II Women

Background

Life in a war period is different for almost everyone. Young people grow up fast; old people get older quicker. The basic structures of society are disrupted, and the "normalcy" of peace-time becomes a collective memory. Wartime means faster-paced living, intense emotions, great exhilaration. It is also a time of stress, of tears, and of tension. No one knows in saying good-bye whether it is good-bye forever. The loved ones may not come back.

America was involved in two world wars in this century. World War I was considerably shorter than World War II; fewer troops went overseas, and its impact upon society was less. But both wars had profound consequences for those who lived through them and for generations to come. These were the last wars in which the forces of good and evil were clearly defined and in which there was a strong national consensus supporting them. Young men and women rallied behind the country. The prime of the nation's youth was in uniform. War colored the landscape of America.

News of tragedies came with casualty lists, telegrams, news no one ever was prepared for. Sons, husbands, lovers. The pride and exultation that had accompanied sending soldiers off to war turned to grief and despair.

There is more to waging war than just putting men in uniform. The industrial base to manufacture guns and equipment for the armed forces must be kept operational. There was more than one war to gear up for—there were half a dozen fronts, each with different needs. Then there was the infrastructure of society to keep functioning—the farms, essential urban services, public utilites, the transportation system.

Women were called upon to help keep the country running. Women who hadn't worked at all or outside the home since they had been married put away sewing machines and vacuum cleaners to don overalls and welders' goggles. They responded to their country's call enthusiastically and poured into factories and government offices.

In the epidemic of patriotism that was sweeping the country, women could not do enough. They surprised everyone, including themselves, with their skill, fortitude, and determination in meeting the new challenges. Before, women had not had the opportunity to express their patriotism in so many ways. Their willing response during the world wars bespoke a readiness to take on expanded roles in the so-called man's world.

World War I played a major role in uprooting attitudes and laying the groundwork for institutional changes. Many of these changes affected women. For one thing, they were brought into the labor market on a hitherto unprecedented scale. The contributions that women made to the successful outcome of the war, including the participation of over twelve thousand of them in military service, did not go unnoticed. President Woodrow Wilson called upon Congress to enfranchise women. Otherwise, he suggested, they had fought a war to safeguard a democracy that was not yet created.

So few American women participated in the military services during World War I that hardly anyone noticed their presence. Many of those recruited into the Navy were in civil service jobs and continued to do the same kind of work while wearing the uniform. However, their enlistment was a breakthrough in bringing women in a nonmedical capacity into the military service.

The passage of the Nineteenth Amendment in 1920 certainly can be considered one of the by-products of the shifting attitudes precipitated by World War I. A similar phenomenon occurred in Great Britain. For some years before the outbreak of World War I in 1914, women suffragists in England had waged a vigorous campaign, only to be met with violence and abuse, which escalated on both sides. British women made important contributions in the war and could not be ignored. The vote was a by-product of those contributions.

Less than twenty-five years later, the outbreak of World War II produced the same labor shortages and therefore the need for women's participation in both the civilian and defense sectors. While it seemed logical and natural for women to be called to the factories and other sectors of the economy, to invite women into military roles was another matter. Despite the historical evidence of the successful enlistment of over twelve thousand women in World War I, women's entry into the military during World War II met strong resistance on many fronts. Upper echelons in the War Department and many members of Congress resisted the pressures from high officials who requested extra personnel to take over the clerical and administrative duties from men who were about to be shipped overseas. It took a year, from 1941–1942, for the bill authorizing the WAAC to be passed. Deeply ingrained attitudes resistant to changing women's traditional exclusion from military service stood in the way of early passage of the legislation.

Once the WAAC became a fact, recruiters were faced with similar attitudes from the public. Even though patriotism was the overwhelming sentiment of the American people, there wasn't great enthusiasm in most families to send their daughters off to war. To lure young women into the WAAC and into the other services which opened their doors to women in 1942, recruiters emphasized the new skills and training that would be available to those who signed up.

During the course of the war, almost a half million young women did join the services. Why did these women join while most of their sisters did not?

> I was going to go into service. If my brother did, why couldn't I? I wasn't going to sit home and be Polly by the fire.

During the years between the world wars, it was still traditional for young women to live at home until they got married, even if they were working at outside jobs. Those who moved away without getting married were the exceptions; if they did, it was because of a job in another city.

Young women with high school education were likely to be engaged in routine clerical positions or in unskilled factory jobs. They were easily impressed by the new kinds of experience the services were publicizing. The film industry, meanwhile, was turning out romanticized versions of what war was like, shrouding its realities in Hollywood tinsel. Normal social life was largely absent during the forties when young men served in the military; young women were faced with a vacuum at an important time in their lives. Some solved this by marrying early the boy next door or a high school sweetheart. Others joined the services as it seemed to them an attractive course of action.

> Americans were joining up. Women had red blood as much as men.

Married women also joined up; enrolling in the service made them feel closer to their loved ones. Some fantasized about being reunited with the beloved overseas. Since the WAAC took women up to the age of fifty, there were women who joined because their sons were in service.

As was true with many men, there were those who enlisted because of a personal trauma, the loss of a loved one, or the breakup of a romance. Certainly, a sense of adventure motivated some young women who joined. Some thought this was to be the biggest thing that would occur during their lifetimes, and they wanted to be a part of it. For others it was a chance to expand their horizons beyond their wildest imagination, an opportunity to break out of the narrow world they grew up in and had expected to remain in. Signing up for military service was an acceptable means of going out into the world. It was a permissible way for a woman to spread her wings and contribute to the national purpose.

Moreover, the boredom and monotony of the wartime civilian world in the mid-forties influenced some women to turn to the services. Fantasies probably outdistanced the reality, and led young women without direction to don the uniform. Those who were in conflict at home with one or both parents, or who were simply unhappy in their environment, saw the services as a salvation. For some it was a way out of responsibilities they either didn't want to assume or wanted to shed. No doubt there were the few maladjusted ones who enlisted to get away from it all, or to find some new unknown direction for their lives.

Was the proximity of men a factor in women's choice of military service? Perhaps for some it was both a conscious and an unconscious motivation. It might have been a wishful attempt to bring a degree of normalcy back in their lives. For those who served, the military turned out to be a mixed blessing. The work environment had pitfalls they couldn't have anticipated—sexual harassment, the abuse of command position, the lack of recourse. For others, the work environment was challenging and rewarding.

The overwhelming number of men overseas compared with the small numbers of women became at times an enormous burden upon the women. Particularly when the women were stationed near the front lines, with the concomitant dangers, fear, and deprivations, they encountered quick emotional attachments that took a tremendous emotional toll. Yet despite the circumstances, the morale of women in and near combat zones was high; it was rewarding to participate directly in the accomplishment of a military mission.

Some women took the recruiters' messages seriously. Either they stopped their educations involuntarily, or they had no chance for further education. Even in the forties women saw the military service as a chance to gain new training, to further one's education. While they probably were in the minority, there were some who had hoped to improve themselves, particularly in terms of a future labor market, when they enlisted in the service.

There were those who joined up because they had special skills that were being sought. The largest group was nurses. Even then, there were not enough nurses to answer the needs of the services, especially overseas. Toward the end of the war, in the mid-forties, the shortage of nurses was so serious that a draft was contemplated. It is quite possible that, if the war had not ended in 1945, such a draft would have been instituted.

Older women with professional training and experience answered the call because they were told they had something special to offer to the war effort. Most of them became officers, even if they didn't initially enter as officers. They had professions as writers, broadcasters, specialists in public relations, teachers, linguists. Only a few women enrolled who were in scientific and engineering fields. Because of their credentials, those who received the invitation to serve as officers found it difficult to refuse. The WAVES recruited most of its officers this way.

Overriding all these personal and social reasons for joining the military services was the call of patriotism. Historically, females had not had many opportunities to express their patriotism by actually becoming part of the armed forces. This was a novel experience, although it is doubtful that they were aware they were pioneers in this enterprise. The equalization of men and women that the all-out war effort entailed propelled women to assume new roles with equanimity and confidence. Patriotism was the cloak of legitimacy for women to become "citizen soldiers" and to participate actively in the defense of the country.

*   *   *

An experience as different from routine life as military service was bound to have enormous impact upon the lives of the women. While war itself—as many believe—may have promoted early maturation, the demands and rigor of military life added new facets to servicewomen's personalities. As one young woman put it: "If I could live through boot camp, I could live through anything."

Self-discipline was one of the spinoffs of military service. Women learned how to organize tasks, how to cope with dissatisfactions and frustrations. They developed the patience and will to achieve a goal, no matter how difficult the roadblocks. They learned how to arrange their time, how to mobilize their own capabilities, how to draw upon outside resources. The acquired habits of cleanliness and neatness remained with them permanently.

For those with strong dependency characteristics, they developed independence of thought and action. For others, the service enhanced an already independent spirit. No task was too formidable; no challenge too awe-inspiring. Sometimes independence had to be put aside for the sake of a group effort. There were times to be innovative and daring and times to be cooperative. If they had lacked determination, they acquired it because they needed it to survive.

Self-indulgence had to be discarded; self-pity was equally frivolous. They learned to defer gratification and to survive without the pleasures they had taken for granted in civilian life. They also learned to give more of themselves to others—to be a friend and a comrade.

One of the rewards of the service was a unique camaraderie that developed among the women who shared quarters or orders. Many women claimed that the most important friendships of their lives developed in the service. Experiencing the annoyances, the pettiness, and the unreasonableness of service life was exasperating but brought women together. There were sad and gentle moments too, of reaching out and of being reached out to. Even though women were not in battle, or dependent upon their "buddies" for survival, the bonding of military life was strong and lasting. Like ex-servicemen, ex-servicewomen learned to see themselves as a distinct group.

Women in the service found a diversity of people which they had not encountered. The mix of different ethnic, racial, religious, and geographical backgrounds broadened their knowledge of this country's inhabitants. For the women as for the men, the melting pot aspect of the service developed new appreciation and tolerance of differences.

The geography of the country became real to those whose orders took them away from their hometowns. The world opened up to those who went overseas—to North Africa, Italy, New Guinea, Burma—all the places that were previously just globs on a map. Not only did they see far-off lands, but they had a chance to observe the people who lived in them. The world became considerably larger than Smithtown, U.S.A.

Many women in the services went to school and acquired skills that they could later use in a job or career. Some who acquired skills in nontraditional fields never used them again. But most found they could learn things and be productive in areas they never dreamed possible.

Perhaps more valuable than anything else was the increased sense of self-worth that the service experience engendered. The servicewoman developed confidence in her own abilities. She found she could learn, if taught. She discovered she could overcome, if tested. She realized she had strengths that had never revealed themselves before. She could follow orders and she could give orders. She could rely on her own judgment and make decisions that would affect others. She could make mistakes, correct them, and accept the consequences. In some instances, she learned how crucial it was not to make a mistake. She learned to accept and rely on herself.

Almost as important as this sense of self-worth was the pride of doing something worthwhile outside the family and community. To be able to make a contribution, to be appreciated by the larger world reinforced her self-esteem. She was important not only to her family but to her country as well. By participating in its defense she saw herself as a full member of society. If she was imaginative, she believed she was playing a part in history—and she was.

Naturally, there were those who were not changed much by their military experience, which did not work miracles. The maladjusted did not adjust. The malcontents continued to make life miserable for themselves and others. Unhappily, the few who did not comport themselves the way that was expected, or whose problems were translated into antisocial actions, were the ones who got publicity. Throughout the World War II years, women in the services had to contend with undeserved bad publicity. But the record was abundantly clear that this group of women had as good a record as other parts of society.

* * *

Women who served during World War II became a part of their country's history. They had taken on the larger world in their stride and did it proud. Without even knowing it, they became pioneers in redefining women's roles in the modern world. For them the rewards were immediate—the satisfactions of being part of the action, of making a direct contribution to the war effort. For their country, they had stepped into a breach and performed admirably. They might have made the difference between victory and defeat. Some historians have suggested that the Allied utilization of women in so many capacities, in contrast to the sex stereotyping by the Axis, was a key factor in the outcome of the war.

Could World War II women who served go back to Smithtown, U.S.A., and pick up again their preservice lives? Some did and married their hometown sweethearts—if they survived. Their wartime service was a high point in their lives. At reunions they would try to find the women they served with. Most of the time they didn't find them, but always hopeful, they went to the reunions anyway.

Many did not go home again, except to say hello to the folks and pack up their bags for their next ventures into the world. Having gained confidence in their own abilities and having developed new skills to earn a living, many left their hometown for other parts of the country, returning only for visits.

Marriage was the end product for many women. Either they married a GI they met in the service or shortly thereafter, or they married the one they had been waiting for. Those who had previously married picked up the threads of married life. Often the woman settled down in the man's hometown, or together they put their roots down in a new place.

The postwar period saw this turbulence of people moving, leaving the farms and towns of their parents. Whole new parts of the country developed from such population migration of ex-servicemen and ex-servicewomen. No longer were people staying where they were born. America's borders had expanded.

Some did not marry by choice. Newfound independence was not easily given up. They found a richness in life outside the traditional framework of marriage and child rearing. Able to earn their own livelihood and to purchase the amenities they sought, they prospered on their own. They found companionship, travel, and community work immensely rewarding. Many went on to promising careers; a few made waves on local and national scenes as newspaper reporters, poets, judges, and deans.

Expectations had changed for many of the women who joined the military services. What had seemed an acceptable future no longer fit in with their new perspectives of the world. The offices they left, the stores, the farms, the small towns they grew up in— all seemed too confining. Some had already ventured forth before they joined up; they had already taken untraditional paths. More choices were on the horizon; choices that added knowledge and increased self-confidence opened up for them.

The military connection proved to be an important one for some who stayed in the Reserves and continued to serve until retirement. Others who married GIs who made the military their career found that the postwar world for them was not too much different from what they had experienced during the war.

For a few women the military service became a career. Although that option was not available immediately, with the passage of the Integration Act of 1948 women had that choice. Since the postwar economy did not offer the same opportunities that were available during the war, some women opted to go back into service. Even women college graduates had a hard time finding suitable employment which matched their background and which offered them leadership roles for which they qualify.

An unexpected bonus was the GI Bill of Rights. The Servicemen's Readjustment Act of 1944 provided to ex-GIs a number of benefits to "make up for time and opportunities lost." The ex-servicewomen, like their male counterparts, could go to university or to vocational school and receive an allowance to cover tuition, books, supplies, as well as living expenses. Former GIs poured into the nation's colleges, transforming the educational profile of America.

Though a number of women used their benefits, most probably didn't. Those who got married and raised families didn't have the time or the energy to go to school. Too often their eligibility for the benefits expired before they could use them. Even among those who stayed single, only some took advantage of the benefits, as single women veterans were self-supporting and needed to work. Perhaps also their aspirations had not been stretched enough for them to try and advance their professional careers, or perhaps they felt there were no careers to work toward. No data are available on women's use of veterans' benefits because the Veterans Administration kept only a 2 percent sampling of all veterans. Since women were less than 2 percent of the armed forces, they fell by the wayside in the VA sampling procedures. It seems unlikely that we will ever be able to determine how meaningful the GI Bill was to the servicewomen of World War II.

•SARAH•

The deep voice with the Texas drawl belies the small, soft feminine person that goes with the voice. Sarah, the intimidator of presidents, the one-woman oversight committee, the thundering feminist, is recognized by her piquant presence and curly red hair. Her eyes are like a Diogenes lamp penetrating hypocrisies and facades. Her almost biblical sense of right and wrong moves her to denounce those who have transgressed. She has learned to make herself heard above the mostly male voices around her at press conferences. She will not tolerate either evasion or obfuscation. For four decades she has galvanized the Washington press corps with her courage and perseverance, and has served as a model for those who still believe the Fourth Estate can be a force for the public good.

Are newspaper reporters born or made? However they are created, Sarah* is of that rare breed who have stories coursing through their veins. It took a lot of guts for a woman to be a reporter before the Second World War. There weren't many in those days, but Sarah was one.

From a family of lawyers and judges, Sarah was the youngest of nine children. There weren't any arrows pointing toward a newspaper reporter's career, but Sarah went to the University of Missouri School of Journalism to launch one.

A ten-year stint on a small newspaper gave her the breadth of experience that would hold her in good stead in the future. She covered several cities, specializing in what transpired in federal agencies and federal criminal courts. As a reporter, she felt she was in a better position to do good than if she had been a lawyer.

Why did a woman reporter already launched on an unusual career join the WAAC during World War II? When she was a small child, Sarah saw her brothers go off to fight in World

*Sarah McClendon

War I. The rest of the family did everything they could to support them. That experience left an indelible impression on her, and she swore that if there would ever be another war, she would go too.

Unhappily, there was another one, even bigger and longer, involving the entire country. Her boyfriend went off to war, as did almost all the young men around her. This time Sarah would not be left behind. She wanted to go immediately into intelligence but she found she had to be in uniform first, and the only way a woman could do that was to join the WAAC. So she did.

It was particularly ironic that Sarah signed up in the WAAC because she had not initially taken it seriously and indeed had made fun of it. But she wanted to get into intelligence, and that was the way to do it. She was always the first to admit that she had made a mistake—the women who joined the WAAC were a great bunch, as she discovered. Her respect for them grew as she went from being a private into the OCS and on to a commission.

Being in Fort Des Moines in winter for OCS was an experience Sarah will never forget. The drilling in the ice and snow, the courses in map reading, and the rough schedule wore her to a frazzle. To this day she can't read maps, and she marvels that she got through OCS. She'll never forget those days of training, and the dread she felt then that perhaps she wouldn't make it. But she did. She recalls that one of the three platoons in training consisted only of black women. Thereafter, the black women were integrated into the regular units.

Because of her years as a newspaper reporter, Sarah was in demand for special assignments. She was called upon to do public relations. That appealed to her, particularly because it meant a transfer from the ice and snow of Iowa to the warmth of Fort Oglethorpe, Georgia. She finally got used to the bitter cold weather of Iowa, but the more moderate climate of Georgia was a welcome change.

It was in Georgia that Sarah became aware of the spate of ugly rumors that were circulating about the WAC. One of the stories was that the WACs were given contraceptives. This turned out not to be true. Sarah conjectured that one of the male officers in high office was trying to hurt Director Oveta Culp Hobby's reputation, and this was one way of getting to her. When the local editor called Sarah to find out if the rumor was true, the editor took Sarah's word that it wasn't and did not print the story. Her good relations with the editor, which she had worked hard to establish, had paid off.

Ever since women participated in the military, they have been maligned by men who could not tolerate their presence in their hitherto exclusive world. Throughout World War II and later, servicewomen were plagued by false reports calling their morals into question. The simplistic thinking that women went into service for one reason enjoyed high currency. There were those who wanted to believe that and they spread all kinds of rumors.

One woman veteran put it well: "You came out just what you went in." Since the services were taking from a cross section of women, as well as a cross section of men, there were bound to be all kinds of women, including the so-called "bad apples." But it was the women who got the attention. They were the ones breaking new ground, and inevitably, their course was not going to be easy.

Military women have had to put up with all kinds of sexual innuendos, slander, and defamation of character. Usually they didn't strike back and tried to be above it all. Sometimes high government officials spoke out to deny the allegations maligning women. But the two sides were unequally matched. The ugly stories that circulated imposed hardships on the women and their families, as well as on their lovers and husbands who were sometimes thousands of miles away.

One unpleasant phenomenon was the fact that civilian women, particularly in the South, were not nice to the military women. Either they believed the stories that were circulated, or they were confused or simply jealous. Whatever the reasons, at various times nonmilitary women made life difficult for those in uniform. Part of Sarah's mission in her public relations job was to knock down the falsehoods about military women.

It wasn't long before Sarah was called to Washington, D.C., for a challenging and satisfying assignment in the Surgeon General's office. The Army was concerned that the American population be prepared to deal emotionally with the kinds of wounds and disabilities they would face when the men came home from war. Their loved ones were going to have to take care of them, give them emotional support, and come to terms with the injuries.

It fell upon the Surgeon General's office to address the issue. It reviewed how other countries had coped, what kinds of information were available, what kinds of services were needed, and how the population was to be educated so that it wouldn't be a complete shock. Sarah found out what the advances were in Army medicine in treating burns and wounds. Much of this new knowledge acquired by the Army Medical Corps needed to be disseminated to the public. The Army burn center was to help in civilian disaster situations. Sarah found this assignment immensely rewarding.

Like hundreds of other WACs in Washington, she felt the capital to be a lonely place for women. Men in the military had enough of uniforms and for relaxation turned to civilian women in dainty frocks. Furthermore, WAC officers were enjoined from drinking in public, which put a crimp in after-hour activities. Sarah and many WACs worked late hours and found there was little time for enjoyment.

In her different assignments Sarah was often called upon to work Sundays to brief visiting advertising executives who had been hired by the Army to develop recruiting campaigns for women. She couldn't believe the Army would contract individuals who knew nothing about the Army, nothing about women, and nothing about recruiting. To this day Sarah is suspicious of all military contracts.

Sarah knew how hard the WACs worked from her own experience, how often they were called upon to give up their free time for special assignments. The slurring campaigns on the WACs' reputations were even more onerous to those who had firsthand knowledge of how competent and hardworking the women were, and how little free time they had. There was hardly any time or energy left for any low-key recreation, and even less for amorous escapades.

Sarah's military service changed a lot of her attitudes toward other women. She saw women undertake tasks that in their wildest dreams they never would have thought possible. Nothing was too difficult or complicated. The women were willing, hardworking, and gutsy. She began to realize that women could do anything they set their minds to.

Then Sarah met and fell in love with a man and married him. It was a short-lived marriage because the man she married went back to an earlier relationship. Sarah found she was pregnant and had to leave the Army. This was a heavy blow to Sarah, who loved her work in the Army. She concealed her condition from most of her superior officers, although she was often sick. In her eighth month she went to her commanding officer and told him that she was going to have a baby and that she had better leave. Somehow she managed to remain in uniform until after she had the baby, a girl who was delivered at Walter Reed Hospital.

It was a long struggle to raise her child, but she did. Not long after the baby was born, Sarah went down to the Press Club and found a job at a small newspaper. Her job permitted her to work and raise her child. Thereafter, her newspaper career was on track. She now runs her own news service and is an independent, highly respected columnist and writer in Washington.

The going was rough during the years she was bringing up her daughter. Yet she found motherhood rewarding and has a wonderful relationship with her daughter, who is making a name for herself in Canada. Sarah is enjoying the warmth of grandmotherhood and is particularly proud of her granddaughter, who is in the air cadets. With some help from her family, Sarah went it alone as a single parent—in those days a remarkable feat for a single woman with a high-powered career.

Sarah had come to Washington with the Army and never left it again. As she said, if it hadn't been for the war and her joining the WAC, she probably would never have left Texas. Military service did other things for her as well. She claims that whatever the Army taught an individual will come in good stead some time in life. You learn how to try to prevent crises, but you also learn how to deal with them. The Army taught her how to get along with people, with subordinates and superiors, and how to get things done. It taught her self-discipline.

Her years in Washington taught her the workings of bureaucracy. She had a hard time with that and still does. It has helped her to become a discerning critic of the government and bureaucratic waste. She is put off by its evasiveness, its wastefulness, and by how it "passes the buck." Sarah's military experience prepared her for a distinguished career. She listened and she learned, always making the most of her opportunities.

• AUDREY •

A large, dignified woman with short white hair met me at the back door as I pulled behind the storybook-looking farmhouse at the end of the long driveway. Despite her simple dress, with her dog at her side, she could have been the grand lady of an English manor. Sitting in the kitchen on a summer's afternoon, looking out at the shade trees ahead and the verdant fields beyond, there was a sense of complete tranquility in harmony with the person who had graciously invited me to lunch. She and her late husband had deliberately chosen this life.

How does an artist turn into a soldier? Quite easily, because artists have to be tough in order to survive. The Army recruiter was askance that Audrey,* an artist, told her she wanted to be an officer. An artist an officer? No way. Audrey decided to enlist because she didn't intend to sit out the war when her country was calling for women to serve.

Audrey, the only child of an artist father, had never wanted to be anything but an artist. She studied for several years at the Academy of Design in New York City in preparation for entering the field. It was a shock to her to find out there were no jobs in art for women. Even a woman mural painter had turned her down because she was a woman. Audrey could not understand why her gender disqualified her from practicing her art for which she was well trained.

When she decided to be where the action was, Audrey was living at home, decorating pots, discouraged by the lack of op-

*Audrey Archer-Shee

portunities she had encountered. Her women artist friends also had only found minor jobs vaguely related to art. Audrey was strong, adaptable, talented. Her father made a decent living as an artist. Audrey had spent enough time walking the streets of New York City to recognize it was a no-win situation for a woman.

Her family had been surprised at her decision but supported her fully. Her father didn't see any reason why girls couldn't do most things. Somewhere back among the ancestors was a soldier who fought in the Revolutionary War. Besides, the family had always kept up a connection with West Point. Newburgh, New York—where Audrey grew up—was not far from the military academy. She could remember the dances and parties she had gone to, though she had not been too impressed with the cadets. Her mother, trained by her own West Point father, kept a tight ship at home. Audrey knew how to be on time, to take orders.

The sixty-first person to sign up in the WAAC in New York City, Audrey did well in basic training which took place in the old stables at Fort Des Moines, Iowa, at one time a cavalry school for the Army. Faced with the choice of becoming a cook or a baker, or going to an administrative skills school, or learning about motor transport, Audrey opted for the latter.

Her art background took her next to Fort Oglethorpe, Georgia, where she was assigned to help with the training aides and with map making. Fort Oglethorpe turned out to be a mixed blessing. Because she was not a commercial artist, she was getting the most boring of details. While the base itself was pleasant enough, the Southern city it was near, like most Southern cities, did not tolerate women in uniform. Military women were highly uncomfortable in such places. Also, because of an incredibly changeful weather, there were constant epidemics of colds and flu, even measles. Audrey remembers being sick but preferring to report for duty rather than be on sick call in cold barracks.

It was time to move on. Audrey applied for OCS, much to the astonishment of her commanding officer who could not really see an artist becoming an officer. Audrey did made OCS and went back to Fort Des Moines again for officer training. This time she learnt how to teach in order to teach motor transport to enlisted women.

This was a phenomenal event for Audrey, who throughout her

childhood was horribly shy. She never thought she could lecture in front of a couple of hundred women. But orders are orders; and teach she did, better than she ever would have thought possible. In fact, she was giving a lecture on leadership when an inspection team visited her class. With the adrenalin pumping she managed to pull through with flying colors. She recalls the cold sweat of fear that had soaked her right to her skin.

Two-and-a-half years of Audrey's tour were spent in the Pentagon, in various kinds of office work. She was one of the few WAACs who received a Washington assignment, and she found it stimulating. She had to deal with all kinds of people, a good number of them high brass. When demobilization occurred she left as a captain, although she would have been prepared to stay on. Later she did try to get into the Reserves, but an old back condition which she had before she enlisted disqualified her.

Not long after she returned home, she met her husband-to-be, who had served in the British Expeditionary Force. After getting married, they thought they would try to go to Mexico, she to art school, he to photography school. She intended to make use of her veterans' educational benefits. The school they both wanted to go to, San Miguel de Alliende, was in a small town about three hours from Mexico City.

It seemed like the ideal setup. Neither of them liked big cities. San Miguel was quiet and had a good photography as well as a good art department. However, unknown to Audrey and her husband, the Veterans Administration had discovered that in the fifties the Institute had invited a muralist, an avowed communist, to lecture there; as a result the VA had blacklisted the school for educational benefits. Since this was the place where Audrey and her husband really wanted to go, they decided to forego the benefits. Audrey never used her GI Bill after that, although she was in the service almost four years.

Neither art nor photography were going to put bread on the table, so the young couple, wanting to carve out their kind of life, decided instead to become turkey farmers on the eastern shore of Maryland.

Unaware that as a veteran she was eligible for all veterans' benefits, Audrey did not apply for a farm loan. Instead, her husband traded in part of his forthcoming inheritance to pay for the farm. With hard work they were able to create a rural setting they both wanted. When her husband passed away, Audrey returned to her art to have an income. Now in the same farmhouse in which she has raised two sons, she is making a living from her art. She is restoring old paintings in her studio, and her reputation is growing.

The military service taught Audrey a lot about herself. She found that, as an artist, she could do a variety of things, that she was as practical, adaptable, and capable as anyone else. Without the officer experience, which pushed her into leadership and teaching roles, she might not have had the confidence to do the teaching she later did. Gone were her shyness and timidity. She now has the strength and the conviction that she has what it takes.

The WAAC (and later the WAC) experience brought her into contact with so many interesting and different individuals, forcing her to learn to adjust to all kinds of people. After she left the service, Audrey felt she could get along with anybody.

Audrey learned to respect and appreciate other women as a result of being in the WAC and still corresponds with some of them. Audrey is convinced that her life would have been quite different, were it not for her service. The WAC changed Audrey's self-image; no longer would she take a put-down or a rejection either because she was a woman or an artist. If anything, the combination had a lot going for it, and if other people didn't appreciate that, it was their loss.

Audrey was proud of being a veteran and, when she first got back to Newburgh, immediately responded to a neighboring village's call for veterans to set up an ad hoc veterans organization. The men were shocked to have her appear in their midst. Not only was she a woman—she also came from up the Hill, whereas all of them came from the village. She was the only woman who had ever approached them as a veteran. They goodnaturedly accepted her, and Audrey continued to be active in the unaffiliated organization until she left for Mexico.

Audrey and her husband had a special bond because they had both served in the military. They could relate to annoying and humorous incidents in their separate careers. It was a close and companionable marriage of two ex-soldiers.

•PAT•

A petite attractive heartbreaker, this enormously capable woman could pull a machine apart as easily as she could grace a ballroom. Her looks belie her iron will. With the energy and the spirit of a thoroughbred, she knows no boundaries to her learning or to her activities. She is the great earth mother to the veteran population in her position as editor of a leading veterans' newspaper. To get her to sit down and be interviewed, to shut out all the people and issues she was involved with, was a major feat. Mercurial, tempestuous, daring, she probably would have been the first woman in space if the rocket age had come a little sooner. She has made her mark in a man's world more than once, and is the most ardent of champions for women.

No was not in her lexicon. Pat* learned at a very early age that there is no such thing as not being able to do something. If you stand your ground, you don't have to take *no* for an answer. If you can't work within the system, you work through it. There was always a way if you looked for it.

Pat was a pilot in the WASP (Women's Air Force Service Pilots). Diminutive, feminine, assertive, this Irish-American lass flew in dangerous conditions in the most unstable aircraft imaginable in secret missions the WASP carried out for the Army Air Force. She was among eleven hundred who performed legendary flying feats for their country during World War II.

Pat was still in high school when Jacqueline Cochran's first letter of invitation to join the WASP arrived. Determined to become a doctor, at the time Pat was fully occupied in taking science courses in order to qualify for a medical school scholarship. But the war was on, and everyone in her family was doing something for the war effort. She took her letter and went to Cochran's office.

*Patricia Hughes

"Who the hell are you?" Cochran asked the small girl with braids who looked about fourteen. Pat, with great dignity, turned on her heels and walked out of the office. Such was Pat's first encounter with the unique woman who had overcome innumerable roadblocks to establish a woman's flying corps to ferry and deliver planes to air bases, and to supply the personnel when male pilots had to be sent overseas to fight the Nazis.

When the second letter came from Cochran, Pat was ready to join. The age requirement had changed, and she could qualify. Pat spent over a year in the WASP before it was disbanded at the end of 1944. She trained at Avenger Field in Sweetwater, Texas, with the rest of the incredible flying women. Besides ferrying planes, Pat became a trainer of Army Air Force pilots, and taught tactical gunnery and instrument flying.

How does a strictly brought-up Catholic woman from a family of educators become a flying ace who could take an airplane engine apart and put it back together? Pat had never had an unchaperoned date before she signed up for the WASP. She came from generations of strong women, women who could raise families of nine children under the adverse conditions the Irish have known for centuries. These were women who could sail across the Atlantic in their ninth month of pregnancy and buy land that would become the homestead of their offspring. How could Pat be other than strong, resilient, and resourceful?

There was no question when America went to war that Pat would take part in the war effort. Everyone in her family was doing something. Her father, a Marine reservist, raced to his unit on the day Pearl Harbor was bombed and spent years in the South Pacific. All the men in her large extended family joined up; the women did all kinds of volunteer work. For Pat there never was any other choice. She would do her share also.

It was her father, though, who taught her early in life not to take *no* for an answer. Born with a twisted foot, Pat might have been crippled for life. But her father would not let her accept her birth defect as a permanent disability. He drilled her, exercised her, had her operated on so that her foot would not be disabling or noticeable.

When Pat was turned down by the Civil Aeronautics Administration for a pilot's license because of her foot when she was a precocious schoolgirl, her father marched her back the next day with another physical for them to give to her—a Marine physical. She passed it and became the pilot that she still is today.

Pat had so completely overcome her bad foot that no one noticed it when she went into the WASP. She had one close call when she was two weeks from her graduation at Sweetwater. Up in the air with a male pilot who couldn't pull the airplane out of a spin (part of the routine flying test), she had to put so much pressure on her foot to help pull the plane out that she sprained her ankle.

The flight surgeon who X-rayed her foot because it was so swollen could see the aberration in the bone structure. Pat was petrified—her secret was exposed. He must have sensed what kind of woman Pat was because he let her go with the admonition to rest her ankle for a period of time. She flew dozens of missions after that without any mishap, and no one else ever knew about her foot.

Being a WASP was one of the great experiences of her life. To this day, getting together with the other women who served with her is like being home. Pat never feels so much herself as when she is with them. They shared so much that was intense and exciting. They had to give so much of themselves, had to mobilize every fiber in their bodies, every faculty of their minds, to survive. The women depended on one another, drew strength from each other, helped one another in such an intense way that nothing afterward in their lives could match the camaraderie.

There were causalties. Two of Pat's bunkmates were killed in a midair collision. The casualties were one of the reasons the Army kept quiet about the WASP. Public opinion probably would not have tolerated the Army Air Force's placing women in dangerous situations and giving them arduous missions.

"They couldn't get away with it today," Pat muses. "It was outrageous, the kind of aircraft the women were trained in and then asked to fly in. Their primary trainer was an unstable aircraft which was used by the men in their advanced training. The WASP were test pilots for aircraft men had refused to take up. Someone had to try them out to find out what was wrong. The WASP took on the most dangerous and difficult domestic flying assignments.

They didn't expect rewards or medals; they did whatever was asked of them."

One of her most dangerous missions was to tow targets so that embryo fighter pilots could practice their shooting in preparation for their dogfights with the Germans. Being shot at by novices was, understandably, scary.

Along with the tragedies and the near misses were human comedies, the funny incidents to look back upon and laugh at because they turned out all right. Like the time when one of the WASPs in a mixed crew passed out on the improvised john—"the thundermug"—when her oxygen ran out, and the young man holding the tarp up in front of her was too chaste to find out why she was taking so long. To save the girl's life the pilot had to make an emergency landing. There were many more heart-warming and unique stories of the WASP's escapades and near mishaps.

If the WASP experience revealed anything about men and women working together for a common goal under difficult, often dangerous conditions, it is that sex is not a consideration under those circumstances. No WASP members, according to Pat, ever had a problem getting along with the men on the flight line. All were too preoccupied with trying to survive.

New cadets at Sweetwater were shocked to find out they were going to be trained by women pilots. "Some of those guys were petrified when they saw who was going to teach them," Pat laughingly reminisces. "I must have looked like a mushroom, close to the ground, swallowed up by my jumpsuit and my parachute."

Pat has thought a lot about women in relation to flying. For her, flying is a poetic experience, like meditation. She thinks women have a knack for flying because they are intuitive, and intuition is important for flying. She also thinks that women's emotions are an energy source which when harnessed properly will give women the edge.

Pat has a lot of theories about the differences between men's and women's performances. In emergencies, women are apt to explore more alternatives than men. For men it is usually an either-or situation. Too often a man's ego will get in the way whereas a woman will direct her attention solely to what needs to be done. Furthermore, women tend to be more inventive—

they will keep on trying new ways until something works. Pat's theories were derived not only from her flying in the WASP but from her involvement in emergency rescue work as well.

One of the things the WASP experience taught Pat was that one has to be totally involved to do something well. This is a "given" that most women do not know. The demands that the WASP made on the women taught them to learn everything they could about their aircrafts, the weather, geography—everything that had to do with flying their missions. They couldn't know too much; their survival depended on their knowledge.

There are no barriers too great, no fences too high. Pat's philosophy has always been that there is always a way. If there was something she didn't know, she would learn it. If there was a skill needed that she didn't have, she would acquire it. She faults women for accepting too little and for not being willing to do the hard work and put forth the energy required to overcome their deficiencies. This requires patience and commitment. Women need to learn to utilize their potential and assume responsibilities in the male world.

Another result of Pat's WASP experience was in her perception of herself in the world. She saw herself as valuable in making an important contribution to her country that very few people could make. Service in the WASP gave Pat an extraordinary self-confidence that nothing thereafter could diminish. It also enhanced her patriotism.

After the WASP was demobilized, Pat continued to fly. She ferried airplanes for commercial companies, took on contracts to deliver goods to a diamond mine in South America, and was involved in other unique missions. Wherever she went, she observed. Whoever she met, she found interesting. Every new place and experience was challenging. Nothing was too strange or unfamiliar for her to deal with. Whatever she needed to know, she found out.

One achievement she is most proud of is when she succeeded in getting the FAA to adopt a new rule. She found the fatality rate in general aviation horrendous. The number of deaths due to pilot error was high. As the director of general aviation of the Flight Safety Foundation, Pat lobbied for a rule that would require pilots to have a biennial flight check. The fatality rate decreased after the rule went into effect.

Pat believes that flight instructors too should be checked more closely. Her experience in military flying convinced her that more stringent regulation in general aviation is necessary. The kinds of safety procedures at Sweetwater gave her a standard which she believes should become more operational in civilian aviation.

Pat knew at an early age that traditional roles for women would be too boring for her. So she has managed to expand her roles in a predominantly male field: as pilot, aviation safety specialist, horse trainer, search-and-find rescue pilot, and editor of a prominent veterans' newspaper. Pat has been a one-woman dynamo.

Through all of this, she has raised four sons and a daughter and maintained a household with an extended family. Her children are very close to her—two of her sons work with her on the newspaper. There has been no contradiction in her life in being a woman and making her mark upon her environment, no matter what it happens to be.

• IRENE •

Tall, red-haired, gracious with a penetrating look, she might have been your favorite brownie mother. A shy, low-key manner hides a keen intellect and a passionate sense of social justice. One senses she would have liked to have done more to express her deeply felt convictions. An ardent feminist, she has made important contributions to public policy scholarship. The energy that lets her bicycle to work and participate in bike marathons she has often mobilized for the things she believes in.

If it hadn't been for the war, she would not have landed an editorial research job at a prestigious magazine like *Newsweek*. But World War II had begun to take men away into the service, and the magazine editors had to turn to women. In normal times women would not have had much chance to break into a citadel of journalism like *Newsweek*.

Irene,* a college graduate, had been the editor of the *Barnard Bulletin* and had presented excellent credentials to the magazine. Irene was fresh out of college, but this was not the first unusual thing that she had done. As the youngest of three daughters from a tight-knit family on Long Island, Irene took a look at the mass education scene at Hunter College in New York City. Her sisters had gone there, but she decided it wasn't for her. She had something different in mind. After high school she went to work and saved her money so that she could go to Barnard.

Irene was in the first class of WAVES officers. Since she had a position at *Newsweek* that promised to lead to the kind of career she had been preparing for—that of a political reporter—one might wonder why she joined up. After all, she was launched in a new profession.

Always a free spirit, always someone who was willing to take risks and who had a strong belief in social justice, Irene was not content to just sit out the war in a magazine's plush offices. She was totally supportive of her country's involvement in the war and saw herself in an active role.

As Congress debated the formation of the women's corps—for months after the introduction of the bill in 1941 by Mrs. Edith Nourse Rogers—Irene followed the progress of the legislation until its signing into law by President Roosevelt.

Having grown up near water, Irene always loved to be near it. This was one of the reasons she chose to join the WAVES when it was formed in July 1942. The Navy had more appeal for her, so she waited past the birth pangs of the WAAC and answered the Navy's call when it began commissioning women as officers.

Irene found out that she was not the only Barnard woman who had that idea. In the first officers' class were several of her classmates, so it was not so stark a transition to military life. Furthermore, that first officer class was quartered in relative luxury at Smith College at Northampton, Massachusetts. Her barracks were a local hotel, and the food was not Navy food.

She admits that she and her classmates were in a unique situ-

*Irene Murphy

ation. Later she was to become familiar with the housing and the restrictions of enlisted women; she marveled at their fortitude in accepting the crowded, harsh conditions. She admits that the perks, privileges, and privacy of the officer corps made military life easier to take.

Irene honestly wonders whether she would have been able to tolerate the much more restrictive circumstances of the enlisted women. To this day she carries a dislike of the caste system, which continues to operate in the Navy and the other military services. She questions whether it really has to be so. While she has not admitted this, perhaps she feels some guilt about being one who benefited from that caste system.

Being in the Navy was not quite what she had hoped for. Opportunities for women personnel, even for officers, were very limited. The way policymakers had envisioned women's roles in the services was for them to take over routine support-service slots from the men who could then be released for sea and combat duty.

Irene felt that the women were ghettoized and given few chances for challenging work. Shunted into communications, as most early WAVES officers were, Irene was bored by her duties. She had very little choice although she was given a chance to indicate her preferences for geographical location. It was a waste of her skills and the skills of many of the other officers.

But they all volunteered and did what was asked of them. In Irene's case, she got to see the country, which in itself was enormously broadening. Her vision had been bounded by being in New York City and Long Island.

However, Irene's editorial background showed up on an early computer, and she spent the last eighteen months of service working on the Navy magazine, *All Hands*, in Washington, D.C. She ended her Navy career in a public relations capacity in New York at the time when the ships were returning from overseas, many with badly wounded men. One of her agonizing tasks was to have to tell a mother who had received conflicting messages about her son that indeed the boy was dead. Irene's commanding officer could not face doing this. Thus she had to do one of the hardest tasks of her Navy career.

Irene felt closer to the war effort as a WAVE officer. This

experience heightened her social consciousness, and strengthened her convictions about the need for strengthening a democratic society. Her horror of dictatorship, her close observation of what the Hitler scourge meant for mankind, and her firsthand experience of the suffering war creates were all gelled by these years in the WAVES.

Also, she became aware of the narrow stratum of society from which WAVES officers were drawn. This was mostly a privileged, white middle-class group. And although Irene relished the different friendships she made from those of different backgrounds than hers, she was strongly aware of those not included in the elite group she found herself in.

When she was released in 1946, Irene decided that she wanted a broader education. Even though she had reemployment rights at *Newsweek*, she did not use them. Irene's decision coincided with her employer's policy of rehiring the *men* who had left for war.

With her GI Bill educational benefits, she enrolled in Columbia University's master's degree program in political science. In fact, she began to take courses during her last months in the Navy, while she was stationed in New York. She concentrated on international relations and later entered the Ph.D. program. While a graduate student at Columbia she met her future husband, and ended her stint in the Ph.D. program. The war had changed her. It had moved her to thinking deeply about herself and her society. Being in the service had a very strong influence on her views and, hence, on her actions. Her husband, who also served, had some degrading experiences which similarly stimulated him into becoming a more rebellious and socially conscious person.

With the knowledge of what had really happened in Europe— the Holocaust, the mass slayings and extermination camps, horrors heaped on horrors—Irene's strength of purpose deepened. She would try to understand how such a monstrous scourge could achieve such power and wreak such destruction. And she vowed to do her part to be sure that nothing like that could happen again.

Some years later, after her marriage broke up and she was raising her two children, she went back to school and finished her Ph.D. The GI Bill had long since expired, but she had saved money to pay the tuition. For her Ph.D. dissertation Irene wrote a landmark study in public policy regarding women's social gains—which to this day belongs with the standard literature on the subject.

Fortunately, with her advanced degrees, Irene had choices as to jobs and where she could live. She found that her education was an excellent investment, as was her service experience. During her years in New York, she had become active in Democratic politics and enjoyed the precinct work. Perhaps it was inevitable that Irene would again end up in Washington, D.C., where she accepted a position as a public policy analyst and has worked ever since.

As one who used her GI Bill and also her home loan guaranty entitlement, Irene was very much aware of her veteran's status. As a federal employee, she enjoyed veteran's preference, which puts her in the second least vulnerable group when reductions in force (RIFs) occur.

Yet Irene has never been motivated to join a veterans' organization. She said she did not feel that she or other women would be welcome in the traditional veterans' organizations, nor did she feel that she could identify with their goals. In fact, one of the most painful realities for her has been that veterans as a whole have not learned from the history of wars that using force is not a solution of political problems. She laments that veterans, who have been close to war, have not been as passionate or motivated to work actively to avoid the conditions that lead to war.

While she regrets that there is no overall women veterans' organization, she feels that, with so few women scattered all over the country, it probably is not feasible. However, if there *were* such a group, she probably would join. She has maintained her friendships over the years and considers them one of the fringe benefits of her service in WAVES.

Would she have gone on to graduate school if it hadn't been for her war service? That is a question she has pondered. Participating in the war stirred her desire for knowledge and understanding of national policies and how these lead to war.

One thing of which Irene is certain is that the discipline that she learned in WAVES has been useful to her all her life. When you can't fall asleep on a watch because a boatful of men depended on your accuracy and attention, you rise to the occasion. The knowledge that there are life-or-death situations that may depend on the quality and integrity of your performance is a compelling one. Women are not often in that kind of position. Too often, particularly if women are married and are being supported, they do not give full commitment to their jobs or to volunteer work.

According to Irene, the main lesson she got from WAVES is this: that if women are to have careers, they must be willing to assume positions of responsibility. If they are to aspire to sharing power with men, they must make a total commitment to what they are doing. This may mean putting up with a great deal of nonsense; it may mean being obedient, even subservient, in the beginning. It may mean going through the same process as men do when they build careers. In any case full commitment and dedication is necessary. Irene learned these truths from being in the WAVES.

• YVONNE •

In Yvonne's* day women flyers such as Amelia Earhart and Jacqueline Cochran were turning the aviation world upside down. Aviation had been a male province, but women were making their mark in it. Those pioneer flying women had a lot of fans. Among them were women who in their wildest dreams had no hope of flying, but they soared in their imagination with the stupendous Earhart, the fabulous Cochran.

One of their fans was Yvonne's mother. She was a Danish woman of peasant stock who worked hard all her life caring for her husband and thirteen children. They lived in a small town in New Jersey and had slim resources.

When World War II broke out, two of the sons went off to war—the eleventh and the thirteenth. Yvonne was the twelfth child and she wanted to fly.

She had listened to her mother voice admiration for the women aviators and she had wondered at her mother's admiration for them. She soon developed a wonder and a thirst of her own.

*Yvonne "Pat" Pateman

Aviation was frequently in the newspaper in her formative years. There was wrong-way Corrigan, and others who were taking to the skies and making life on earth seem mundane. Yvonne took her first airplane ride when she was in her teens. It had an incredible impact on her. She knew that someday she was going to be a flyer.

Yvonne thought that if she had been born rich she surely would have been a flyer. However, she knew that Jacqueline Cochran had been born poor like herself, and somehow through sheer willpower and determination had become a top flyer. She even had her own cosmetic business; hers was a rare fairy tale of success. For every Jacqueline Cochran, there were thousands of Yvonnes who aspired to spread their wings and glide like Icarus.

In early 1942 stories appeared of the several attempts to mobilize women to ferry planes from factories to their debarkation points to Europe. America was sending fighters and bombers to help Britain repel the Nazi onslaught. The draft was on. All able-bodied young men between the ages of eighteen and thirty-five who had not already volunteered were reporting to local draft boards. At the onset of America's involvement in the war, there were 1,810,101 men on active duty with the armed forces. By early 1945, 12,124,418 were in uniform, with a constant stream passing from recruitment centers and draft boards through basic training camps to overseas or domestic units.

As men filtered into the armed services, a vacuum of essential labor was created in the weapons making and scientific and technical industries supplying the war effort. America's women were called upon to fill the vacuum . . . and they answered their nation's call willingly and enthusiastically. The film "Rosie the Riveter" is a tribute to the variety of tasks women took over. Nobody questioned whether they could do it. The jobs had to be done, and there were no other individuals to do them.

Against this background Yvonne saw two of her brothers go off to war. She read about the women's air-ferrying service that Jacqueline Cochran was forming. She knew she wanted to fly, and saved up her money and took two hours of flying lessons at nearby airfields. Then she called Cochran and asked her if she could go to Sweetwater, Texas, the service's headquarters, and work and learn how to fly. On meeting Cochran in New York City, Yvonne was told she had to acquire seventy-five flying hours in order to be eligible for the program. Shortly thereafter, Yvonne began to pursue flying lessons with fervor. After much hardship and under a severe time restraint, she accumulated her seventy-five hours.

Cognizant of the young aspirant's lack of money, Cochran offered Yvonne the opportunity to drive down to Sweetwater with another person. Tempting as this offer was, Yvonne could not accept it—she didn't know how to drive! If they found this out, they wouldn't accept her into the WASP, for wasn't flying the next step after driving? So her mother borrowed a hundred dollars from a brother to pay Yvonne's train fare to Sweetwater.

The rest of the family was not that supportive. Her father and brothers couldn't understand the young woman's desire to fly or to join the women's ferrying service. But her mother backed her all the way, standing up for her daughter's wishes before her husband and sons. In their minds, women just got married and raised children.

* * *

"Yvonne is going to do something with her life," the mother told the males in her family, "she is going to do more than be married and have babies," her mother insisted. This daughter was going to have the chance to do something, to be somebody. Her mother, strong and confident, stood up to all the negative voices. It was Yvonne's mother, whose belief gave Yvonne the strength to do this unconventional thing, to aspire to fly and to earn her living as a flyer, who provided the fortitude to overcome the many obstacles that lay in the path to flying. Yvonne remembers her mother's pride when she went off into the wide blue yonder, and that pride became a constant source of courage. Through all her years of flying, Yvonne has been aware of her mother's confidence in her and the aspirations for her for a different kind of life than her mother had had. She was always an inspiration to Yvonne whenever she was flying.

Once at Sweetwater, Yvonne wanted to spare her mother worry, and so she did not send home newsletters that contained stories of fatal accidents and crashes of some of the women in training. Only later, after Yvonne had finished her training, did her mother find old newsletters and discover the dangerous nature of the vocation her daughter had chosen. Yvonne reassured her mother that she would be cautious, that she would never overestimate herself or her craft. She believes she convinced her mother who thereafter was calm and confident. Her mother died soon after— on the day Yvonne left to go to her next station. Yvonne conjectures that her mother was probably ill and did not tell anyone. She was only sixty-three.

Yvonne served with the gallant group of just over a thousand women in the WASP. Although they were trained by the Army, the WASPs were not officially part of the military; yet they lived at the Army base in Sweetwater and were subject to the Uniform Code of Military Justice.

Many WASP missions were extraordinarily dangerous. They ferried planes across the country, flew endless missions, and test flew new planes. They were also called upon to fly planes with targets so that troops could practice shooting at them. There were casualties, both during the training and in the course of their ferrying planes.

Although WASPs had been promised military status and had military-type uniforms, they actually never were granted that status. A complicated political dilemma arose after legislation was introduced. Advocates of the WASPs abandoned their effort when the male pilots came home from their missions without flying assignments. These pilots accused the WASPs of usurping flying jobs. Consequently the WASPs were *not* given military status and therefore its members were not eligible for any veterans' benefits, including burial benefits. Finally, in 1978—more than thirty years after the war had ended—Congress corrected this miscarriage of justice after an intense campaign by the women themselves and their supporters, including General Bruce Arnold, the son of their mentor during the 1943–44 period. When the WASPs finally gained veterans' status, most of the veterans' benefits had expired.

Flying had become a way of life for Yvonne. It was that way ever since she stepped into the cockpit of a plane and was lifted into the atmosphere. It was not only the sensation of flying, it was the people in aviation as well. There was a special bond among them, invisible, unique, and indissoluble. Pilots respected each other for the common danger and love of flying they shared. It didn't matter what else you did, where you came from, what you looked like, how much money you had—pilots felt a strong kinship for each other.

It was natural when the WASP was disbanded in December 1944—before the war was over and after it failed to get military status from Congress—that Yvonne would seek to stay in flying. Her mother was gone, and Yvonne's roots now were in the air. She went to California to look for work. If she couldn't get a flying job, she wanted at least to be near an airport. New Jersey was no longer home to her. However, until the end of the war there was no gas available for nonessential flying. Pilots could only get gas to fulfill the hours required for their professional licenses to be renewed.

Yvonne opened a cafe near the airport at Monrovia, California, and sold hamburgers for several months. She also worked in the aircraft industry. There were no flying jobs for women. The male pilots who were demobilized in 1945 filled the few flying jobs that were available. Then starting in 1946 the aircraft industry boomed. American aviation came of age after the war, and factories were turning out civilian planes for commercial use and for business and corporate purposes. There was again a need for ferry pilots.

Yvonne was among the sixty or seventy women who got jobs delivering planes. Men didn't take those jobs because the pay was not good. But for women aviators who were single the low pay was enough. Yvonne was in heaven—she was flying again.

Then in 1949 the aircraft industry took a dive. No one was buying planes, so factories closed or became involved with building rockets. There was no more need for ferrying planes. Yvonne and the other women pilots found themselves out of jobs, so she reopened her cafe near the airport and flew on the side to keep her license current. Finally she got a job at the Culver City airport teaching flying, and soon became the airport's chief instructor.

Although the WASP was not militarized, the women who had served were offered reserve commissions in 1948 in the Army Air Force. Yvonne was one of the women who accepted the reserve commission, though she didn't ever expect to fly in the military. All a commission meant was attending a meeting once a week. There was no pay, but there was camaraderie and a place in the military.

Then came Korea. America, with only a peacetime military force, suddenly found herself needing troops. The reservists were called up. Ironically, it was the reservists who were on pay rosters who were used to call up all the unpaid reservists. Yvonne—pilot, ferrier, entrepreneur—was called to active military duty as a lieutenant in the Army Air Force when she didn't expect it. She didn't go to Korea, but to the Philippines, Japan and Alaska. Women were not permitted to fly for the Air Force. Instead she was placed in Intelligence and became a specialist in the Far East. When the Korean war was over, she decided to continue in the Air Force. Since the Culver City airport had closed, there was no job there waiting for her, and she didn't believe there were any more flying jobs for women on the civilian side. Besides, she could fly while she was in the Air Force, and during off-duty hours she could be a flying instructor—something she had done during the Korean War.

When Yvonne signed up, it was for an indefinite amount of time; otherwise she would have been released. She hadn't planned a military career or to become an intelligence expert. If it hadn't been for the Korean War, she might never have been called up.

Yvonne thought about what she would face if she left. She would have no job and no place to live. She'd even sold her car. What was there to go back to? Where? She had no college degree. The Air Force, by training her in intelligence and giving her a specialty, had provided her with a career, status, and responsibility. Thus she stayed in service and rose to the rank of lieutenant colonel and became head of her unit. Later, still while in service, she received her B.A. degree.

There didn't seem to be another choice for Yvonne. In the Air Force she was treated equally; she felt that her talents would earn her a position she was qualified for. Weighing what the outside world would offer her, Yvonne knew she chose right. Without a college degree she couldn't possibly get equivalent work of the same responsibility, and she'd certainly earn less. The employment market was not crying for women. Many women had been forced to leave their jobs and return to their homes and child-rearing after the men came home. Women with Ph.D.'s who had been called into defense industries and into the universities to teach were being turned away. What place was there for her in civilian life?

Yvonne never regretted her decision. She continued to fly off-duty, to teach flying when opportunities arose, and to have a demanding, interesting career in which her abilities and intelligence were appreciated. As a captain, she was assumed to have the leadership and intellectual qualities to do the job; in the civilian world, without a degree or experience, it would have been an upward climb to prove herself. And who knows whether she would even be given the chance.

Yvonne spent some time in Vietnam in intelligence before she was released in 1971. She would have liked to have stayed, but the service was letting officers with twenty years of service go to make room for others. Now she is retired, is busy writing, and is engaged in various community projects. And she is still flying.

Yvonne is a military retiree, not just a veteran. Therefore she gets the benefits that retired personnel get, as well as veterans' benefits. She also gets CHAMPUS. Except for the purchase of a home with a VA loan, she hasn't used her other VA benefits.

•NANCY•

Life must be more than going to Foley Square (New York City) everyday. So Nancy thought during the height of World War II, and she decided to do something about it. Recruitment posters for women were everywhere; Nancy's brothers were already in the service. Born and raised in Brooklyn, she was in fact working for the FBI, an agency considered close to the military establishment.

Nancy first tried the WAVES, but by 1944 that service was looking for highly specialized women who were engineers, psychiatrists, etc. Nancy had spent some time at Brooklyn College but did not finish. Her next call was at the Coast Guard; New York was a Coast Guard town and New Yorkers were very aware of it.

Her father, a fire chief in Brooklyn, wasn't thrilled at Nancy's decision since two of his four children were already in the service, but he went along with it. Her mother was very supportive; she thought it would have a stabilizing effect upon her only daughter who had not as yet shown any direction. The youngest boy was to join also, so there were to be two in the Navy and two in the Coast Guard.

The Coast Guard was the only service which sent women officers to its academy for training. Nancy was in the last Coast Guard OCS class for women reserve officers. It was a small service; altogether there were about ten thousand enlisted personnel and one thousand officers. Half of the officer candidates came from enlisted ranks. For someone like Nancy who came from a comfortable middle-class home, the seven-week training program was rigorous. She certainly hadn't been brought up to rise and shine at five-thirty in the morning. But she survived it and to this day feels that enlisting in the Coast Guard was the best decision of her life.

It was a small close-knit service. Strong friendships were easily made that lasted for decades. The SPARs have had reunions every five years and maintained contact through an informal network. After the war the Navy turned its jurisdiction of SPAR over to the Treasury, which was the original agency administering it. Today the Department of Transportation is the parent agency. For twenty-five years after the SPARs were demobilized there were very few women in the Coast Guard. There was no additional recruitment of women during those years.

The women in the Coast Guard were members of the Reserves; they were not regular Coast Guard. It wasn't until legislation was passed in 1973 that the Coast Guard women were integrated into the regular service. The first academy class for women officers began in 1976.

When World War II was over, the Coast Guard Women's Reserve Corps ended. The enlisted women and the officers were discharged. When asked if she wished to keep her commission, Nancy said yes. She wasn't sure what that meant, but it had been a positive experience so far. Then nothing happened. Two years later she was asked if she wanted to be an ensign in the Women's Reserve of the Coast Guard. Nancy had no trouble accepting. In 1951 she had a pay slot in a unit.

However, as a reserve officer she would have no command over men, only over women. In the Coast Guard Nancy spent every

Wednesday night with her reserve unit, and her summer vacations—at least two weeks of it—in Coast Guard training camp.
When she retired a few years ago, Nancy had reached the rank
of captain.

After basic training, she was assigned to intelligence, a logical
choice considering her FBI background. But women in the SPARs
did a variety of jobs, including being gunner's mates, parachute
riggers, etc. The only slots that were barred to women were those
that could only take place aboard ship, such as that of boiler-
maker. Otherwise women worked together with men, although
their schooling was always separate. In addition, Coast Guard
women were trained in a number of specialties with the WAVES.

All her experiences and associations with the Coast Guard were
positive. She used her GI Bill to get her B.A. at Brooklyn College
and an M.A. in education at Teachers College of Columbia University. Looking back, she wonders whether she would have gone
back to school at all if it hadn't been for the service. Before she
went into the service, she didn't have any particular aspirations.
When she left the service, she wasn't sure what she was going to
do. She assumed that, like most of her peers, she would get
married and raise a family.

First she tried her hand at learning secretarial skills at Columbia's School of General Studies and also took courses in Spanish.
After that she turned her education toward teaching, although
she had never shown interest in it before. Her mother was a
teacher, and there were lots of teachers in their extended family.
Teaching was a well paid and respected profession. It seemed like
a logical course of action. She went on to a full career in teaching—first in Harlem, then in Brooklyn, and then in Great Neck
where she taught junior high school until she retired.

Some years after beginning teaching, Nancy got married. Her
husband was a veteran but he resented the Coast Guard phase
of her life—the Wednesday evenings, the two weeks on active
duty. He wasn't a part of that and felt left out. Nancy concluded
he probably would have resented any other aspect of her life. The
marriage did not last.

The Coast Guard experience broadened Nancy's life and out-
look. Over the years, she has been active in community affairs,
in her labor union, and in many other organizations. She is not

one to sit back and let things happen. She was appointed to DACOWITS (the Defense Advisory Committee on Women in the Service) by President Jimmy Carter in 1978.

Nancy lived abroad during her sabbatical. As a retired military officer eligible for available space on military planes, she has traveled extensively, particularly since her retirement from teaching. Most recently, she went to Australia and found that as a veteran of World War II, she was a heroine to the Aussies. It was a nice feeling to be an American abroad and to be adulated.

•LILA•

Perhaps it is the glasses or the intensity of her gaze; Lila looks like she just stepped out of the laboratory or the classroom. The study of medicine was a passion in Lila that was thwarted by the narrowness of the prejudiced. At an early age she learned to seek other outlets for her intelligence. She found these in allied medical fields in which she excelled through work in the Navy. Friendship is important to her, and she has an extended family of friends she nurtures. She is the bustling organizer, one everyone turns to to get things started or to follow through. The Navy connection has been an anchor in her life.

The dean of Lila's college was puzzled when he had to sign Lila's sheepskin: a major in psychology and a minor in aeronautical engineering. That didn't make any sense at all. So he looked at her record but saw that it was true. It was confusing, but she received her degree.

This was in 1947 after twelve months of steady course work as a World War II veteran on the GI Bill. Shortly before that, Lila had taken and passed the test to be a licensed pharmacist. It was also in 1947 that Lila joined the Women's Reserves of the Navy. It was offered to her as to all other enlisted women who had served well in the WAVES during World War II.

Lila was not with the WAVES in the beginning. First, she had a stint in the field of aeronautical engineering. She was at the University of Cincinnati on a scholarship when she was recommended for a six-month training course in aeronautical engineering that the Goodyear Company was providing for select candidates. She lasted three months in the program and left out of boredom. She also felt she wasn't contributing much. She later received those credits in aeronautical engineering in college.

When Lila went back to Chicago after the Goodyear experiment in Akron, she found that her father had taken ill. As an only child she was very close to her parents. Lila felt compelled to stay in the Chicago area where she had grown up. The war was in full force by then, and she mulled over what to do next.

As a child she had dreamed of being a surgeon. She was drawn to medicine and wanted to heal people. But it was apparent that her parents, with limited means, were in no position to support a medical education. There was no question she had to give up the idea of becoming a doctor. She had taken all the science courses her high school had to offer. The next best thing was to be in laboratory work associated with medicine.

Her parents were of European background and were fiercely patriotic. Many of Lila's relatives were, too, and some uncles had gone to war. There were stories she heard during her childhood about uncles who had been gassed during World War I. Winning the war was terribly important; it was dominating the lives of most Americans at that time. In Lila's family it was a personal cause.

It was then logical that Lila should decide to join the WAVES, the women's reserve unit of the Navy, whose largest training base, the Great Lakes Training Station, was in Chicago. She signed up with the expectation that she would be assigned to Great Lakes, and she would be near her parents. She also hoped to get into hospital work that would lead her eventually to working in a laboratory, which was her long-range goal.

Lila primarily wanted to do something meaningful for the war effort. Everything she had heard and read about the WAVES and the training they gave their young women matched her ideal of contributing to the war effort, and also starting on a medically oriented career. She was not disappointed. As an apprentice seaman, she went to Hunter College for her boot camp training, and was launched in what was to be a rewarding career doing exactly what she had hoped to do—to be part of the healing profession.

From Hunter College, Lila was sent to the Bethesda Hospital Corps School where she was trained in a variety of hospital-related areas: in lab work, blood chemistry, and some nursing and medical skills. She came out of school as a Hospital Apprentice First Class. Lila was good at what she did; she was hardworking and courageous.

Her first assignment after Bethesda Hospital Corps School was at the Arlington Farms Dispensary in Virginia, which provided medical services for the WAVES in the Washington, D.C., area. Because the WAVES were being employed at the naval communications and administrative systems at the Naval Headquarters in Washington, D.C., the latter had a large contingent of WAVES personnel. Lila enjoyed her work enormously: hers was a choice billet.

Then Lila's father died. While she knew her mother was resourceful and social, she wanted to be near her. At the suggestion of a warrant officer, she applied for a transfer to Great Lakes, a far less desirable post than where she was. The transfer was approved, and Lila found herself back in Chicago.

Because of her excellent record, high grades, and enthusiasm, she was placed in charge of the pharmacy for the dependents of naval personnel at the Great Lakes Training Center. This position involved considerable responsibility—she was her own boss on a day-to-day basis and reported only to the captain. She was the only female among the pharmacists; she had regular hours; she finished work at four-thirty. She remained in this job until she was discharged in 1946. There was every reason then to accept a post in the reserves when it came up in 1946. She knew she loved the Navy and wanted to stay a part of it.

Peacetime for Lila meant going to school, getting her B.S., working as a placement counselor, and attending her reserve training once a month on a voluntary basis. This time being in the Navy reserve even included going on board ships, which was fun. When they opened the reserve program and began to drill women, she volunteered for a paid billet. This made her feel a stronger connection with the Navy, even though the pay wasn't much.

Reservists were called for the Korean conflict in 1950. As a reservist, Lila was called up and was happy to go as a First Class Pharmacist's Mate assigned to Great Lakes. This was her second stint on active duty and it was as successful as her first.

Fully trained herself, she was assigned to train others. She became an instructor for the hospital corps. This was the first time that an instructor was appointed who was not from the nursing staff. Lila took to teaching and enjoyed the contact with the corpsmen and -women, who went overseas soon after training. Her chief regret was that the information filtering back from Korea indicated that most of the casualties were corps personnel—men and women who had been her students.

Peacetime returned and Lila returned to the employment counseling career she had begun, this time in the medical field. She began taking courses again, this time in subjects she knew little about; in particular, public relations and the mass media fascinated her. She probably would have kept on taking assorted classes if the VA had not pressured her to have an educational goal.

Lila looked around and found a department she thought she would enjoy and to which she could make a contribution—the Committee on Communication. She worked out a program with them for an M.A. This made things okay with the VA, and Lila came up with a thesis idea: "Navy Recruiting and Retention." This was approved by her department, the Navy gave her carte blanche to use any material she wanted, and Lila began collecting data. After she had finished her research for the degree, the Navy changed signals and wrote her that she couldn't use any of the figures unless those who were going to see them had security clearances. This was probably the only time Lila can think of that the Navy fouled her up.

This left Lila out in the cold—no one in the department had a clearance. This was the end of her thesis and that degree. By that time the department had gone out of existence, and she wasn't about to begin a new program of courses and research.

Lila continued her work in the employment counseling field and, of course, her activities as a reservist. Someone suggested she apply for a commission, which she did. In 1956 she was granted a commission as a lieutenant j.g. in the reserves. From then on promotions occurred regularly so that in 1975 she became a captain.

From 1960 on Lila accepted some short-term active duty assignments, which she squeezed into summer vacations and in between clients. By this time she was in her own consulting business. As a reservist she could refuse orders when it was inconvenient. She had unusual opportunities offered to her, including one working in the Office of the Secretary of Defense. Lila is approaching her retirement as an officer, but this doesn't mean she will sever her connection with the Navy.

Because of the various fields she was in, Lila often found herself to be the only woman on assignment or the first woman to have done something. While she had little to complain about in regard to the treatment she received in the Navy, she is the first to admit that there were many commanding officers who couldn't abide women working on their staffs. She can recall staff meetings in which women were left out. The old boy network was there, but, happily, the young women's network is beginning, she says.

On reflecting how military service affected her life, Lila is simple and direct. She can't imagine living her life without the Navy. The experience exposed her to things that as a civilian she would never have encountered. It contributed to her growth in ways that were not possible if she had stayed at home in Chicago. The service changed her educational and career goals, providing opportunities for skills training and helping her discover her own abilities.

One aspect of the naval career she feel most positive about was the new social growth she experienced. She couldn't have found a finer group of women to serve with. The friendships she made during her tours and reserve training have been constant and enriching. She and her colleagues—particularly those who served with her for long periods of time in the same unit—have a bond of sharing that is indissoluble. One often hears of the strong bond that men have with their units in service, especially if they have been in combat. Lila and her sister hospital corps mates had similar, long-lasting friendships.

When there is a draft the only true volunteers are women, Lila says. Lila is an example of an individual whose military experience formed the framework for the rest of her life. Not only was she able to pursue a career that suited her, she was able to engage in more than one calling. The GI Bill was invaluable to her in furthering her education and permitting her to explore more than one occupational field.

Lila does think of herself as a veteran. While she has not joined some of the larger veterans' organizations, she did join the Navy Clubs of America when she first enlisted in 1946. Later on she became active in the predominantly male Naval Reserve Association. She served as an officer in that organization, then as national vice-president for women. Her recommendation that they didn't need a separate officer for women led to the organization finally eliminating this category.

A woman who always felt equal with men, Lila was insulted when she flew across the country for an NRA convention only to find that it was held at a men's athletic club that barred entry to women. Lila let her ire be known; since then, this kind of exclusion has not occurred again. More women are joining it now and are beginning to play more active roles.

• FREDDIE •

She is slight, intense—with a gentle manner that makes the stranger completely at ease. Her large eyes search for the facts of every situation. We sat in a crowded restaurant recalling her military career, which continued until her recent retirement as an Army Captain reservist. Only her precision of speech reveals the military background; it is marked by her midwestern twang. Always the reporter, searching for the what, the how, and the why, she takes in her environment with ease and curiosity.

Freddie's* childhood dream was to be a reporter in a newsroom. She had her first essay printed in the local newspaper when she

*Freddie Boyle

was thirteen and had written for student newspapers throughout school. After college, in good faith, she applied for a job as a reporter, which she was eminently qualified to be with her talent and passion for journalism. This was when the rude awakening set in—that she was born into the wrong sex. There were no openings for her. Opportunities for women in the newspaper business were almost nonexistent.

Freddie was born and spent most of her formative years in Ohio, where she got her B.A. from Marietta College in Marietta, Ohio. For some years she lived in Kansas, where her father was in the oil and gas contracting business. Soon after college, and her disappointment in not finding work on a newspaper, she went to Washington, D.C., to continue her schooling at George Washington University.

World War II was in full swing. She found employment as a Public Information Specialist with the federal government. While this was not newspaper reporting, at least she was writing, even if they were only radio scripts. As the recruiting campaign for women to join the military services stepped up, Freddie thought she would like to take part in the war effort. She signed up in the WAC. She was single, free, and adventuresome. Why not?

Her leadership qualities were soon recognized, and Freddie was sent to OCS and then to advanced OCS. One of the things she learned was that the officer's only excuse for existence was the welfare of the enlisted women under her. That lesson made a deep impression upon her and inculcated a sense of responsibility that stayed with her throughout her life.

One of her hopes in joining the Army was that she would go overseas. The WACs were the only branch that could be sent abroad. But she didn't get the chance as she continued to serve in public relations, recruiting, and public information. It wasn't until after she left the Army as a captain in 1945 that she did get to go abroad.

The Nuremberg War Crimes Trials were taking place, and the Army was looking for Public Affairs specialists. Freddie's Army background helped her, she was sure, in getting the job. For twenty months she covered the trials for the Army as a civilian and published numerous articles for the European edition of *Stars and Stripes*. This was one of the most rewarding professional assignments she ever had and the turning point in her career. Now she had the experience and the writing samples to help break into the newspaper business.

The editor of the *Hartford Times* was impressed by Freddie's Army credentials—she was a captain—and by her experience at Nuremberg. He took her on as society editor, making it completely plain that there was no way for her to use that position as an entrée to the newsroom. He was never going to hire a woman in that capacity. Some time earlier this editor had hired a woman reporter who later tried to unionize the paper. He never forgot that and would not hire a woman again as a reporter. Freddie found out that if one woman did something they didn't like, they didn't want any more women. If a man did something they didn't like, on the other hand, they didn't vow never to hire another man. Freddie learned one of life's lessons on that job. Deep down, of course, she wanted to move beyond the society page, but she was confined to such trivia for the time being.

Getting the story and finding out the facts was deeply ingrained in Freddie's nature. She always wanted to probe what was going on, what really happened, because she was a newspaper person to the core. She was never satisfied with shortcuts, a credit to the profession that had spurned her initially.

When she was hired by the *Camden Courier Post*, some years later, she mostly did rewriting, but also acquired a taste for more general writing. Shortly after that she went to the *Philadelphia Bulletin*, where she served as a roving reporter and covered all kinds of stories and situations.

Returning to Washington, D.C., in the mid-seventies, Freddie had another interesting stint doing free-lance stories on national disasters. This was another assignment she believes she would not have gotten without her Army past. After her years in journalism, Freddie turned her talents to real estate. Freddie continues her hand at public relations and free-lance writing, as the spirit moves her, but she doesn't depend on that for her income.

Freddie is extremely proud of being a veteran and identifies strongly with other veterans. Staying in the Reserves, she retired after twenty years as a major and has been enjoying the benefits of that military retirement. She was recalled during Korea and served again in public relations from 1951–1953. An active member of the American Legion, she was the first woman elected as the Commander of the National Press Club Chapter of the Legion.

An ardent feminist, Freddie volunteers and works hard for women's rights—for ERA and for all the legislation and policy initiatives to grant equity to women. She knows what it is to be penalized on account of sex and wants to see changes so that young women do not have to deny their innermost being because of their anatomy. For Freddie, military service was the magic door that let her into the world where she belonged.

•ALICE, JUNE, FLORENCE•

We sat in the basement of an American Legion hall in Nassau County, Long Island. The members of this all-women's post welcomed this stranger into their midst, anxious to talk about themselves as veterans. They found out a lot about themselves, and about each other's 'war' experiences; they had never talked this way before. June, warm, gregarious, and outgoing, had arranged the meeting—and was anxious for the evening to be a success. Alice, the nurse, brusk and efficient, direct and generous. Florence, the New England matriarch, incredibly bouncy and youthful for her 80 years. Also a veteran from a later war, Edith who radiated a strong sense of self, was with us. A few months later, on a warm summer's evening, we met again in Florence's living room. We could have talked for hours more, discovering new information and insights about the women who served . . . I felt privileged— they had let me share their memories.

•ALICE•

A daughter from a large coal-mining family, Alice studied nursing to break out of her narrow environment. When World War

II broke out, she was working away from home. It was the most natural thing in the world for her to sign up. There was an acute need for nurses, particularly those with some experience. She was grabbed up by the Army Nurse Corps, and was given a commission.

There was not too much enthusiasm from her parents because one of her sisters already was a WAAC and a brother was in the Navy. But Alice wanted to do something different, and she wanted some new experiences. Joining the Army Nurse Corps was a golden opportunity for her to do just that, as well as to contribute to the war effort. She was strongly patriotic and convinced about the rightness of America's involvement. It was a privilege to take care of the boys who were getting hurt in order to stop the Nazi scourge. She saw service overseas in England, France and Germany, attached to the 81st Field Hospital.

Military service was a high point of her life. She met her husband while she was in service. He was an enlisted man; she was an officer. That kind of fraternization was frowned upon, but love won out. She got married and she was then discharged; this was compulsory. She has raised a family and has also resumed her nursing career. Now a widow with her children grown, Alice is even more certain that her military service did well by her. She feels she learned a great self-discipline that has been useful to her in all her later pursuits. Besides, she came in contact with people she never would have before. And she was one of the lucky ones who got overseas.

•JUNE•

A traumatic experience has been a well-known reason to prompt men to join the Foreign Legion. There were certainly enough movies to mold such a myth. Disappointment and despair have been known to motivate young men to enlist, and also young women.

A deep personal loss was the immediate reason for June's* signing up in 1944 in the U.S. Marine Corps. She needed to do

*June Donahue

something radically different from what she had been doing; to get away from the environment which was associated with her loss. Besides, she was an adventurous young lady who had a mind to see a little bit of the rest of the world. She had never been away from home, New York City, and she wanted to find out what it was about out there beyond. Here was a chance for her to find out about other people, to learn other things which there was no way of her learning where she was.

June had been doing clerical/secretarial work with the telephone company when she joined the Marines to do her part for the war effort. But there was no way that she wanted to do office work in the Marine Corps; that is not why she joined the Marines. When she filled out the papers, June did not tell them that she had any office skills; she wanted almost anything else.

June could drive—which was rare in those days for a young city woman, so they put her in the motor pool. This was much to her liking since it brought her in contact with all different kinds of people, including high-ranking officers. Her time in the Marine Corps was a spirited and exciting period in her life. It gave her the new contacts she yearned for. It opened up a world she had never seen and her life touched lives of others who would have been remote, history-book figures.

While June does not think of herself as a pioneer particularly, she was the only one in her group to join up. Her family was surprised but they supported her in what she wanted to do. They always did. Her sister was a nurse, and her grandfather had been a veteran. Her friends' husbands are veterans, while they themselves are not. While she didn't meet her husband in service, he also served. They had mutual friends and they were bound to meet sooner or later. She has raised a family—two children, and has resumed her work part-time at the telephone company.

But June was never the same after her military experience. She would make an excellent recruiter, she is so positive about the values of joining the service. Girls have such opportunities today, she feels, way beyond the very limited ones that were presented to her and her fellow Marine women. She marvels that they can learn so many skills, they can enter so many new fields and go to so many places around the world.

No doubt if June had entered service as a member of this

generation, she would have been an MP outside an American Embassy in the Middle East or a volunteer for the space program. Military service, she feels, is a way to get beyond your upbringing, to stretch your perspective, to find out about the larger world. It was for her. She is a woman veteran who is persuaded that all young women should take advantage of the military experience.

•FLORENCE•

Those "damn Yankees" are always likely to do something different. Florence,* born in New Hampshire and raised in Vermont, developed those strong resourceful traits that have grown to be identified as New England's special contribution to the American character. At the age of 42, with two sons in the Marines, Florence enlisted in the WAC. The year was 1944. The reason she joined the WAC and not another service was that it was the only one that would take a warm body up to 50 years.

Why does a mother of three with two sons already in service sign up? Her family had a tradition of giving its sons for military service, and now the country was screaming for women to help in the war effort. They desperately needed nurses. Although Florence was not a nurse, she always wanted to be one. When she was a housewife-mother raising her kids, she was also the neighborhood "home nurse," the one the neighbors called upon when Johnny broke his arm or Janie bloodied her nose.

Florence was just recently separated from her husband. It had been a gloomy marriage, with her husband an invalid a good part of their 27 years of marriage. Her mother had died when she was 10. She had married to get away from her stepmother's home at the age of 18, as so many girls did in times past. Florence's character was molded from her mother who had been college educated and was a strong, independent person who had no doubts about her equality. The stepmother was of another vintage, and life had become miserable for Florence. Marriage was the only way she knew to make the break.

Despite the problems of the marriage, Florence bore and raised

*Florence Picard

three children. As she reminds us, if a mother left a marriage in those days, she would lose her children, and Florence was not going to do that. So she stuck it out until her husband found another woman who he felt would be better for him. For Florence, this was a tremendous relief and gave her the opportunity to be her own person.

During these many years, she supported herself and the family as a worker in the needle trade. When she was filling out the application in the Army recruiter's station, she asked for Medical Service. Not knowing what to do with an accomplished needle-trade worker who wanted to go into the Medical Corps, they put her down for orthopedic appliances. Of course, after she finished her basic training, they still didn't know what to do with her, so she was placed in an orthopedic ward.

It was just like being back on the block for her. She became "Ma" or "Pete" (her married name then was Petersen) to the boys, and those boys became her boys. It wasn't long before she became a Wardmaster. If she had her way she would have gone overseas. But the war ended before Florence got to Australia which had been her dream.

Her service experience was invaluable to her, Florence believes. Though her character and personality were pretty much formed, the service gave her an opportunity to get on her own feet after a long, unhappy marriage and separation. In a sense, Florence found herself during those three years in the Army. Besides, it gave her great pride and satisfaction to continue her family tradition and serve her country. She was also able to realize her life ambition, to be in the medical field. If she wasn't a nurse, she was the closest thing to it, and she knew her presence on the wards meant a great deal to the guys who passed through them. They made a difference to her too. She could fulfill a strong part of herself that had not had the opportunity to emerge or blossom. She was never the same again after her years in the WAC.

A fringe benefit was that she found a new husband while she was in service. He was a cook and had a similar New England background to hers. This marriage was a very happy one, and lasted 22 years till he died. Now Florence is in business with her daughter—at the age of 80!

•HARRIET•

When the invitation came to join the first officers class for the WAVES, Harriet applied. To meet the requirements she added another year to her birthdate. To be accepted was a great honor, for this was an elite group of women chosen to be in the first WAVES officers class. One had to be a college graduate or to have had at least two years of college.

Harriet was a leader; she had been president of her student class in college. She had been fine-tuned to leadership by the circumstances of her life. Raised by her mother who was deaf, Harriet had learned to be her mother's ears; to interpret what was going on for her. Harriet majored in broadcasting when she was in college. Even before she got out of college, she received some professional broadcasting experience since many men had already left their jobs and gone to war.

The first class of WAVE officers went to Hunter College, New York, for training. The purpose of having women in the Navy was to release men for shipboard duty. No WAVES, officers or enlisted, were allowed on board vessels or out of the country. In the first few months of the WAVES, the women did not have uniforms. They were not the first women to serve in the Navy. Back in World War I, the Navy had 10,000 women as Yeoman-ettes.

Most of the women from that first class were sent to Washington, D.C., where they were assigned to communications and operation of the code room. That was highly important work, where their precision and accuracy were essential for the lives of the men at sea. Harriet recalls the great pride in what they were doing for the war effort.

The WAVES had an easy berth in Washington; they could live where they wished. Washington had become a city of women during the World War II years—and many of them were in uniform. Harriet lived in a group house in Chevy Chase during most of the thirty months she was there; that was before group houses were known. That kind of communal living was a rare and exciting experience for her, one that demanded responsibility and consideration and managing of a household.

After a stint in the code room, her background and talents were recognized and she was put into the Public Relations Section. She interviewed local people who came back from the fleet—on radio. Anything that went on the air related to the Navy came through her office. There were journalists and editors, and filmmakers seeking information about what the Navy was doing and what it was thinking. Harriet was at the center of that universe; she met dozens of interesting media people of the day, some of whom were to become famous later; David Brinkley was one of them.

Another important experience came her way. For about a year she worked on the "Daily Digest," which served a similar purpose as the Gallup Poll. Her job, together with one colleague, was to go through 50 or 60 local newspapers and scan the editorial pages to find out how the public was perceiving the Navy role in the war effort. If there was an unfavorable editorial, the Secretary of the Navy wanted to know about it. It was felt that a bad press was bad for morale, both for recruitment and retention. The Navy was very sensitive about the public's perception that it wasn't treating the boys "right." Harriet recalls that in those days nobody worried much about treating our girls "right."

Harriet had another career experience in the Navy that was to serve well later on. As the war phased down, she was an "Educational Services" counselor. With demobilization in the offing, the Navy command, at the behest of the government, was giving some thought to what was going to happen to all the young women that would be sent out into civilian society. While Washington had been concerned about the demobilization of the millions of men, the relatively small number of women had not been taken into account. Although the GI Bill was going to be available, there was no way of knowing how many enlisted women were going to use it and go on for college degrees.

It was expected that many women would get married and raise families. Many were already married. But because of the large numbers of casualties, and because some of the women were still very young, there was bound to be a glut on the job market of young women veterans who might be competing for the same jobs as the men. After all, many women had learned the same skills that men had and performed well.

Employers were required to take them back after their military service during the war. However, most of the women did not have jobs to go back to, or if they did, they were low-paying jobs. After the military experience with new skills, women were not going to be content with what they had before.

Yet very little thought had been given to this kind of post-war manpower situation as it pertained to women. Harriet was recruited to bring all her skills, intelligence, and resourcefulness into play to help meet the challenge. She conceived and implemented a program that would bring in industry's representatives and company executives to Washington to interest them in what these young women veterans might have to offer to their companies. She may have set up the first Job Fair, or at least the prototype of the Job Fair, which became an extremely popular device for matching the private job sector with potential applicants.

Besides employers, she brought in the trade associations, the business schools, journalists and other media people. Her aim was to provide information for the young women being demobilized, most of whom had only high school educations, about the employment market for them. Some would choose to beef up business skills they already had; others took other directions.

Harriet put it very well about the women coming out of the military experience of World War II: "No one wanted to shuffle back to the broom closet." Of course, a lot did. Many married the beaux they were fortunate enough to come back to. Those that were married took on the traditional role of wife and mother. The early post-war years saw the baby boom burst on the American scene.

But those who didn't marry immediately had had their expectations raised. Some took advantage of the GI Bill. How many, no one knows. No one will ever know, because the VA did not keep statistics on the use of the GI Bill by women.

Unhappily, Harriet's pioneer program was never followed up, so there is no data on how many of the women got jobs or were put on career tracks through her program. The women in the defense industries and the other support industries were replaced by the men who had left those jobs vacant to fight. They and their military sisters did return to the broom closet. But women had achieved equal pay for equal work. They had also acquired the taste for responsibility and for doing important work which they would not forget.

Military service left its mark on everyone who experienced it, including women. Harriet recalls the eight-mile marches while at Smith College, no matter what the weather. She recalls the flat oxfords, the lisle stockings, the mittens and galoshes. One could never be out of uniform; one didn't put on an exercise suit or jog. This was not being female in the way she was used to.

There were a lot of things taken for granted that were given up when the women donned their uniforms. Harriet recounted how you had to roll out at 6 A.M., no matter how you felt; others depended on you. There were heavy responsibilities, and lives were always at stake. Harriet had to learn how to land on her feet under incredible circumstances. Always there was the discipline and the training which became ingrained in the women and benefited them in the years to come. The responsibilities they carried matured them quickly. Harriet recalls many instances where that kind of training helped her deal with complex, frustrating situations years later. She could recall the long hours of standing watches that toughened her.

Some years after the war, Harriet went back into broadcasting. She interviewed people on tops of buildings, in the middle of lakes, in cable cars, on the ocean. She doesn't think she would have had the courage or the trepidation to carry out those assignments but for her experiences in the WAVES.

Physical fitness was emphasized in the Navy, something many women did not pay much attention to. Traits of neatness and organization were stressed. Women learned to pay attention to their grooming in order to be a credit to the service. One developed a pride in being a part of an honored institution with a history and a tradition. One learned standards of conduct in public so that you were a credit to your Service. These learnings served her well in later years.

Harriet spent some years in the broadcasting world where women were few and far between—she found she held her own. She knew she could handle responsibility, that she could take charge, that she could work hard and perform as well as a man, if she were properly trained.

She could be kicked down, stepped on, humiliated, tricked, hurt and kept back, just because she was a woman. But because she knew her own worth, she persevered and did not let herself be discouraged. She had a unique career in broadcasting in Ohio, at a time when women had not crashed that media.

When she had to go out to work unexpectedly, she met the test, found employment and kept the family going. The broadcasting, editing, and experiences of the Navy helped her immeasurably.

Seeing that she probably would be put out to pasture at a relatively early age in the broadcasting business, she decided to prepare herself for an academic career. She went to graduate school, earned a Ph.D. in sociology and found a job teaching sociology at a southern state university.

Military service meant some wonderful friendships, friendships that are still cherished. She got to see some of the country also, since military personnel could hop military flights on a space-available basis. The country opened up to her and she used that fringe benefit as often as she could.

Harriet is proud to be a veteran, proud to have served. She considers it an honor, a unique opportunity. During the World War II years in the Navy, women were very restricted in the Navy as to what they could do. They certainly couldn't enter any of the non-traditional occupational specialties that young Navy women can today. And they were ghettoized. The women officers, of course, commanded and supervised enlisted women. But occupations were so segregated that rarely did men and women work together.

As a veteran, Harriet recalls that she got very little counseling about benefits before she left service. The only GI educational benefit she used was a course after the war in cooking and in home management. She had never taken home ec, because her mother who had been a home economics teacher persuaded her not to take those courses in high school or college. They turned out to be very useful when she became a woman's editor later.

Only eight years ago, Harriet bought a home using her VA home loan guarantee program. She felt very grateful for that because it was a great help to her. But she didn't feel that it was coming to her, or that other benefits were owed her by the government. Her view was that she served voluntarily, and that it was an honor to serve.

Harriet herself never felt personally put upon about the gossip that hangs around military women's morals. Women have a great deal to be proud of in the way they served their country, in uniform and out. She feels that innuendos that creep in when the subject of military women comes up are due to ignorance. This bad-mouthing, the slanderous gossip, is a method of social control that occurs when women have entered an area in which they had not been before. They are not accepted and the negative things said about them are attempts to keep them out or from fulfilling their roles successfully. From her experience, the vast majority of women who served were patriotic, hardworking and anxious to be a credit to their country.

Another important learning that Harriet ascertains was derived from her Navy experience is that one has to be ready to change careers or vocations. The military experience certainly helped her to adjust to new lines of work. She had several changes. When the military needs you somewhere else, they pick you up, train you, and you start a new occupation. She thinks that kind of flexibility—the ability to adapt to change—is an important fringe benefit of military service.

Harriet does not hide her pride in being a Navy veteran, but she has never joined any of the established male-dominated veterans' organizations. She was resentful when the American Legion and VFW would not let her march in the parades with the men. She felt that if the men could appear in uniform on certain occasions, there were no valid reasons why women veterans were not permitted to do so. Furthermore, she didn't feel she was welcome in those organizations.

Harriet, wife, mother of two, has already had several careers and is well into her current one. Besides teaching sociology, she is also working on a longitudinal study of the first Navy WAVES officer class, of which she was a member. The thrust of the study is to see if these women as a group have been more successful negotiating the aging process than might have been expected. That study is well underway with Harriet seeking out the classmates—over 700 of them.

•LUCILLE AND EDNA•

*They span two wars and are close friends. Lucille, small,
feisty, moves quickly and directly to the point. She sees
the WACs as special, role models for future generations
of young women. Wherever she would be, Lucille would
be a pioneer. Her buddy, Edna, deep throated, more
sedate, is a conciliator. She is equally fervent about the
WAC experience, though she served later in Korea. Their
enthusiasm is infectious; their camaraderie with each other
and their fellow WAC Vets heartwarming. They have a
strong sense of their femininity and still are leaders.*

We sat in a comfortable bedroom suite of the Hyatt Regency
in Columbus on a gracious August day during the WAC Vets
Convention. It was the fortieth anniversary of the founding of
the WAAC and the two former chairpersons of the WAC Vets,
Lucille and Edna* were enthusiastic about the pride they felt in
having been a part of the WAC. Their feelings for the WAC Vets
Association were warm, sentimental, and contagious.

Lucille had entered the WAAC during World War II. She had
rushed down to Naval Headquarters the day after war was declared. "Take me," she said to the astonished recruiter. But there
was no corps that took women at that time. She had to wait,
and she did. If her younger brother could serve, so could she.
There was no question in her mind that she wanted to be
where the action was. She wanted to go overseas, in particular,
to France.

Her parents were against her enlisting, but Lucille was determined. It was something she had to do; she didn't care whether
she got married or she didn't. To serve in the military forces
during WW II was number one on Lucille's agenda.

Eventually, her parents came to terms with her decision and
supported her, but not initially; there were giant battles. Not only
did Lucille go overseas; she was stationed at Rheims, France,

*Lucille R. Tauscher and Edna Dryden

close to the front lines during the Battle of the Bulge. Many times, she asked herself under terribly scary conditions, "What am I doing here?"

Lucille married while in service; her husband was shipped to the South Pacific to do his share of the fighting when she was sent to ETO. They were separated for three years. But Lucille never faltered in her conviction that this was where she belonged. Even during those tough moments near the fighting, when they might have been overrun at any minute, Lucille retained her sense of purpose and commitment.

Hers was one of the happy love stories of the war. She and her husband were reunited at Fort Dix to be discharged at the same time, ecstatic to be together and then to turn away from war and toward the business of building a life together.

Lucille admits that her years in the WAC were precious; she wouldn't trade one moment of it. She grew up fast and had to learn to do everything, to stand on her own feet, and not turn to home for support. No longer intimidated by anyone, no matter what their position in life, she mingled with people of all kinds.

Edna is younger; she enlisted during the Korean War. At twenty-one, she had passed up college and was working as a keypunch operator in her home town in Connecticut. She hated her job. When the Korean War broke out, in back of her mind was the thought—WW II had a GI Bill, there will probably be a GI Bill for this one. She enlisted; her family was stunned.

The chance to go overseas came; she spent three years in Germany and had a brief stint in France as well. This was the kid in high school who never raised her hand or opened her mouth.

But the Army saw leadership material in Edna and sent her to leadership school, to an NCO school and to recruiters school. After ten years in service doing a variety of things, and ending up as a recruiter, Edna got married. She had intended to make a career out of her military service. In those days, it was difficult to combine marriage and a military career. After ten years in the Army, Edna left to become a military wife. Her husband remained in the Marine Corps until he retired several years ago.

It is hard to think of Edna as the shy and retiring girl she describes herself. Just that morning that we conversed, she had chaired a session of the WAC Veterans Association through a

complicated session involving considering parliamentary maneu-
vering. Edna had conducted the session with the ease of one born
to lead; she kept the session going smoothly, with a firm but not
obtrusive hand.

The two women, Lucille and Edna, veterans of different wars,
are like schoolgirls, giggling and having fun together in sheer
exuberance. They have become close friends through their years
of participating in WAC Vets and try to room together at the
annual reunions whenever possible. Edna has enormous respect
for those who paved the way—the women who served in WW
II. Lucille agrees that the WWII vets paved the way—they were
the pioneers, the role models.

Lucille tries to explain those warm feelings that the ex-WACs
have for each other. They all went in together, total novices, and
didn't know what to expect. They experienced something in common which has created this unique bond. The "girls" can use the
same phrases and each will know what the other is talking about.
It's a kind of shorthand only ex-WACs can understand.

This enormous pride in the WAC keeps the WAC Vets together; a lively, gregarious bunch, they meet together in chapters
around the country and reunite every year. Those annual reunions
are a high point in their lives. Happily married, with children,
Lucille and Edna are still reverent about the "special" nature of
their WAC service. Both became leaders of the WAC Vets.

The service was not a bed of roses. Lucille recalls that the
WACs were fair game, and that the less sophisticated girls had a
hard time dealing with all the "bad stuff" around. Overseas,
conditions for the girls were even worse, because of the pressures
of numbers, the closeness to the fighting, the isolation. And of
course, the reputation of the WACs was hurt because of a few
bad apples. Lucille recalls that there was resentment too from
some of the men who were being shown up by the fine job that
the WACs were doing. Edna had her downs in the WACs too but
took them in her stride. They all grew up quicker for the experiences, good and bad.

They laugh together easily—friends, ex-WACs, women who
tried something different and met the test. They are proud of
their veterans' status. Neither of them used their GI Bill of Rights.

Before they knew it, their eligibility was up and they no longer could use it. They had been raising their children and keeping the families together. Both think that if the eligibility were longer, they might have taken advantage of it.

•BILLIE, TARA, ELAINE•
(Navy Nurses)

Their buoyant enthusiasm for their professional lives in the Navy eclipsed the difficult conditions of interviewing in a crowded, noisy restaurant at lunch time. Two of them had been "flight nurses" in the Navy who had served in Korea and Vietnam. The third had been a Navy nurse during World War II. Their positive attitudes toward their nursing experiences continued into their retirements. They were positive about everything they were involved with.

Now they were planning the 75th anniversary party of the Navy Nurse Corps, to take place May 14, 1983, in Bethesda.

Billie is slim, athletic looking, a sailor and a pilot. Short gray wavy hair frames the alert eyes that take in everything. Her little dog accompanies her everywhere and is a fine sailor also.

Tara is more quiet, but she gets things done. Her small stocky figure does not give evidence of the great energy she commands. She loves the sea also, shares a house with Billie, and is the crew for Captain Billie's sail boat.

Billie wanted to be a Navy nurse since she was five years old. Why? She doesn't really know, except that it was almost an innate drive. She loved water, grew up on a lake in Pennsylvania. It was what she had to do in life. She fulfilled her dream and gave over twenty years to being a Navy flight nurse.

Flight nurses in Korea were the medical personnel on the aircraft that pulled casualties from the battleground to Honolulu and then to Travis Air Force Base in California. An elite corps, specially trained to do tracheotomies and other emergency methods, there were only 80 of them with this specialty.

Since she was a pilot herself, being a flight nurse was a little bit of heaven to Billie. She could practice her profession nursing and fly too. Occasionally, the crew let her get some flying practice during the mission. She says she was unofficially the first girl to fly a Navy jet fighter.

By the time Vietnam came along, the Navy flight nurses had been disbanded and the Air Force Nurses took over their duties. Billie herself was the first Navy nurse to volunteer for duty in Vietnam. She was coopted to help with the flight nursing in Vietnam because they were so short-handed. Officially she was stationed at the Naval Hospital in Saigon, where she met Tara.

Flight nurses are like the modern nurse practitioners, with their specialized training. Besides the extra intensive training that they get for doing dangerous and difficult jobs, they were also given first-rate survival training in jungle, arctic, sea. The aircraft they flew in had the most sophisticated equipment imaginable, like a modern operating room. This was the way thousands of American soldiers' lives were saved. It was during World War II that many of the procedures of air evacuation of the wounded were learned. But it was in Korea that the techniques were refined and fully used.

Tara's specialty was anesthesiology. She had been specially trained and was a crucial figure in the operating room. After her stint in Vietnam, she helped set up a school for anesthesiology training in Virginia. She had always wanted to be a nurse, and she decided she preferred the Navy uniform when she thought of military service in 1949. Tara gave up a good salaried job in the civilian sector to enlist. But the security and the benefits appealed to her, as well as the possibilities for change and adventure. Tara got to Cuba (during the Korean War), Alaska and Vietnam.

Elaine sends beacons of warmth through her light blue eyes, which are set deeply below the high forehead framed with upswept light brown hair. Tall, almost stately, she could be the headmistress of an English boarding school. She has a shy smile, but her outgoing nature contradicts that signal. She cannot do enough for you. Everyone is enthusiastic about her. She must have been a great chief nurse to serve under. There are other contradictions as well. The regal bearing hides an impish humor. Though she looks like she was born to command; she strikes one as someone it would be easy to tell your troubles to. If Elaine didn't see herself as a bedside nurse, her ease and openness draw people to her.

Brought up in Tidewater, Virginia, Elaine always wanted to be a Navy nurse from the time she was very young. There were no military members of her family. In 1944 she decided to join the Navy Nurse Corps and found it to her liking and made it her career. Although she didn't get overseas during World War II, later she was sent to Guam, Japan, and Iceland.

Making changes as a nurse was acceptable in the Navy; after two or three years in one place, it was likely that you would move on. In the civilian sector, a nurse who changed jobs often was suspect. For the Navy Nurse Corps, it was de rigueur. Furthermore, as a military nurse, one would be able to start a new assignment of the same pay and benefits. In fact, it was likely she would get a promotion.

When World War II ended, Elaine was chagrined because she thought she would have to leave. Happily, she learned in time that she could switch over to the regular Navy, which she did in 1946. Knowing that her forte was not being a bedside nurse, Elaine sought to become a nursing administrator. One of the fringe benefits of Navy service was the in-service schooling that it provides. Elaine was sent to the University of Indiana to study administration where she took a degree in educational administration and then went on to become chief nurse of several hospitals, retiring 26 years later. She had served her country during three wars.

Afterward

When World War II ended in 1945, it was expected that women would willingly vacate their factory and other jobs so that the men whose jobs they had filled could resume their traditional role as breadwinners. About one million women did leave the work force, but the vast majority did not. Some women were reluctant to give up their newly developed economic independence, while others could not leave their jobs because they were the sole supporters of their families or of themselves, having been widowed by the war or having husbands who were disabled. Still others continued to work to supplement the family income. Many women were forced to take jobs that paid less and that required little skill. During the post-war period the image of women as homemakers was widely promulgated, and the idea of women having a right to work was not generally accepted.

The end of the war meant the total demobilization of women in the military services. This was mandated by the legislation passed in the early forties that had opened the doors to them. Most women, like the men, were glad to leave the service after having done their duty, and were ready to return to their traditional roles—that is, they would not have stayed in the services even if they had been allowed. There were others who would have chosen to stay in if they could have.

While there was no clamor for women to remain in the military service, there were high-level officers, including General Eisenhower, who supported the concept of a permanent women's component in the services. These officers had been impressed by the performance of women during the war, and saw women as an important human resource.

Even before demobilization took effect, the War Department had recognized the serious personnel deficiencies that would occur. There were a considerable number of postwar administrative tasks, including staffing an Army of Occupation. So despite the mandate small numbers of women were retained in all the services except the Coast Guard. Within a couple of years, the passage of the Integration Act of 1948 created a permanent place for women in the military services during peacetime. This was a major departure from the old policy in which women were tolerated in military service only during emergency wartime situations.

In the late forties and early fifties, both men and women slipped back into accepting traditional divisions of rights and responsibilities, even though the events of World War II had made some of these social mores obsolete. It must be remembered that women were still prisoners of biology. Before "the pill" women had little control over their pregnancies and were continually vulnerable to child bearing. It is not surprising that women assumed that their primary functions lay in the domestic sphere only.

Therefore, although many married women worked after the war, and their number continued to rise during the fifties, they shared the view of their husbands—at least outwardly—that their work was important only for supplementing the family income. Generally, women had "jobs," not "careers" or "positions," which were secondary to their primary homemaking and child-rearing roles.

Despite the breakthroughs women had achieved during World War II, they did not seem determined to consolidate their gains. Even in view of their successful participation in the hitherto exclusively male military establishment, women did not take the initiative to push for equal status. An editorial in *Life* magazine (October 21, 1946) marveled that women did not press for full equality: "Yet instead of resenting the way they are patronized or feeling challenged by the opportunity of their new and legitimate power, women in general show a surprising lack of interest in it."

There was a dispute among social commentators and historians as to whether the changes in women's status as a result of the war were to be as pervasive and permanent as they appeared, or whether these were only superficial and that basically women's roles had not been radically altered. Whether women's overall position was improved as a result of the social upheavals of the war is a different question from whether their position had changed.

Women who joined the military had probably taken the largest step in changing women's position, in the sense that they entered an alien and completely masculine world. The nature of military life meant being cut off from the civilian sector. Women had not only left their families and communities; they had taken on a new life-style in the midst of an an environment fashioned by men who had little time or no inclination to adapt to the feminine presence. There was no external support system for women in the services; any support had to be found among themselves.

Perhaps one of the reasons that women in the services returned to traditional roles was that while perceptions of themselves changed, their understanding and acceptance of their roles in the family and in society remained the same, reflecting the unchanged view that society had of those roles.

It is most probable that the great majority of women who joined the military services did not view themselves as the vanguard of a social revolution storming the bastions of male privilege. They were helping out their country in wartime and were caught up in the fervor of patriotism. For them, signing up was a temporary measure in an emergency situation.

Women who joined the services had not joined to seek equality in all areas of life, although they did want to share in the defense of the country. Yet they laid the foundation for a later drive for women's equality. Indeed, the emergence of the women's liberation movement almost two decades later would have been inconceivable without the road clearing and preliminary steps taken by women during World War II—especially by those who entered the military.

The goal of equality in the women's movement of the sixties— political, social, and economic—was not the primary concern of the World War II generation of women. Consequently, it is not surprising, as *Life* pointed out then, that the female is "still not a full partner in the national scheme of things. The immense and positive power that women should exert is still not effectively applied over the full social and political arc." Except for a minority of women who did see themselves as trailblazers, women in the services shared the perceptions of other women of their generation—that what they did for the country in time of war was the feminine thing to do. It was an extension of their supportive role in society. They did not have parity with men in many areas and did not expect to have it. It was not difficult, then, for them to accept the second-class status they had while they were in uniform and also afterward.

Since to be "giving" was supposed to be their true nature, women who gave up comfort and the security of home to accept the restrictions and rigors of military life did not expect anything in return for their contributions to the war effort. An example of this mindset is the fact that many, if not most women in the service were not aware of their eligibility for veterans' benefits. They also did not expect any changes in their civilian status, any rewards, or any advantages because they had served. They considered themselves true volunteers and were grateful that they were permitted to express their patriotism.

The strong self-image developed by women who served in the military had repercussions in their roles at home. Their daughters were bound to acquire from them a broader sense of their capabilities as females. Their sons would also see women in a different light than their fathers, whose mothers probably had a different self-image. These new perceptions on the part of the younger generation helped create the climate that made possible the women's drive for political and economic parity in the sixties. A World War II woman veteran reflecting on young women's achievements nowadays in the military mused, "We were the first; we paved the way for them."

What set off the women who served in the military from other women of that generation (who had also penetrated the male world in dramatic ways), was that the former had developed strength and resiliency that surpassed in achievement the economic independence that the wartime condition generated for civilian women. While nonmilitary women also found that they could perform in areas that men had not thought possible for them, the military women had participated in an ultimate male endeavor— the process of warmaking itself. The last myth of man's uniqueness was shattered by the substantial numbers of women who were invited to assist in the endeavor of war.

This is not to say that women who served became leaders of feminism two decades later. Possibly there are not more feminists among women veterans than there are proportionately among the general population. What is more important is the symbolic value of their military service.

Social revolutions are not built upon one event, nor do they occur overnight. Events and activities accumulate to reinforce the foundation; the stage has to be set for any radical transformation of attitudes and mores. Betty Friedan, who is credited with sounding the clarion call for the women's movement in her book *The*

Feminine Mystique, was preceded by Margaret Mead, the Menningers, the social and psychiatric innovators of the forties, and the work and thought of early American feminists. Friedan's social manifesto had been prepared for by the multiple political, social, and economic occurrences since the suffrage movement. In particular, World War II had precipitated profound transformations in the economic and social roles of men and women.

Women's participation in the military services was one such transformation whose implications have not been fully recognized. No longer were the separate spheres of male and female clear-cut and intractable. Women had proven that there was no area at all in which they could not make a contribution. Though direct combat has been set off limits to women, military service no longer is an all-male citadel.

Characteristic of the late forties' atmosphere was the military women's willingness to step aside and allow the men to take the limelight completely. Even though they might have been overseas and faced danger and deprivation, women veterans did not dwell on their experiences nor did anyone ask for their war stories.

Although society also changed its perception of what women were capable of doing, there has been an ongoing resistance to the emergence of women as equal partners with men in all areas of life. The willingness to let women share in the winning of a war did not continue into a willingness to let them share in the process of building a peaceful, just world. *Life*'s 1946 editorial would not be justified today when women have a strong interest in exercising their "new and legitimate power." The forgotten heroines of World War II played important roles, even if unconsciously, in changing social attitudes.

Profiles: Women in the
Military After World War II

Background

From 1948 on, after the passage of the Integration Act, women could have a military career if they desired. This was the first time that women were allowed to serve in the military services during peacetime. A woman had the option, like a man, to sign up for a three- or four-year period of their young adulthood, or make a longer commitment.

During the late forties and fifties the percentage of women choosing to go into the military on either a short- or long-term basis remained low. Among the women who did join the services in the post–World War II years were those who had served during the war. Among these were some who had difficulty getting relocated in civilian society or were unchallenged by the kind of work that was available; they remained in or embarked on a military career.

Even though an attempt was made during the Korean War to bring in larger numbers of women, the services did not find many willing to enlist, although reservists, including women, were called up at this time. The Korean conflict was not a popular war, and it did not arouse the patriotic feelings that the two world wars had.

A decade later this was to be equally true of the Vietnam war. But with Vietnam the disinterest in military service was compounded by the hostility of large segments of the population for the war and the consequent divisions throughout society about the war. Enlisting or not enlisting was taking a stand on the war and was interpreted as such.

Beginning with the peacetime army in the late forties, patriotism was no longer the dominant reason for going into military service. Until the expansion of opportunities for women in the late sixties, the few thousand women who went in wanted change and adventure, a new perspective and self-development. The personal reasons that motivated them were similar to those of the women during the World War II period. Those who were officers found chances for command positions that were not open to them in the civilian sector.

Throughout the fifties and sixties military service for women became closely tied to the possibilities of broadening one's educational and economic horizons. Military service also became an avenue for pulling oneself up socially, educationally, economically, and professionally. Women were also guaranteed another kind of equality: "equal pay for equal work."

There was, therefore, a large pool of qualified women who sought entrance into the services during the late sixties, despite the unpopularity of the war. Women had a tendency to be better educated than men and to have lower disciplinary rates. However, women had to meet higher standards than men to get into the service: they had to have a high school diploma. The opening up of many more occupations to women in the services in the late sixties and early seventies emphasized the career possibilities that the service offered.

Since the All-Volunteer Force changed the character of military service to an occupational model, the major attractions for both men and women have been job possibilities and post-service benefits. With high employment in the mid-seventies, however, the number of men volunteering dropped off, and the number of women went up. In a 1977 study the Secretary of Defense indicated a plan to double the 1976 number of women on active duty by 1983. Women's importance for the success of the All-Volunteer Force was increasingly emphasized by the Defense Department throughout the rest of the seventies.

In a personal message to field commanders in 1977, General Rogers, Army Chief of Staff, emphasized that women soldiers were an integral part of the Army. He assured them that they would be deployed with their units and that they would serve with the skills in which they were trained. General Rogers further enjoined the field commanders to train women adequately and hold them responsible for the full range of duties prescribed for their assigned positions.

Programs such as ROTC and the College Junior Program of the WAC also provided incentives for young women struggling to get a college education and attracted high-ability women. These programs provided a free education, officer's training and a commission with an obligated period of active duty military service following graduation. Some of those who initially thought of a short-term enlistment found opportunities for challenging work and remained in the service. In the second half of the seventies, with the opening up of the service academies—Air Force, West Point, Annapolis—to outstanding young women high school graduates, women had one more road to a successful career through the military.

With the eighties the hopes of women with military careers have been diminished as the Reagan administration retreated from the previous commitments made under the Carter administration to bring women's participation up to 12 percent. Despite evidence of that retreat—the end of integrated basic training and the reduction of the number of occupational specialties open to women—the current administration claims that it is not pulling back the opportunities for women in the military. Since this chapter is not closed, it is difficult to evaluate at the moment what the future holds for women in military service.

•CAROLYN•

The strong leadership qualities are not immediately visible in Carolyn's slight, low-key demeanor. Short, straight tawny blond hair frames a reflective face. Her speech is precise and thoughtful, matching the clear and direct nature that has taken her from military leadership to activist in the nation's capital. A child of the sixties, she took a different route from most of the women of her generation. She is a Vietnam-era veteran, but she has not defined her

*life by the war. A wife and a mother, she responds at her
best when she is most challenged.*

Today Carolyn* heads the Woman and the Military Project of
one of the largest and most active women's organizations, Wom-
en's Equity Action League (WEAL). Her evolution as a feminist
was a slow but sure one. Being a Captain in the Medical Specialists
Corps of the U.S. Army early in her adulthood helped the process.
Becoming the Chief of a section in a large 1,000-bed hospital at
the age of twenty-three with a staff of ten pushed the evolution
further. Carolyn took charge at an early age, and it is not likely
that she will sit back and settle for a bit part wherever she
may be.

The Vietnam War was in progress when she was finishing her
junior year at the University of North Dakota in 1965, but it had
not yet stirred the ferment on campuses that characterized the
next few years. A nutrition major, Carolyn was looking for an
internship after college, although there were not many to be had.
However, her father, who loved the Army, identified an internship in her field given by the Army. Bold but cautious, Carolyn
first tried out a six-week practicum given by the Army to test the
waters.

It worked for her, so she signed up and got her senior year
paid for, with an internship after graduation which meant an
obligation of three years. Commissioned as a second lieutenant,
Carolyn became an expert in diabetic and renal nutrition, working
hard and capably under the direction of the head nutritionist, who
acted as her mentor. During those first couple of years as an
Army dietitian, Carolyn learned her skill well and assumed more
and more responsibility. After a fruitful tour in Denver, she was
sent to Fort Devon where the challenge was less and there was
little opportunity for her talents.

This was a difficult period for her, but she did what she could
and managed. In the meantime she met her husband-to-be and
was married shortly thereafter. He was in armor; they became a

---

*Carolyn Becraft

couple and suffered the problems of trying to get assignments together and of finding suitable housing. Carolyn learned the hard way that the female military spouse was not eligible for the same kinds of quarters or allowance as the male. It was a hard lesson in second-class citizenship, one that she would not forget easily.

At the age of twenty-four, she became Chief of Food Services Divisions at the hospital in Fort Devon, the youngest person in the Army to be in such a position. At the 500-bed hospital, she had ninety people working for her and a budget of a third of a million dollars.

The next tour, two years at Fort Knox, Kentucky, was less felicitous. While she was chief dietitian in the hospital there, she had no colleagues of her own age. She felt like a freak in the small town near the Fort. When her husband was about to be shipped to Vietnam again, Carolyn was at a crossroads and didn't know what to do. She didn't want to be at Fort Knox herself— she knew that. Meanwhile there was pressure from her family and husband to start a family. While she reflects that she herself did not have a tremendous motivation to embark in this direction, she didn't know what she wanted to do. She was certain she didn't want to be in Fort Knox alone.

Pregnancy meant that she had to leave the Army. Carolyn went home to North Dakota to have her baby while her husband served in Vietnam. This was the most difficult transition that Carolyn ever made, becoming a military dependent spouse after having been a military member—a captain. She compares it to going from a participating adult in the community to becoming a child.

There were several other moves in the States for the dependent wife with a child. During the year Carolyn was in Phoenix, Arizona, she took a course in real estate selling and learned how to market a product. This was the best transferable skill she ever learned, she feels. She then sold real estate and was successful at it. This increased her self-confidence so that she could be out in the business world. Up to then she considered herself an introvert despite all the successes she had had as a dietetian and as a manager.

It was the experience of being a dependent wife during the three-year tour her husband did in Germany that convinced Carolyn that she really didn't want to be a housewife. She now had two children, but could not work in the economy of the country as she was blocked from getting a job in the civilian community. She chafed at her status, her isolation, and all the time she had on her hands. Not one to let things just happen, Carolyn found she could take a master's in education. With a little ingenuity and managerial skill, Carolyn took her master's degree in one year which kept her mind going.

The thesis she wrote for her master's—"Measuring the Effect of the Woman's Movement on Wives of Military Officers"—was another step in the direction her life was to take. On her advisor's advice, she began to speak to officers' wives' clubs, and federal women's programs, about the data she had compiled. She found the response astonishing: it seemed she was verbalizing what many were thinking or feeling.

At this time she had not even read Betty Friedan's *Feminine Mystique*. After her thesis she plunged into all the feminist readings that she could find. But this wasn't enough to keep her busy. Carolyn managed to find the one federal job that was available, a GS–7 slot to create a learning center for military training materials. The Army had developed a good model for training, but they had not explained how to use it. Carolyn brought her organizational skills to bear on the problem and set up the center so that officers could be trained how to use the materials. She was so successful that the business at the center increased from one thousand to ten thousand visitors per quarter.

A year or so later, when she and her husband came back to the States, Carolyn did not stay home. As a volunteer she organized a Family Committee for the Army which had a large impact on policies concerning military families. Her dual experiences as a military spouse and a regular service member gave her the insight and the background to bring the Army's attention to some of the most nagging problems that military families were experiencing. The committee, which she chaired for over a year, explored the problems, brought them to the attention of the right officers, and also developed models to solve the problems. To this day Carolyn regards this as one of the most important things she ever did.

Carolyn thinks of herself as a veteran, even if she doesn't dwell on it. Through both the Family Committee and her work as the

Director of the WEAL Project, Carolyn has had to stay in close touch with the military, and hence she has more of a military orientation than a veterans'. However, she used her GI bill to get the master's degree, and she may still use her home loan provision. Carolyn went into service for economic reasons. It was not an easy path to take during the mid-sixties, but she took it and made a success of it both for herself and for the Army.

Military service not only provided the career path that Carolyn embarked on with zest and competence; it also helped her to find herself. It was not only the professional successes that shaped her; it was the double standard for women, both as military members and military dependents, that brought her face to face with a reality that she had not grasped before. Her innate managerial skills were brought to the fore by the Army. This same Army also activated the feminism that was to become such an important part of her life. Carolyn found many parts of herself through her Army experience. Now she is bringing all those parts to bear on another important mission in her life.

• LINDA •

Military service gave Linda* a chance to finish college without killing herself and to move on to a new career and new sense of self. She was in financial trouble during her junior year at Riverside College in California, supporting herself with a fulltime job while pursuing her college program. However, this treadmill was wearing her down, and she knew she'd have to drop out unless she found another way.

They called her *Doc* because she was always ministering to and taking care of others. In fact, she planned to be a doctor and although that changed later, she would always continue to take care of others.

She had long been attracted to the military—maybe because she had been a tomboy. Thus when she stopped at the recruiting office, the College Junior Program of the WAC (the ROTC for women) seemed the logical solution. Among two thousand ap-

*Linda Cormany

plicants Linda was one of the one hundred fifty chosen for the program. That summer she took the three-week minibasic training course at Fort McClellan.

It didn't take Linda long to realize that she had come home. She knew it when she first saw a parade at Fort McClellan—the feeling was in her gut. This was real to her, in contrast to the college life she had been living, which seemed more of a fantasy world to her. The Army experience, beginning with that junior year at college, developed a sense of discipline and personal worth that she liked. The Army made the kinds of demands upon her that she could respond to with pride.

The Vietnam war was at its height when Linda joined the College Junior Program. Right after the Cambodia invasion, Linda had to address her psychology course and justify herself. It wasn't easy—the student body was in an uproar, and the campuses were a hotbed of antimilitarism. But Linda stood her ground. Yes, she told them, she had a purpose that was moral and just. She reminded the students that neither she nor the military leaders made the war. In our democracy the civilian government declares war. The war was a political tool and had been engaged in by our political leaders. She was only going to do her job in the best way she could.

Most of her experiences in the Army were good. She did her job and was appreciated—she never had the hassle that some of the women before and after were to have. She got some marvelous training, and studied military intelligence. She met her future husband. Her family had been supportive; she had developed a new confidence in herself and knew where she wanted to go and what she wanted to do with her life.

After she had her first baby, Linda and her husband decided to leave the service. However, she continued in the Reserves and has found it rewarding and very much a part of her life. She constantly urges young women leaving the services to join the Reserves. She has continued with her plans to be a counselor and volunteers to assist with terminally ill patients. She hopes to continue with her studies—and use her GI Bill, the way her husband did to get his Ph.D. But raising two small children and participating in the Reserves and her volunteer work delay her studies for a while.

Linda doesn't mind and is confident she will do as she has planned. The Army taught her how to prioritize, how to discipline herself, how to accommodate new realities, how to get the best out of herself. Before she left, she trained two units of new women recruits and saw the same metamorphosis that she participated in. She saw them emerge and mature and cope. She saw them grow up and take on responsibilities. She also found that for some of the new recruits she was the first person who ever cared about them.

Linda was in the WAC before integration, so she experienced both situations—women in the separate Corps and women in the integrated military Army. Maybe because she experienced both, her attitude toward the "new integrated Army" is different from those young women who entered after it was integrated.

For her, the WAC was ended by men to get women to shut up. Without a WAC staff the women didn't have advisers or advocates—they had no voice. She is convinced that it is harder for women in the Army now, without the WAC.

Linda participated actively in the WAC convention in 1982 in Columbus, Ohio. It was very important to her; she took great pride in the WAC veterans' organization and spoke of it as the heritage. She felt humbled and honored to be working for the WAC vets, in the presence of history, as she put it. The original members of the WAC (many in the original WAAC formed in 1942) were giants, she felt, even though most of them don't feel that way. She was struck by what appeared to be the attitude that anyone else could have done what they did. Linda knows that it was a lot harder back then during World War II than it is today or when she went in. She has a great sense of history and admits to being awed by being a part of that history.

Linda never wavered, either then or now. She claims that her "togetherness" came from the Army training. Certainly, her sense of purpose, her self-esteem, her organizational abilities, were all fostered by the military experience.

Linda would like to see the WAC Vets organization become the advocates for military women. She feels that in an integrated Army, which certainly has many pluses, women are at a disadvantage. However, advocacy is needed and given her commitment, she is likely to be involved in such a project in the near future.

•SALLY•

A strong jaw and penetrating look mark her the leader that she is. Committed to the study of history, she has made a little history on her own, by achieving many firsts as a woman officer in the Army's first integrated companies. Her intense concentration makes her seem a little aloof, but the warm smile is reassuring. She is gracious and anxious to communicate. There is a hint of the inner strength that goes with a deep commitment to equality and human rights. She is gearing up to meet her newest challenge, proving herself in civilian life without bars on her shoulders. No doubt she'll take it on with the same intelligence and determination that she took on an unpopular military career.

She was trained as a soldier and evolved into a feminist. She thinks of herself as a pioneer, and many of her accomplishments in the military were firsts. Sally served in the Army as a captain during the Vietnam War. She entered the WAC's College Junior Program in 1971, while a junior in college, so that her parents wouldn't have to pay for all her college education, since there were two siblings yet to go on to school. To her and her parents' surprise, Sally took to the military like a duck to water. Her roots were in a traditionally Catholic, close-knit family where the emphasis was on education and learning; her father was a high school principal, and her mother was a librarian. There was neither a glorifying nor a decrying of the military in her background.

Sally had to have been a fighter to survive. She was born with a rare birth defect—no opening between her nose and airways; she was hospitalized for the first year of her life. Afterward it was touch and go whether she would be able to talk. However, the devoted care of her parents, and their patience and constant training in getting her to speak, ensured her complete recovery. One of the greatest satisfactions of her life was when she won the debating contest in her high school. For the baby who might never speak, she had come a long way.

Going into the Army in 1971 was not an easy decision to make, with college campuses the playground of student demonstrations. Sally was the only one who chose to go into the WAC Program from Bellemon College, a small, recently integrated Catholic college in Kentucky. There were no friends, no peer pressure, no background of marching parades or intense flag-waving to encourage her. Only Sally went into the Army. The others, on the whole, opposed the war.

Why did she choose this path? Because she had studied political science and black studies in college, and because of what she knew about race relations, she believed she could make a unique contribution. There was also the opportunity to experience a different life-style and work with different people. When she attended the four-week orientation at Fort McClellan, she felt sure her decision had been the right one. The whole thing—the esprit, the parades, the camaraderie, the other women, the sense of commitment, the being part of a group with a purpose, the opportunity for leadership—intrigued and satisfied her.

Sally was in the very last officers' training class at Fort McClellan in August 1972 before the WAC became integrated in the regular Army. It was the largest WAC officer class, and it produced the first woman instructor at West Point. Sally remained at Fort McClellan for six months as a basic training officer. Then her minor in black studies showed up in the computer. She became the only white woman race relations instructor, dealing with individual cases of discrimination and other race relation problems as they came up, of which there were many.

Although her title was "race relations officer," Sally had to deal with women's problems also, as there was no one else to serve as their advocate. There was the case of a military couple of different races who wanted to get married. This was Georgia, after all, shortly after the civil rights turbulence of the sixties. The local laws had not changed. Sally was the one to deal with that one, as well as problems that involved women's issues. It was at this time that she realized she was becoming a feminist. She lectured to women officers not only about race relations, but about women. "We must be aware of what women have done in the past in order to be good leaders of women," she urged her sister officers.

Not all of her female colleagues appreciated her conviction, although some did. Being a feminist in the Army was not an easy role—not only because of the male traditional world that she was part of, but also because of the resistance and fears of other women. She received terrible peer ratings; she was considered too liberal, often too radical. *Feminist* was a bad word in some circles and the Army was one of those circles.

Yet Sally thought of herself as a soldier. She dove into the role she had chosen with passion. It was a commitment, a calling, a moral obligation that she had accepted. She gave her all to it and yet she still experienced all the limitations placed on women in the Army. She couldn't do a lot of things that male soldiers could. She couldn't be photographed with a weapon, she couldn't march in parades in fatigues, she couldn't pull duty, she couldn't go into the field later than 10 P.M., she couldn't attend VD briefings.

There were many things to fight against and for. Sometimes this meant she had to fight members of her own sex, such as the time when she was at Fort Lewis and noted that the women enlistees were getting away with murder, breaking all kinds of rules. The male noncoms didn't know how to deal with the situation. These were the beginning days of integration of male and female into units, and the noncoms had no experience in knowing whether a woman's uniform was properly smart. Furthermore, there was fear that attempts to make the women shape up would be interpreted as sexual harassment. Sally and another woman organized classes for noncoms and instructed them in proper decorum and dress for women. She did not win friends for this no nonsense, all business approach. That was okay though, she was a professional, she was doing her job, and that was more important than anything else to her.

As time went on she found plenty more challenges for herself. Sally learned that women had not been allowed to attend VD briefings for thirty years. The implicit assumption was that, if the Army permitted women to attend, they were making the judgment that their military women were of loose morals. Therefore, if a WAC went to a VD clinic, she was stigmatized for the entire time she was in the military. For years men had been given prophylactics. It was assumed that boys would be boys. Women were given neither the education nor the means to protect themselves from pregnancy.

Sally suggested that women should be allowed to attend the VD briefings or that there should be separate briefings set up for women. The Army refused to sanction such briefings but did give her permission to set one up herself. With some other women Sally finally got lectures on VD for the women. It was a do-it-yourself operation, but it provided an important educational service that had been missing for military women.

Another victory for Sally and some of her colleagues was their protest of Japan Air Lines' reference in their ads (on the bases) to the hostesses as *girls*. Those in command—males—couldn't see what the fuss was about. Just a word. Weren't they "girls"? Nevertheless, as a result of the protests JAL pulled the ad and no longer referred to them in this fashion.

Then there were ads for *Playboy* and other semiporn magazines that were shown in between listings of available space on Army flights. Sally and other women found them offensive. She called upon the manager and asked him to delete the ads out of respect for the military women. The manager was aghast at such a suggestion. He told her "the troops" wanted them. Sally retorted she was a "troop."

There were lots of skirmishes, lots of letters, lots of protests about the way things were done that either slighted or ignored military women. Being the professional she was, she didn't abide any discrimination against women soldiers, nor any special treatment either. She was prepared to pay any price for equality. She had been at Fort Lewis for four months when she noticed she was not put on the duty roster. It was not exactly a sought-after job; it meant being on duty twenty-four hours at a time, checking barracks. She suspected that her fellow officers resented the fact that she had been spared that onerous duty. Sally requested and finally got it. Then, there was contempt for her seeking out something she had not been forced to do. It was a no-win situation. Yet Sally was sure that she had earned some respect for her action, even if it was a grudging respect.

Once Sally found herself in the position of acting company commander. During this period there was a review parade. Company commanders led their troops out front and on the right. However, even though women were part of the troops and were acknowledged for their contributions to the military, they were not supposed to be seen. Therefore, when there was a review parade they were always supposed to be on the left and as far away from the reviewing stand as possible. Furthermore, they were to be in dresses, not fatigues, and they must not carry weapons. As a professional and as company commander Sally was prepared to take her place up front, on the right. Her colonel backed her.

Later on, she wondered whether it had been a pyrrhic victory. Perhaps no one in the reviewing stand had noticed she was a woman: in fatigues, hair up under cap, no makeup. Then Sally remembered that when she saluted, she had smiled. The women who had been trained in the WAC had been taught always to smile when they saluted. Men did not smile. Everyone must have known who the company commander was. Yet she learned that a high-ranking woman officer visiting the bases criticized her for marching on the right. This was difficult for Sally to take; it was not just men who were keeping women in an unequal position.

There were plenty of challenges to keep Sally hopping for she was young and energetic. Then the unplanned happened. She fell in love with another soldier and married him. When he got orders for Korea, naturally Sally did what she could to be sent where he was. At first the WAC would not let her go. She cites instances to support her theory that the WAC command did not look favorably on marriage. Perhaps there was the belief that, if a woman married, her loyalty to the Corps diminished. Sally had to leave her race relations MOS and went into transportation in order to get orders for Korea. Although they both were assigned to Korea, they did not know if they would be able to see each other. Still, each went off to her and his own unit to perform their obligations. They accepted their separation like the good soldiers they were.

While in Korea Sally found herself once again commanding male troops while she was Executive Officer to the commanding officer of her unit. For her such a position meant she had to desex herself; it meant she had to make her fellow officers who were male think of her not as a woman, not as someone who used her sex to get her way or to get special dispensations. She had to prove constantly that she was a professional so that the male officers would take her seriously.

The image she projected was an asexual one. She never wore makeup—except with dress blues. She would not wear civilian clothes, short skirts, or her hair down. She was married—everyone knew that—but there was no way she was going to project a sexual image. She never cracked a smile. She almost tried to dehumanize herself because most of the time she was just plain scared. She was in a totally new situation, and she was breaking new ground for women. She wanted desperately to succeed—for all women, for herself. Her aim was to be a professional in a man's world, to accept the full responsibilities and problems that went with being that kind of professional in that kind of world.

Those were difficult times for her. Although her husband was always there in the background offering his support and confidence in her, she suffered enormously. It wasn't until after she left the Army that she learned how much of a toll it took and how many psychic scars she incurred in the battle. After five years in the Army, Sally decided she had had enough. She had to get out to find herself once more. Fortunately, her husband had arrived at a similar conclusion, and the two soldiers turned to civilian pursuits.

They both enrolled in graduate school—Sally in history, her husband in pharmacology. Now that Sally was a woman veteran, it turned out that she had more problems than she expected in returning to the civilian world. In the service her bars had told her and the world that she was a leader. Who was she now? Her personal identity had been so tied up with the military that she found she was lost outside its world. Her husband's support was there, but there was no supportive female peer group that she could identify with, such as the women officers' "round table" which had been so important to her in her early days.

There were also the "ghosts of Army past" to cope with: the memories of all the tearing down, of all the lack of understanding, all the hurts, the aloneness of those years as a pioneer which had to be dealt with. Fortunately, Sally found a feminist counselor, and she began to work through her readjustment problems.

Sally had not been to Vietnam, but she was a Vietnam-era veteran. She had made the decision to join the military during one of the most stressful periods in American history. Even before she encountered the hostility of an institution reluctant to accept women into positions of integrated leadership, she had to face the hostility of her peers on campus. Still, Sally did not think she had the post-Vietnam Syndrome that many Vietnam veterans were experiencing although she did encounter overt hostility because she had served during the Vietnam War.

After she received her M.A. in history, Sally got a job as an assistant archivist at a southern university, where her husband now held a job. It was then that she experienced what so many Vietnam veterans had experienced in heavier and more frequent doses. "Why did you want to kill babies?" her boss asked her one day, out of the blue. The woman had marched in antiwar demonstrations in Madison while Sally was marching in uniform on parade. That was the beginning of a civilian ordeal for Sally which led to her decision to leave that job. As a reservist she applied for orders to serve a 180-day tour at the Center of Military History in Washington, D.C. Happily, that assignment came through, and Sally spent six months researching material on women in combat for the Army.

The Army is still a part of Sally. The connection is still there and will probably always be with her. She has buried the ghosts of Army past now and has come to terms with the good and the bad in her military career. Now she is a civilian-veteran, and she is beginning to learn who she is without her uniform and bars. She is proud of being a veteran and will tell anyone who asks that she is one. She believes she provided good service to her country and will continue to do so: "I have made and am making a contribution to my society."

• CLARA •

Clara was a nurse in Vietnam. She was in nursing school when her parents got divorced. Faced with a choice of going out to work and earning the money to continue her schooling or joining the military, she signed up in the Army. This would allow her to finish nursing school, incurring an obligation of two years' active duty. She had always wanted to join the military, she admits. She had grown up in the military—so it seemed the right thing to do. When she enlisted, she knew she would be going to Vietnam. The nursing training she received prepared her for the ward. But there was no way they could prepare her or any other nurse for war.

The year in Vietnam was a mixed bag for her. It was not like it was in M*A*S*H, she assures you. For one thing, she was in a fixed hospital at Longbinh, where she felt safe, not vulnerable to enemy bombardments or guerrilla incursions. The work itself was very rewarding, and she found that the relationships—the friendships she had as well as the colleagual relationships—were quite remarkable. For her and the other women, it was their first exposure to being around so many men. There was great warmth and caring.

There have been different reports as to what that has meant for different individuals. Some of them have complained bitterly of sexual harassment; others have noted all kinds of unpleasant-nesses. Clara did not have this experience—she said the men could not do enough for you, and they were exceedingly protective. It was like being "queen for a day" for a year.

What remains with Clara about the relationships she had in Vietnam were that they were so honest. Everyone she knew was open and honest; each moment counted so. There were no social trappings; the only thing that mattered was you as a person and how you did your job. The economic or social class or possessions you had weren't important.

Clara admits that they were the closest relationships she ever had. Her husband never wanted to hear about them. Until she took part in a rap session run under the Vietnam Veterans Readjustment Counseling Program by the VA within this past year, she never talked about that part of her experience in Vietnam, or for that matter any other experience there.

For Clara the nursing experience in Vietnam was challenging. She planned to make a career of it until she and other nurses were informed that, if they wanted to stay in the Corps, they would have to get degrees. The women like her who were graduates of hospital programs weren't wanted any more. To this sudden development Clara reacted angrily. She felt betrayed, bitter, let down. Her training was as good as, if not better than, the university graduates', and she saw no reason to be forced into going for a degree. Besides, at that particular time, she did not want to study for a degree.

She left the Army Nurse Corps and got married. In the months before she went to Vietnam, she was on duty in New Jersey and met her future husband, a conscientious objector. After she was married, she tried to get a nursing job in New York and couldn't. There was never any explanation. So they went back to Tacoma, Washington, where she was from originally. She eventually found employment as a civilian nurse in an Army hospital. She explains that the military environment was more satisfying for her because the doctors give the nurses credit for some intelligence. This was not what she found in civilian hospitals.

After her second child was born, Clara quit her job and went back to school on the GI Bill. She got her degree and is now working on her Ph.D. in medical cultural anthropology. Both her master's thesis and her doctoral dissertation are on women veterans.

What was it like being a Vietnam veteran and returning to the United States? Did the nurses suffer from the same kind of delayed stress syndrome as the fighting men? Did they experience the social rejection, the stigma, the alienation that the male Vietnam veterans experienced? Did they have delayed stress syndrome, sometimes called post–Vietnam syndrome (PVS)?

Clara reported that, after she came back, a lot of people asked her if it was like M*A*S*H. When she would begin to tell them, they would turn away or say, "Isn't that interesting," and not wait for an answer. After a while she stopped telling people that she had served in Vietnam. This was easy because most people didn't realize there were women in Vietnam. In fact, besides the nurses there had been a WAC detachment on Longbinh.

Coming back seems to have been as traumatic for the women who were in Vietnam as for the men. This has not been recognized until recently. For a long time Clara didn't want to be around anyone or talk to anyone. There was too much going on in Vietnam that was important to her. She felt she didn't belong here; that everything in the world around her was trivial. She began to have all kinds of doubts about everything, even her marriage.

It took several months for her to calm down enough to resume her life again. She did get married and then went back to nursing. Life began to seem normal, but there was a whole world of experience in Vietnam that was tightly closed off from her consciousness, as it was in so many of the men and women who served in Vietnam.

However, you can only bottle up the genie so long. Three years ago she went into what she calls her "nervous breakdown." This was such a depression that she was unable to function or to study. She took the summer off and pulled herself back together with the support of her husband and without outside psychiatric help. Clara discovered that another nurse also went through something similar at about the same time.

One of the pressures on her was the limited eligibility of her GI Bill of Rights. This limited eligibility of ten years after discharge applies to all veterans. But for women like Clara who marry and have children, their eligibility is essentially less. Also, she needed money to start a new life. She couldn't go back to school right away. Indeed, Clara was worried about being able to utilize those GI Bill benefits. That, after all, was one of the precious rewards of her military service. Her crisis passed after a few weeks, however, and she was able to resume her studies.

Yet there were many unresolved doubts and anguishes that still lingered. The rap sessions that just recently let her bring out some of her ghosts, and those of the other women veterans who were in this session, have been very therapeutic. One of the great frustrations for the nurses, when they finally could reflect and admit this to themselves, was not knowing what happened to their patients. There was no continuity of care, so the nurses were left hanging, never knowing the end results of their care. A lot of the nurses, Clara reports, came away with strong guilt feelings about what they gave to the patients. She and others in her group are plagued with feelings that they didn't give enough of themselves emotionally to the patients and didn't show enough caring. This is a catch–22 situation for a nurse. Professionally, she must keep her distance if she is to be effective and carry out her duties in the best possible way.

In one rap session held jointly with the male Vietnam veterans those who had been patients expressed how they felt in their position. The nurses came away feeling very good about themselves, that they had really done something very worthwhile. Clara noted that being a nurse in Vietnam was probably easier than being attached to a WAC unit in Vietnam. Nurses had their professional mission; they were with others they knew—the boundaries were clearer than for the other women, Clara conjectured.

Another plus of the rap session Clara was so involved with was that it helped put her in contact with feelings she hadn't dealt with. Somehow, talking it out with others who had experienced something similar is making it easier to talk to people close to her. For Clara and the others in the rap session, more than ten years later, they are working out the buried feelings of rejection, disapproval, guilt, anger, and bitterness that overwhelmed them when they returned to the States.

One negative experience that was unique to the women was the categorization of them as "whores." Clara said she heard this over and over again, and this pained her greatly.

A benefit of her military experience was getting over her shyness. She felt that her horizons had been broadened, that she had grown as a person. She wished she had kept in touch with more individuals. When she appeared on a recent CBS program on women, she had hoped her former friends and colleagues would see her and contact her. Unhappily, her face didn't show.

How did Clara, a nurse who served in Vietnam, feel about the war when she came back? She expressed great bitterness against the government. She felt cheated that there was no peace with honor. It was very difficult to understand why most of the protests were not directed against the government, but they were directed against the veterans. She simply could not comprehend why the people of the country, particularly the protesters, were not directing their anger against the government.

•EDITH•

She is the first woman commander of an all-male American Legion Post, and she had to fight her way in just to become a member. Edith, like many other women veterans, was told to join an auxiliary when she applied, but she stoutly defended her rights: "I am a veteran, just like you." Now she is a respected, sought-after head of a Long Island American Legion Post.

A coalminer's daughter, Edith hasn't made the hit parade as a country singer, but she has made hits in many ways, besides becoming a commander. She grew up in a small coalmining town in Pennsylvania in a family that did unusual things. She was not raised with the philosophy that girls don't do "such and such"— "It's not right for a girl; it's not proper for a young lady." Edith was therefore one of those rare females who did not have a mind set that "women didn't do those things." She was convinced that she was equal to men and she always behaved that way. She asserts that she never ran into any trouble with this approach.

As soon as she graduated high school, Edith didn't waste any time getting started on a life of her own. She found a job in Harrisburg in the Bureau of Vital Statistics and supported herself. She even sent money home to her family, since coalmining was not one of the occupations that produced heavy income. She also continued volunteer work in the Civil Air Patrol which she had begun when she was fifteen. Her family was terribly proud of her vigor and independence, as well as her generosity toward them.

When she turned twenty-one, Edith signed up for the Air Force. The Korean War was on, and she wanted to do her part for the country of which she was exceedingly proud as well as wanting to learn communications. Her family was a little shocked. No other girl in her school, or in her community, had done such a thing. Actually, her Civil Air Patrol experience, which gave her a taste of a paramilitary institution, had told her she would be comfortable in the military framework. But as Edith has characterized herself, she was an oddball—she has always marched to the tune of a different drummer. So her family was surprised but not astonished.

Edith had wanted to learn communications, so when she signed up requested training in that field. Unfortunately, there was a shortage of people with clerical skills, so they immediately put her in office work. This was not what she had in mind, but consistent with her philosophy of life, she made the best of it and, over all, her thirty years in service were interesting and profitable.

It is always conjecture how much we bring to our experiences and what our experiences do to our personalities. In Edith's case she brought a strong will and determination that was only reinforced by her military experience. Her theory was that if you can't get through something, you walk around it, or you climb over it, or you crawl under it. When you have a goal in mind, there is always a way to arrive at it. This attitude served her well in the service; she was neither rattled nor thrown by the frustrations she encountered, and there were many. Along with this equanimity went a logical mind.

Edith did not care for the usual evening carousings in the bar or the barracks; drinking was not her thing. However, she loved dogs and decided she wanted to spend her spare time with one. Of course this was not the kind of thing that was allowed on base. However, she had discovered that one of the older noncoms had a dog.

Without a second thought Edith went to her superior and asked her if she could have a dog, assuring her that she would give the animal careful supervision and that it wouldn't interfere with her work, or that of any of her companions. She spelled out her reasoning so convincingly that she got her dog on base.

While she was disappointed that she didn't get the kind of training she would have liked, Edith found her service experience invaluable. It gave her the kind of self-discipline that has remained with her the rest of her life and has been an asset in everything she has tried to do—from raising a family of six children to running an American Legion Post to taking over a business she knew nothing about.

Besides this invaluable character-strengthening her military service gave her, Edith had the opportunity to meet the kinds of people she would have never encountered and also to spend some time in California. Long-lasting friendships emerged from the experience that have been a great source of joy. She also met her husband in service.

As you might expect, Edith is also active in community affairs.

She is gung ho for young women to join the service. However, her daughters see things differently, and she respects that. After all, she had her own steps, and they were different from those around her. Why shouldn't her daughters have their own tunes to dance to?

•RUTH•

Ruth* was a war baby—born in the deep South but raised among the urban poor in New York City. Her father died when she was ten and had played little part in her life, for when he came back from World War II, he spent the rest of his life in VA hospitals. And so it was her mother that raised both Ruth and her older brother in a housing project in East Harlem, sustaining herself and her family by hard work and religious beliefs. As her mother was determined that her daughter should go to college, Ruth was sent to Washington Irving High School, an all-girl school known for its strong academic achievements. After she graduated, Ruth's mother made applications for her to several of the best black colleges in the South.

But Ruth had other ideas. She had fallen in love and wanted to get married. However, the object of Ruth's infatuation had other ideas too—he planned to join the military. It was the only legitimate way he knew how to break out of the poverty cycle. In the service he would learn skills, receive the GI Bill of Rights, and be able to further his education. Ruth was in love, but the boyfriend wanted a better way of life most of all. She told him she would wait for him, but he didn't encourage her because he didn't know how long she would have to wait. Ruth suggested they go into the service together, but he thought that it was not reason enough for her to go in—just because he was. But she was not to be discouraged.

With some asking around and looking in the library, Ruth found where the WAC detachment was located and went there to get all the information she could about joining up. To her surprise, Ruth found many other young black women talking to the WAC

*Ruth Young

recruiters. She didn't expect to find this, since none of her friends had an interest in the service. But these young women, like her boyfriend, were hoping the service would lead to a better way of life.

Ruth's motivation was perhaps more romantic, but it was just as strong. Studying the recruitment literature carefully, she found that the service sent people to many different places. Since coming to New York as a small child, she had never been outside the city. Ruth took the tests and passed them.

Still, her mother was dead set against the idea, and all her friends and relatives tried to discourage her. While her father and uncles had joined the military, there was a general disapproval of a young woman joining up. They told her all the negative things they had heard about women in the military. Only her brother supported her desire. He had been in the Air Force for four years in England and was now studying pharmacy with his GI Bill. He suggested that she might meet different kinds of people whom she would never otherwise have the opportunity to know. This was the kind of support Ruth needed although her mother still refused to sign the paper giving her permission to enlist; she wanted her daughter to go to college, for which she had worked so hard. Ruth was underage—she wouldn't be eighteen until the following December.

For a spirited eighteen-year-old, her mother's thwarting her wishes was intolerable. She would not go to college. Even though she knew how hard her mother had worked, scrimping and saving in order to send her, she was not going to go. She had her own ideas about her future, even though it meant she would be disobeying her mother for the first time. On her eighteenth birthday Ruth enlisted in the WAC and it wasn't long before she was in basic training at Fort McClellan, Alabama.

What an eye-opener the camp was for her. Here were young black women from all parts of the country, and they were all strangers. Their backgrounds and experiences were as different from each other as they were from the young white women who also came from vastly different places and backgrounds. Most of them, white or black, had had very little, if any, contact with other races. Ruth was amazed and pleased because this was the melting pot that America was supposed to be, a mixture of all kinds of races and colors and ethnic origins. Her brother was right: she was going to meet all kinds of people.

But this was the deep South before the civil rights movement. The NCOs and the senior officers warned them that the blacks were not to venture alone into the nearest town of Anniston. After Ruth's one venture there to buy shoes, she was only too glad to return to base, never to go back.

Basic training is not something that anyone, male or female, forgets. The high and rigorous standards as well as the physical schedule of exercise and marching found all the young trainees in the same boat. In order for them to make it, the young women from all walks of life, from all areas of the country, had to help each other. The basic training routine that stretched them to their physical and emotional limits was the great equalizer. What had to be done, had to be done right. There were no second bests or second chances. The quarter had to pop from the made bed the first time; the white gloves had better not be dirtied. Ruth learned like the others that there is no right way, no wrong way, only the Army way.

Out of mutual need a great camaraderie sprang up among the young women, forging friendships that have lasted for years. Under these circumstances the recruits got to know each other—their good and bad sides. Ruth met the different kinds of people she hoped to find: there was a former nun, women who had left marriages, others from farms and factories. And there were young women like Ruth who came into the WAC right out of high school.

Although Ruth scored very well in the mechanical area, she wanted to get into clerical school and did so. She did well and was assigned to Intelligence at the Aberdeen Proving Grounds. It was a dream come true when she was assigned to Orleans, France.

One of Ruth's fondest dreams had been to go abroad. Soon after she arrived at the base in Orleans her excitement faded. She found that in this particular WAC detachment black and white did not mix. Not only were they never assigned together as cubicle mates, there was no socializing between the races. Ruth had not encountered this in the WACs before. Also, of the number of black women there, none had been promoted while stationed in

Orleans. This was Ruth's first encounter with blatant racial discrimination in the military. She was miserable. She was shocked and discouraged as incident after incident occurred, and there was no one to appeal to. She tried to contact the NAACP, but the base was too remote. Since Ruth was not one to stand for what she didn't believe was right, she was considered a troublemaker.

Ruth calls the Orleans situation a failure of leadership. A major problem was that, in these days before Equal Opportunity Officers, there was no one in authority who could deal with these kinds of problems—because they were part of the problem themselves. Since they were overseas, there were no outside organizations or agencies that one could call upon. Ruth wagers that most of the less-than-honorable discharges and AWOLS given service people occur outside the continental USA. She found the overseas situation shockingly different and certainly disappointing.

To get away from the uncomfortable tensions and problems in the WAC barracks, Ruth took herself off on French trains and traveled the countryside on her passes. At least this part of her tour fitted her dream of what it would be like to go abroad. She found the French pleasant and open, and she communicated with them easily. Finally she got herself transferred to Special Services, which provided entertainment for the American troops in France and Germany. For the next eighteen months she helped put on musical and theatrical performances that kept the troops and Ruth happy.

If she hadn't had the experiences in Orleans, Ruth might have reenlisted. But when the time came, she chose not to, even though her initial reason for signing up—to be near her boyfriend—had ceased to be; they had each gone their own way.

Her veteran's career now began in earnest. Like many other Vietnam era veterans, female and male, when Ruth came marching home she suffered readjustment problems. The country had changed; the civil rights movement, Dr. Martin Luther King's march on Washington, the turn toward the black Muslims, the new black consciousness, Malcolm X, the Afro style of dress had all happened while she had been away. Being overseas had kept her from being part of the civil rights movement.

Back in New York City she felt like a stranger. She and her old friends had changed so that she thought some had become quite radical. She had had many broadening experiences too: She had been abroad, had traveled and had got to know the French and Germans—and had outgrown many of her old school friends. Things had changed at home too. Ruth's mother had gone to school at night and got her nursing degree, as well as moving into a co-op that had mostly middle-income people as residents. Her brother had a good job in pharmacy at a medical center after graduating at the head of his class from Columbia University. Ruth seemed to be the only one without a college education.

As always, Ruth surveyed the situation and decided she needed to have a job first of all. So she started work as an office assistant for a construction company. Her military service had given her good skills and good credentials. Her boss, recognizing her worth, worked her to the bone and paid her little. Her brother convinced her that she was being taken advantage of, so she quit.

Having passed the Post Office exam, she shortly thereafter got a job there and enrolled at Baruch College at night. However, the Post Office shifted her schedule constantly, so she could not finish a semester. She worked at a meaningless job in the Post Office for several years until finally her family persuaded her to resign because she was getting nowhere and was unable to continue her schooling. It didn't take much to convince her—she knew she didn't want to be packing mail the rest of her life and so she resigned.

Her next job was with a Queens Community Action Program. The pay wasn't very good, but she liked the work. Her boss was very impressed with her and introduced her to an official of the Department of Labor Veterans Employment Service. He wanted to make some history by being the one to help hire the first female Veterans Employment Representative. Ruth had impressed him, and he saw her potential and her leadership.

This introduction was to be the turning point in her career. He pointed out that in a year or so there were likely to be more Vet Rep appointments and that she ought to be ready to apply when that occurred. This meant getting a driver's license and a car. The Vet Rep needed to be mobile; this was an absolute prerequisite.

Although Ruth had no money, she was able to borrow, study driving, and get her license.

Once more, the friend who had been her boss at the Community Action Center came to her rescue by moving her to an evening shift. She rejoined the Post Office and carried two fulltime jobs for six months to save up the money to buy a car. When openings did come up for the Vet Rep, Ruth was ready and was hired. On February 9, 1974, she became the first female veteran hired to be a VER—Veterans Employment Representative. A press release was sent out announcing her appointment.

The official was jubilant. He had achieved his objective. Ruth was ecstatic. She had an opportunity of a lifetime—she was a professional. This appointment was particularly welcome since Ruth was passionately concerned about veterans and their problems and would give it her all.

They made it very clear to her that this was no easy task, that it was a demanding, challenging job that would infringe on her personal life, that she had to be willing to work extremely hard and put her work first. This was the reason he had seen her, a single woman, as the right person. She was to be a pioneer—she was the "first"—and with that office and position came heavy responsibilities.

Under Ruth's wing were Suffolk and Nassau counties on Long Island, two of the wealthier suburbs of New York City, where there were thousands of veterans in the two million population. This was a heavy load. Here she was a woman—and a black woman at that—assigned to serve this vast community of veterans, most of whom were white and male. Furthermore, she would have to work with the organizations on Long Island who were the powerhouses of veterans affairs.

There isn't a thing that Ruth sees is needed that she won't follow through on. She joined all the veterans' organizations and became as active as her time permitted. She noted that the American Legion has several women's posts, and she has tried to spark them into more active roles. She only regrets that in all the years that she has been in this job, only one woman veteran came to her asking for assistance.

•MARIA•

A young woman born in Puerto Rico of a very strict Catholic family wants more freedom. Maria graduates high school and looks at her options. Her parents have modest means, they can't afford to send her to university. For her to go on to higher education she would have to work first and save the money, or try to work while going to school. Jobs are scarce on the island for the unskilled.

There are relatives in the States, so Maria asks her parents if she can go live with them, find a job and perhaps be able to go to school. Opportunities in the States are known to be better than on the island, she points out. The States have been a mecca for opportunity. Her parents have enough to contend with other children, one retarded.

Maria goes to New Jersey and lives with her aunt and uncle. Her conversational English is almost nonexistent so the only job she can find is in a factory doing piece work. She is disappointed, but she is in America. So she works on her conversational English, meets people and wonders what she will do next. After a year of doing this work, she decides it is a dead end—this is not what she came to America for.

Since her relatives have a grocery store in which she sometimes helps them out, she hears bits and pieces of all kinds of information about American life. One lady who has come in tells her that she is signing up with the Air Force, that they are going to send her to school where she will be trained.

Meanwhile, Maria has found out about social work. This appeals to her; she would like to go to school for social work. The lady suggests that maybe the Air Force will send her there. So Maria goes down with her to the Air Force Recruitment office, takes the test, and indicates that she wants to go to social work school. Unhappily, she finds out that that is closed, so she gives up the idea. She continues to work at the factory, unhappy, depressed, with a seemingly bleak future. America has not been the land of plenty or opportunity for her.

Shortly thereafter, an Army recruiter calls upon her; recruiters from the different services share information about applicants.

The recruiter points out the benefits to her: that she'll learn a skill, that she will get the GI Bill, that she may go overseas. To a young woman without a prospect of an education, without any skills or the prospect of getting any, the pitch of the recruiter sounded good. Besides, she was missing her family and finding the factory work onerous.

Maria got the permission of her family and signed up in the WAC for three years. She was sent to Fort McClellan for basic training, an experience she would prefer to forget. Not only was the training difficult, but there was nothing to do off-hours, people were unfriendly. But somehow she managed to get through it. With secretarial skills that she was taught she was assigned to Fort Mead, Maryland, where she stayed for the rest of her tour. She was very disappointed that she didn't learn other skills, nor get into social work or any other type of school. She was chagrined that she never went overseas. Because she was a good and reliable worker, her commanding officer did not want to part with her and refused to let her go "on orders." With these disappointments, Maria did not think about reenlisting.

While the military experience didn't fulfill all her expectations, she did learn a marketable skill—secretarial—which she has been able to use anywhere. She also met the man she would marry just before she completed her tour. She was looking forward to her marriage and to having a family by this time. What she had seen of the Army did not convince her that staying in the Army was a good idea for the new kind of future she envisaged. Her husband-to-be was in service and she didn't see how she could accomplish her other objectives if she stayed in.

Despite the disappointments, the military experience was an important one for Maria. It brought her out of a dead-end situation and opened up new doors for her. Today, she is an executive secretary for one of the Government agencies in Washington, D.C., with three children. She is now separated from the husband that she found while in service.

One of the best things about military service, Maria concludes, is that you grow up fast because you are responsible for yourself. That is a rude awakening, a reality that you have to come to grips with. She reported that many girls had problems with this type of shock. They had problems, many went AWOL, many didn't make it out of basic training. For Maria, it was rough—particularly the beginning—but she made it and was glad that she did. As far as she was concerned, she made a commitment and she was going to see it through, no matter what the obstacles.

She speaks fondly of the many different kinds of people she got to meet, of the many new friendships she made. And her English became exceedingly good. She found that her fellow soldiers were a great support group. They were in it together, and they helped each other out. That in itself was an important experience, one that was unique in her life.

Maria used her GI Bill. She had delayed using it because of her pregnancies. She has amassed 100 credits when the time eligibility ran out. She is very bitter about that, because she was so close to getting her degree. Now it is very difficult to pursue the degree since she holds a full-time job and is without funds for tuition, books, etc. If she were writing the GI Bill, she would not have any time limit. She feels that she earned the entitlement and that she shouldn't be denied it because she couldn't use it right away.

Maria doesn't think of herself as a veteran. She never joined any veterans' organization. While she remembers her friends from the service, she has not been asked to join any WAC alumnae organization, or something similar nor has she had the motivation to seek out a veterans' organization. Basically, she saw her military service as a way to get out of the box she was in and to advance herself. While it fell short of her hopes, it certainly led to a new life. Most people do not know she is a veteran.

• EMMA •

She was all of 18 and had just graduated high school in a small bedroom suburb of New York City. College didn't appeal to her at all. What she wanted to do was see the world. So Emma joined the Marines and became a woman Marine.

It was 1964. The war in Vietnam had not yet escalated and the country was not struggling with the agony of the wisdom of our involvement in Southeast Asia. Emma had no relatives who had ever joined the military service. She was the first and the only one in her family to put on the uniform. Her family was completely surprised at her actions but supported her nonetheless.

Emma's dream of sailing across the seven seas and seeing far-away places didn't materialize. Her tour of duty for the four years she was in the service was mainly at Cherry Point, North Carolina, where she served as an NCO in barracks duty, data processing and document control. By the time she left service, she was a Staff Sergeant. Still, she was able to visit many parts of the United States during her military tour, which was a major step in broadening her horizons.

Boot camp was a testing of her mettle, of her ability to work hard under difficult conditions. Emma claims now that if you can make it through boot camp in the Marines, you can make it through anything in life. Four years in the Marines helped Emma grow up fast. They also helped her grow sure of herself and her own abilities to meet whatever came along. She was stronger and tougher and wiser.

Emma married while she was still in the Corps. Her husband was a civilian, and he joined the Marines to follow her. Usually it is the other way around; the wife joins up to follow the husband. But in Emma's case, her husband was the civilian. As a Marine, he was sent to Vietnam and had a narrow brush with death. Neither of them can ever forget that. She left the Corps first, he shortly thereafter. Neither of them decided they wanted a military career.

Emma chose to raise a family shortly after service and has been busy and satisfied with the process of being a wife and mother. There hasn't been any opportunity to use any of the skills she acquired while in the service. Her family has been the chief focus of her attention and energy. She has never used any of her veterans' benefits although she might have tried to continue her education if they were still available. The way the GI Bill is written, those benefits only last for ten years after leaving service. While her children were small, Emma did not want to dilute her energies and attention by going to school, so she lost those benefits.

Emma became active in the Women Marines Association, recently served as president; and is very active in her own local chapter of the WMA. While she has not been active in other veterans' organizations, many of her fellow WMA's are. Being in the leadership of WMA has been both a rewarding and challenging opportunity for Emma.

Having served in the Vietnam era, her attitude is: "Let's get on with it." History will render its verdict about the rightness or wrongness of it, is her philosophy. She is somewhat disturbed by the emphasis being given to the "so-called problems of Vietnam veterans." Her feeling is that they did their jobs; they need to continue their lives and put the war behind them. Emma is convinced from her own and her friends' experiences, that most of the veterans did get on with their lives and are now contributing to society. They have not sought to capitalize on their Vietnam veteran status.

Both she and her husband came down to Washington, D.C. for the National Salute to the Vietnam Veterans, November 11, 1982. They were interested in the dedication of the Vietnam Veterans' Memorial and were upset at the acrimony and the carping by dissidents after the design was chosen by the Fine Arts Commission. She saw Jan Scruggs, the chief mover behind the memorial, an example of the achievement of Vietnam veterans. She was resentful of those who were critical of the memorial and was particularly disturbed by the nasty comments and prejudiced statements made about the architect who conceived the design, Mai Lin. Altogether she found the site of the memorial very beautiful and felt comfortable with the memorial itself.

Mentioning that she had just finished Jeanne Holm's book, *Women in the Military*, Emma reported that she was shocked to find out what had been going on behind the scenes regarding women in the Air Force. There were many negative things that she encountered while in the Marines, but she never thought about them, nor did she imagine they could be otherwise.

•ZOE•

Her smile and bright eyes are immediately disarming. There is a warmth that lights up the dark face that invites friendship. But they are wise eyes as well, eyes that have taken in injustice and intolerance and cried inwardly. Why can't I be judged for myself, not for the color of my skin?

*Why, why, is the world the way it is? It must take a
solidified prejudice not to want to meet her on her terms.
She has grown strong and resilient over the years. More
important, she has learned to wait. Now she is out in the
civilian world again, tokenly equal. But she is quick to
recognize the subtle slight, the exchanged look, the
innuendo. She still has no illusions about the ways of this
America.*

Her family did not want her to have to clean houses, so at great
sacrifice they helped her through two years of community college.
Despite the Associate of Arts degree, the prospects for a liberally
educated young black woman in Detroit in 1961 were zero, so
Zoe joined the Navy.

With many naval stations up north, she thought she'd be better
off in the Navy than in the other services. Besides, she liked the
Navy uniform. She had no illusions about what lay ahead of her,
but she didn't see any alternative. Many times she wanted to give
up, but she wasn't much of a quitter. These were the days before
the civil rights marches in the South and Martin Luther King's
March on Washington.

After she finished at boot camp, Zoe asked to go into one of
the training schools the Navy was famous for. But despite the
fact she had the intelligence and the background, she didn't get
into any training school. Instead, she was assigned to general
duty, which meant cleaning the barracks.

Sent for after a few weeks, she got launched on a typing career,
first at the Bureau of Naval Personnel, then at the Pentagon. Her
typing, which had been nonexistent, improved so that she was
considered a yeoman in training. After a year, Zoe thought she
ought to go to school. She asked to go to Yeoman school and
shortly thereafter had orders to do so. She returned to her administrative duties after that.

In the back of her mind was the desire to go to nursing school.
She went through all the application stages till the last one when
she was turned down. That prompted her to consider getting out
of service. It had become apparent that the Navy had limited

opportunities for black women. On home leave, she tried to track down a civilian job, to no avail. Three years later, the situation hadn't changed for Zoe as far as job opportunities were concerned. She began to have second thoughts about reenlisting.

Meanwhile, back at her unit there was some guilty feeling about Zoe not getting into nurses training when she had been so close. She was offered an assignment to go to Paris if she would reenlist. That was hard to resist, particularly when there were no prospects of earning a decent livelihood in the civilian community.

Zoe was never sorry that she did reenlist. This time, the promise was kept. Zoe spent the next three years overseas—first in Paris near SHAPE headquarters, and then at Stuttgart. She thoroughly enjoyed the overseas assignments. When she came back, she was sent to Yeomen B school and had been promoted to an E-7.

Then came several years at Norfolk and then in Washington. Before she knew it, Zoe had already invested more than ten years in the service. Women were being channeled into positions supervising other women and Zoe, now with seniority, became Master at Arms for a barracks of over 250 women. She played no favorites, with either black or white. Being in the military doesn't change your biases, she was quick to point out. If you were prejudiced before you went in, you continued to be prejudiced. If you were always above board and observed the law and regulations before you joined up, then you were likely to behave just that way while in service.

Zoe had a series of interesting administrative assignments after that, including a stint at the Industrial War College at Fort McNair, which she enjoyed tremendously. Always willing to learn and to experience, Zoe made the most of all her orders. Whenever she could, she took courses on her own to improve herself and to add to her skills and knowledge.

Her first enlistment evolved into a military career. In 1980 she retired from the Navy and once more turned to the civilian sector to see what it had to offer her now, twenty years later. She was much better prepared to deal with the limited opportunities that were still facing her. She has bought a house and created a home. Generally, she is optimistic about finding the kind of work that she would like to do. Counseling appeals to her because she is people-oriented. With one career behind her, and a retirement cushion, Zoe is going to explore and test. She still has a lot to give and she is looking to help other people.

The world has changed for her. She is wiser and more skilled with many successful working years behind her. But she has no illusions that people have changed that much. She felt prejudice in the Navy, but she knew it before and after Navy service. And she is sad about it because she doesn't expect it to change much. She sees it as a weakness of this country which diminishes its potential.

Zoe does not think of herself as a veteran. The military service was her employer. She never identified with the military as an institution and even less with the veteran population. Her military service was a job to her; it never became an emotional attachment. Perhaps because she knows it so well and has some ambivalent feelings about the Navy, she advises people never to go in as an enlisted person, but to get an education first and go in as an officer.

And Now . . .

The military services, with a diversity of opportunity in traditional and nontraditional fields, siphoned off ambitious, bright young women into both its enlisted and officer ranks during the seventies. It was the one area where "equal pay for equal work" was insured. While there were inequalities of opportunity and other problems including sexual harassment to cope with, the military world held out a chance for economic stability and upward mobility that was not matched in the civilian sector. ROTC programs, the academies, OCS and other leadership schools, further enhanced the military services' offerings to ambitious young women. A young woman without opportunity or direction could start and continue a career path in one of the military services. Women, like blacks and Hispanics, soon discovered that the military sector provided an escape hatch out of poverty and social closure and gave them a new dignity in an integrated work force.

The passage of the GI Bill of Rights during World War II and the possibility that such an educational package might be available to veterans of other wars, or even for a peacetime period of service, was another inducement for young women to sign up in a service slot. While some young women had passed college by, others would never have the chance to obtain any kind of higher education and this was a way to complete or continue one's education under positive conditions.

Besides the GI Bill, young women sought the training that was part of the service career. Whether they wanted a secretarial background or a radar operator's skill, young women were drawn to the possibilities painted in glowing colors by recruiters. Unhappily of course, there were many disappointments as well as success stories as far as these opportunities were concerned.

Boredom, a thirst for adventure, a desire to find oneself, an urge to break away from family ties in a socially acceptable way— these were also reasons for young women joining the military services. A three- or four-year enlistment could provide the space and time a young woman needed to find out who she was and what she wanted out of life. Military service became a transition period for young women emerging into the perplexing world of adulthood with its attendant responsibilities. The military service tour could be seen as a period of testing and learning as well as a preparation for later trials. Some chose to make a career in the military sector.

The phenomenon of the military couple became more prevalent. Sometimes for economic or other reasons, one spouse would follow the military member and join up as well and it was not always the woman joining up after the husband. This pattern became both a headache and a strength for the military establishment. It also helped cement ties for a unique kind of marriage. The military family suddenly demanded attention from the service leadership. Social services were needed; different kinds of housing and other allowances had to be furnished which had important consequences for the logistical and deployment operations of the headquarters planning staff.

Particularly since the All-Volunteer Force came into being after the draft ended in 1974, young women have seen the Army in much the same way as young men have. The services became a haven for jobs, schooling, stability, and economic security. Military service also held the promise of further benefits after service including going on to further schooling through a GI Bill and using the service experience to launch a career in the civilian sector. Ambitious young women college graduates without specific professional training entered as officers and found new challenges for leadership in career fields that would have been closed to them in the civilian world. Former teachers, office managers, secretaries, and sales clerks were attracted to the diversity of occupational specialities that seemed available. The possibility of travel, of going overseas, of meeting lots of new people, were also positive factors for recruitment.

The buildup of women's participation during the mid-seventies, as the pool of qualified young males shrank in an expanding economy, strengthened the image of the military services as a career path for women. With a participation rate of 12 percent projected by 1986 during the Carter years, it looked as though women's roles within the military services would be enhanced and expanded. During the mid- to late seventies, the reports from official documents about women's performances in most of their occupational specialties were glowing. The positive pronouncements from the Defense Department seemed to assure women an important place in the military establishment, one that would be good for them and good for the services, for years to come.

However, with the Reagan administration a new era began that has not proved beneficial to military women. There were rumblings in 1981 that some Army field commanders were concerned about women's effects upon readiness. These numerous reports were never documented, but one high-ranking officer specifically referred to *one* commander's complaints. The Army instituted an overall study, supposedly spurred by the GAO (General Accounting Office) report of 1976 which criticized some aspects of women's performance and complained of high attrition rates for the women. The Army in 1981 set up a task force called the "Women in the Army Policy Review Group" to review the performance and place of women in the Army. This study group's report was delayed several times, with ominous rumors surfacing about their negative findings and portents for women's future roles in the military. Briefings to DACOWITS, the Women's Congressional Caucus, and women's groups confirmed military women's suspicions that the commitment to women expressed during the seventies was being watered down.

The Army Study Report was finally issued in October 1982, and it did indeed put a damper on women's aspirations for careers in the Army. Turning back the clock, the Army closed off twenty-three military occupational specialities to women, bringing the total number of these specialities closed to women to sixty-one. But this was only the beginning for every single military occupational speciality was being reevaluated by the Army to determine what the (upper body) strength requirement should be for a soldier to be able to be assigned to that speciality. Every woman and man would have to meet these specifications.

Another major change in the Army's approach to women's roles in its ranks was the newly instituted *P* factor, which was described as the *Probability* of being in a combat zone. Each speciality was to be rated according to this probability. Women were already, by policy, barred from all specialties that had direct combat roles. With the report of the Study Group, women were now going to be excluded from all specialties that would bring them into proximity to combat zones that were prefigured and designed by the Army review group's team. Dozens of specialties—in chemical, nuclear, medical, biological warfare, and logistic fields were going to be cut off for women. Those women who had been trained and were vital parts of units, here and overseas, were to be removed from those slots.

The Army has used the combat exclusion policy as a justification for its findings and subsequent actions that have literally pulled the rug from under the careers of thousands of military women. While the Army is not statutorily bound to a combat exclusion statute—as the Navy and the Air Force are—it has in the past, by policy, prohibited women from participating in direct combat units.

The new policy announced by the Army, with the release of the policy review group report last year, is an even broader interpretation of the combat exclusion policy. By digging considerably behind the so-called front lines combat zone and prohibiting women's presence in a number of units behind those lines, the Army seems to be pushing out thousands of women who have been trained at Army expense from where they are now deployed. Not only have the Army actions caused military women's morale to plummet, but they have raised serious questions about the "readiness" of the units now stripped of their qualified personnel by the ousting of their women soldiers.

Despite the Army actions that began to take place even before the review group's report had been made public, there is considerable controversy raging about the pullback on women's participation. The official Department of Defense policy verbalized from the Secretary of Defense on down is that women have participated brilliantly and that their contributions are very valued. Defense and Army officials deny that there is a radical change in women's career possibilities in the Army. The words are there, but the actions seem to belie them.

There is no question that, if the present trend of Army actions regarding utilization of females continues, women will not have the career opportunities they had in the seventies. Furthermore, Army actions might possibly provide a model for other services to take similar steps to reduce and limit the opportunities for women in their ranks. At this point, however, there is still debate going on within the Pentagon and only time will tell whether women will continue to find careers and opportunities in military service.

·PART III·

WHAT HAPPENED TO THEM

Women Veterans as Viewed by the Public and Private Sectors

The Broad Picture

Women veterans. Isn't that a contradiction in terms? Men are veterans, not women. Men are drafted; men bear the burden of national defense. Women can provide some support services: They can fold bandages and answer telephones. But who thinks of women as veterans?

It is not well known that there are 1,218,000 living women veterans. The media has presented a modern image of women who are in military service. Drill sergeant and aircraft maintenance mechanic are familiar roles for females today. When women leave the services, they become veterans. But somehow no one thinks of them in that way. It's as though these women wore their uniforms forever.

Women in earlier wars often did more than tend the wounded and staff the communications system. Women have participated in the defense of the nation, even to the extent of seeing action in battle.[1] More often than not, they disguised their sex. They were not many, but they played important roles and demonstrated skills, bravery, and determination which had not been considered characteristic of women.

While World War I brought the first institutionalization of women's support services for the military other than the nurses' Corps— i.e., the Yeomanettes (Navy) and the Marinettes (Marines)— World War II gave women a genuine chance to participate actively in military service when the Women's Auxiliary Army Corps

(WAAC) was created. In 1943 the WAAC was changed to the Women's Army Corps with a projected strength of 150,000 by June of that year.[2] Women served in other branches as well. Altogether, during World War II more than 350,000 women participated in the Army, the Navy, the Coast Guard, and the Marines.[3]

A World War II woman veteran describes her experience:

> I would not take any amount of money for the experiences I had during the nearly four years I was in the Army. As a freelance artist at the time of my enlistment, October 1, 1941, I had the prospect of spending the War somewhere in a studio making maps or other aids. . . . This did not appeal to me. On completion of basic, I applied for driver training. Following completion of driver training I was sent as an artist . . . where I worked in the drafting office. I was accepted by OCS and, on completion of training, was assigned as Instructor to the Driver Training School.[4]

Many of the women who served in World War II joined the services for patriotic reasons—

> I joined the service because I felt that women could replace many men (as I did) in clerical and office positions, leaving the man for the grimmer duties. I replaced a master sergeant and a corporal as Information Clerk and receptionist at the Selfridge Field Hospital. Although it sounds like a "nothing" job, I worked from 7 A.M. to 7 P.M. every day, with a 15-minute lunch hour. In my seven months I had just one 30-hour pass in all that time.[5]

But there were other reasons also. The love of adventure, the desire to travel, the feeling that somehow military service would open up new vistas if not new opportunities—all were incentives for women to join the military. Back in the early 1940s there were few opportunities for women to enlarge their horizons.

> As I had only eight years of schooling it was my chance to try to better myself, giving me a chance to see the country. Perhaps you could call it an escape. But underneath it all, I loved my country and it gave me a chance to do something for all it gave me.[6]

But participation in one of the women's service corps during World War II did not change the roles of women in American society, even though it would seem it had the potential of doing so. Not really—at least not immediately.

> There was a distinct message that we should now let the men take over the real world and we should silently return to our kitchens. Unfortunately, many of us did and we should have known better, for we really were a pioneering, adventuresome lot.[7]

Hasn't this been the story of women since ancient times? To accept the burdens of war as well as of peace, no matter what the consequences—patiently, diligently, uncomplainingly? And humbly, as if that was their due—without any expectations, without any thought of recompense for their sacrifice? Isn't that the true story of womankind? At least, until the recent feminist revolution crystallized in the sixties, it was the picture for most. Anyway, the women went in cheerfully and contributed directly to the war effort. And then they came out of the war—demobilized like their brothers, to return to the society which had called them, as housewives.

The Veterans Administration

Every population group served by a government agency is measured, examined, studied, and evaluated routinely. An incredible amount of statistics is kept. Veterans are no exception. Pages and volumes of data are compiled and made available periodically—monthly, quarterly, yearly—by the Veterans Administration about veterans. The total estimated veteran population (as of September 30, 1981) is 30,083,000.

As an example of this recordkeeping, the VA puts out a statistical summary of its activities every month, breaking down the use of services it offers, i.e., hospital care, nursing-home care, domiciliary care, outpatient care, national cemeteries, disability compensation and pension, and all the other benefits the VA administers. There are dozens of statistics that also give comparative data from the previous two years.

Altogether 107 categories of information on the veterans' population are given in these monthly VA summaries. None of it is broken down by sex. Among the 107 categories in these summaries are the veteran population, broken down by period of service; hospital care, broken down by daily census of those treated in VA hospitals, and those treated in non–VA hospitals and State Home hospitals; outpatient care, service-connected and nonservice-connected; vocational rehabilitation; spouses' and widow(er)s' educational assistance; National Service Life Insurance, for World War II and later; policies in force, term policies, permanent plan policies, and service disabled policies in force; and many others.

Women veterans are left out of important reports on veterans. A prestigious report by the National Academy of Sciences, which examined the VA hospital system, in 1977 stated in its preface: "In this analysis, only *male* veterans are considered because the female veterans amount to less than two percent of the current total."[8]

This study by the NAS was an extremely important critique of the VA medical system which prompted extensive hearings on both the report and the VA's response by the Senate Veterans Affairs Committee.[9] Women veterans who are eligible to use the VA medical and surgical services and do use them were not considered important enough to be included either in the NAS study or in the VA response.

It is particularly unfortunate that women were not studied or considered in the NAS study because women veterans have complained most about the inadequacy of facilities at VA hospitals for their special needs. There also have been reports of insensitivity and brashness toward women—both as inpatients and outpatients.

> . . . most VA hospitals are not totally equipped to handle women and their problems. Many of our hospitals, especially here in Syracuse, are trying to upgrade the service, but there is much room for improvement.[10]

Gynecological services are not routinely provided at every VA hospital. With the small percentage of women veterans, this has not been a service in great demand, heretofore, and hospitals have not set up special units. However, even in other services women veterans have felt shortchanged.

> In dealing with the Urology clinic within the VA hospital, I find them totally geared to men. The rules and regulations governing such conditions are written by men for men.[11]

The same woman veteran complained that VA doctors were uncooperative and pleaded a lack of knowledge about "women's problems" like urinary tract infections. She also found that there was no gynecological follow-up, which is routine with treatment of such infections. When she tried to find out information about obtaining contract services from the VA, she was rebuffed.

The experiences of women at one VA hospital were chronicled recently by two investigators who wanted to ascertain what women patients experienced in the predominantly male environment of the hospital.[12] The researchers sought to find out how the women patients at this VA mental hospital (Brentwood) felt about their treatment and environment. A major concern of the female patients was a feeling of a "lack of personal security" in their home ward or on hospital grounds day or night. Also, a high number of women patients stated that there were incidents of assault, robbery, rape, and "flashing." Another finding of the researchers was that medical care for female health concerns was haphazard. Only half of the women indicated they had been given breast and pelvic examinations.

In view of other verbal and written reports by women of dissatisfaction with the VA's responsiveness to their medical needs, the lack of attention still as reflected in this study is inexplicable.

* * *

Another example of the VA overlooking women veterans was its action in 1977 to 1978 when it commissioned the Bureau of the Census to mail a twelve-page questionnaire to eleven thousand *male* veterans. Since women's participation in the armed forces was by then already 6 percent, certainly some women veterans could have been included. As it happens, a fine opportunity to obtain important data on women veterans was lost.

The purpose of the census survey was "to collect information that will be used to determine the effectiveness of veterans benefits programs in meeting the needs of the nation's veterans and to provide a basis for future planning of programs and facilities." When queried about leaving out women veterans, VA officials invariably stated that they were concerned about the total veteran population of which women were a part. Their thesis was that what is good for male veterans is good for female veterans. This assumption is questionable considering the different positions in society and life-styles of both sexes. While the census was most useful, it would have been advantageous to have more specific information about women veterans.

In 1980, the census queried women as to their veterans' status for the first time. It is hoped that when the census data becomes available, women veterans will cease to be invisible. Perhaps with continuing pressure from women veterans themselves and their allies there will be interest in evaluating veterans' benefits programs for women. Then, too, perhaps there could be policy planning for women veterans as distinct from the total veterans' approach that characterizes current processes.[13] Developments in the eighties are pointing in that direction.

The VA, in response to requests for information about female veterans, provides a collection of statistics called "Select Characteristics of Female Veterans for 1977," and a similar report for 1978. Both sets of data contain breakdowns by marital status, age, period of service, branch of service, and a breakdown of the nation's female population by states. Statistics on current women veterans' use of the GI Bill and women on service-connected disability compensation rolls are available as are figures for DIC (Dependency and Indemnity Compensation) for dependents of female veterans, and dependents receiving death pensions.

Some data on female veterans' use of medical facilities are available for the years 1974 to 1978. They include women's use of extended care facilities and the number of women using VA medical centers as inpatients. Comprehensive data is not available. An interesting statistic uncovered by the VA is that in the one-day annual patient census, there was an average of 1.7 percent females in VA medical centers, out of approximately 77,000 veteran patients.

In addition, current information on women veterans' participation in the following programs is available: home loans, educational and training programs, compensation and pension programs. Some programs that the VA conducts do not have any data on women veterans' participation: the insurance programs, burial benefits, and ambulatory care.

This then is a partial picture of women veterans' current use of veterans' programs administered by the VA. What about the use of these programs by women veterans in earlier years? How about the gallant women who served in World War II, Korea, the years between Korea and Vietnam?

It is on this issue that the VA is most embarrassed. Since this agency, like many other government agencies, could not possibly keep all the statistics they have accumulated over the years on the millions of American citizens they serve, they had to thin out their records—the VA admits that it has kept a 2 percent sampling of their records. Because the number of women who served in the armed services (prior to the modern all-volunteer force) constitute 2 percent or less of the total military population, they did not show up in the records. The 2 percent sampling technique therefore effectively eliminates women veterans from those records. Consequently, we do not and cannot know, for instance, how many women veterans from World War II made use of their GI Bill, or how many received outpatient medical care from VA hospitals. For that matter, there is very little information altogether on women veterans before the Vietnam era.

Current data keeping by the VA still does not break down the veteran population by gender. Besides the monthly summary reports of activities mentioned earlier, the Office of the Controller and Reports and Statistical Services both put out dozens of publications each year. Examples of these, which are circulated among veterans' organizations, Congress, and interested agencies, include such reports as "Educational and Income Characteristics of Veterans," "Data on Vietnam-Era Veterans," and "Disability Compensation Data." These statistical reports are not broken down by gender.

* * *

A headline in a recent issue of the VA newsletter *Vanguard* reads:

WOMEN VETERANS USE OF EDUCATION BENEFITS
UNDER THE GI BILL.[14]

The lead paragraph goes on to state: "This report recently released by the Office of Reports and Statistics examines for the
first time the use of GI benefits by female veterans of the peacetime post–Korean conflict and Vietnam eras." (Emphasis sup-
plied.) As far as can be determined, this is the first time that
women veterans' use of any benefits under the GI Bill has been
reported and analyzed. The report itself related some interesting
things about women veterans of World War II. Not as many of
them took advantage of their GI Bill as did their male counterparts. However, women who did use them used as much of their
entitlement as the men, although they tended to use it later after
release from active duty. Furthermore, they were more likely than
male veterans to use their educational benefits at the college level
and to train fulltime.

In the past six months the VA has put out two more reports
and is planning to do others.

Other Agencies

If the VA has overlooked women veterans as a population group,
what about the other government agencies that administer some
kind of veterans' program?

The Department of Labor is very important to veterans. It runs
the Veterans Employment Service (VES). Within the Veterans
Employment Service, only two women are serving in a professional capacity. The Department of Labor also has responsibilities
for such programs as Job Service; Disabled Veterans Outreach
Program (DVOP), CETA programs (veterans are one of the eligible groups; however, this program is being phased out); Unemployment Compensation for Ex-Servicepersons (UCX); and
the Targeted Jobs Tax Credit Program. No figures on women
veterans' participation in these programs are available. The Department of Labor has funded a number of ad hoc programs
relating to Vietnam-era veterans, but none of them have specifically focused on women. Under the Carter administration a new
office was created—a Deputy Assistant Secretary for Veterans'
Affairs—to emphasize the Department of Labor's commitment
to veterans. That office now has been·upgraded to that of an
Assistant Secretary.

The Bureau of Labor Statistics (under the Department of Labor), which spews forth ominous facts each week about national unemployment figures, also is derelict in its data collecting. It keeps no statistics on women veterans' unemployment. Figures from BLS which have been alerting the public, in particular, to the dire strait of the Vietnam veterans tell nothing about the employment status of the women veterans. The BLS compares veterans' unemployment figures against those for nonveterans by age. There is no comparable breakdown for women veterans as against nonveteran women.

There is a Women's Bureau in the Department of Labor, but only now has it begun to focus on women veterans.

The Department of Education currently is the home of one of the veterans' programs designed to assist veterans go to college, and then stay in college. The Veterans Cost of Instruction Program (VCIP) was legislated by Congress in 1972 to encourage colleges and universities to provide outreach and counseling services for their veteran students. Hundreds of institutions of higher education around the country have participated in VCIP at one time or another. Since 1973 over 6,500,000 veteran-students benefited from counseling and other services funded from the VCIP. Total institutional participation from 1973 to 1981 has been over 9,700 colleges or universities.

It is impossible to find out how many women veterans benefited from the VCIP Program—no records were kept according to sex. Furthermore, there is no breakdown of women veterans' use of any other educational program administered by the Department of Education (formerly part of the Department of Health, Education, and Welfare).

The Office of Personnel Management (formerly the U.S. Civil Service Commission) seems a logical place to find out how women veterans used or didn't use their veterans preference in the federal civil service. In recent years the Commission has been compiling statistics on women. It furnished data showing the total number of women and of women veterans in the federal work force as of March 31, 1977. It also provided the number of women veterans newly hired between 1975 and 1977, by grade. There is recent data for the total number of employees and minority employees— by grades and by different pay systems. There is also a breakdown of women employees according to ethnic background and job grade. However, it has no breakdown of women veterans as a distinct demographic group. Nor could the Commission indicate how many women veterans used their veterans' preference. However, it is compiling 1978 data on veterans' preference by status, sex, and grade level.

Department of Defense

Since women veterans come out of the Department of Defense, it might be presumed that the department would have statistics on them, at least for the periods when they were members of the armed services. This proved not to be the case. Sketchy, fragmented data were available for different periods: force strengths, educational levels in percentages as against the total Army's; attrition rates and educational levels, and reenlistment and first-term rates. There are also current figures breaking down women in the Army by skill, branch, officers, warrant officers, and enlisted personnel. Comparative figures of women's rates as against men's are also available. Complete historical data on women who served in the armed services were either missing or not available. There have been studies on women's performance in the various military services and some policy reviews on women's participation in the armed forces. The most recent one is the background review, "Women in the Military."[15] A striking fact is that the Department of Defense has not been able to ascertain how many women served in Vietnam.

Academic Research

The academic research community has not discovered women veterans yet. Like the government agencies, social scientists who have done research on veterans either include only men or they do not separate the information into men and women. Again, they have been concerned with *all* veterans. There have been no academic studies on women veterans except the ones cited.

One of the reasons that recent studies on Vietnam veterans have not included women has been the emphasis on combat experiences and the consequences of those experiences. Yet, even if women were not in combat, they were exposed to some of the perilous conditions of combat since some were very close to the fighting. Several women lost their lives during the Vietnam War; others were injured. There were casualties in earlier wars as well.

Furthermore, in the case of the Vietnam War, women shared with men the trauma of returning to civilian life (see Chapter 6). Many suffered from the post–Vietnam Syndrome; some had to face the hostility of the civilian population that objected to the war and were angry at the veterans who participated in it. One woman veteran of the Vietnam era wrote:

> . . . we female veterans of the Vietnam era have suffered from readjustment problems relating to the shattered illusion of Patriotism encountered during and after the Vietnam conflict. Though many of us did not see service in Southeast Asia, we were very much affected by the radical changes in attitude and direction of our great nation. We also had to defend ourselves when family, friends, and our communities condemned us for participating in such an unpopular war. The hostilities were vented on us—at home—more so than it was on the government which sent us, or which we served. In this, we share the same burdens and conflicts as our male counterparts.[16]

An important study which compared the adjustment patterns of veterans to those of their peers who did not serve queried only males. The rationale was that only males were drafted. This study, entitled "Legacies of Vietnam: Comparative Adjustment of Veterans and Their Peers," came out last year. It is partially subsidized by the Veterans Administration, and was directed and compiled by the Center for Policy Research in New York City.[17] Since women who served during the Vietnam era shared the agony of rejection with their male colleagues, it would seem logical that there be some study of how those who served differed from those who didn't. There hasn't been any such study.

Another reason that women veterans somehow lost out in the research community's brief and sporadic interest in veterans is the fact that survey research on veterans usually only produces a small number of female veterans, because they have been such a small proportion of the total population of veterans.

Recently there have been studies on women serving in the military, i.e., Binkin and Bach's *Women and the Military,* Helen

Rogan's *Mixed Company,* and Major Gen. Jeanne Holm's *Women in the Military.* With the media focusing on the woman soldier (e.g., the movie and TV series on Private Benjamin), there has been an increasing interest in the military careers of women. As more women participate in the armed services and hence more women will become veterans, the lack of information on women veterans is likely to change. One can imagine in the future the development of the concept of a typical male soldier and a typical female soldier, and that of a typical female and male veteran.

The Overall Picture

The picture that emerges from the investigation of women veterans vis-à-vis government agencies is that they have not been identified as a distinct population group. Government agencies in the past, and to some extent even in the present, have not routinely collected information about them. Historically, there is practically no source of data because so little has been saved. As a whole, women veterans have suffered benign neglect. When women become veterans they often are totally eclipsed by the much larger male veteran population. For now, a bibliographic search reveals that almost nothing has been written on women veterans. There is no individual category "Women Veterans" in the Library of Congress catalogue cards under "Women" or under "Veterans."

∘6∘

Veterans' Benefits
for Women Veterans

A. Historical Background

Veterans' programs have been an integral part of the federal budget since the Revolutionary War. As the nation was born out of war, "citizen soldiers" have been seen as the underpinning of defense. Veterans always have had a unique place among the general population, although they have not always had the nation's gratitude expressed as generously as in modern times.

Initially, veterans' programs were partially an inducement for men to stay in the army. During the Revolutionary War, Continental Army soldiers were promised pensions to help morale and to lower the desertion rate. The first general pension was enacted in 1818; pensions were to be based on need. In 1836 the widows of the Revolutionary War were finally remembered and granted pensions.[1]

During the Civil War federal veterans' benefits were only for Union soldiers. It took until 1958 for the government finally to pardon the Confederate soldiers. In 1866 a system of National Homes that were residential facilities were created for Civil War veterans. Union veterans were also given preference in public employment.

More soldiers died of typhus than of battle wounds during the Spanish-American war. These veterans, who were relatively few in number, received medical care and were awarded a small pension without strings attached. This was to be the last time that a pure pension was granted. Subsequent legislation extended the eligibility for some veterans' programs to the Spanish-American War veterans.

Almost five million veterans came out of World War I. Some benefits were granted them: disability compensation, government life insurance, a family allotment, and vocational rehabilitation. Two hundred thousand veterans who had been wounded were treated by a hospital system for veterans that came out of the Public Health Service Hospitals. Most of the veterans had a hard time finding jobs when they left the service, and the government did little to help them return to a productive life. The march on Washington by World War I veterans for a "service bonus" was not one of the happier occurrences in American history.

The end of World War II brought serious problems to a nation that had been turned upside down by a long war on both sides of the globe. America had never been involved in such a large-scale military undertaking overseas for that long a period of time. Over eleven million men and women served in the armed forces of the nation—a great proportion of the country's youth.

With economic and social institutions drastically altered, the challenge of gearing down from a wartime to a peacetime economy, together with a massive demobilization, was on the horizon. Recalling the sight of veterans peddling apples on street corners after World War I, policy planners were concerned about the integration of the returning veterans into the economy and the social fabric of the nation. New industries had sprung up; there had been changes in the geographical population centers; women had entered the work force in great numbers. America had changed, and it had to find ways to bring the veterans back into the economic fabric.

Americans had changed also. Those who had served had experienced much, learned a great deal, and widened their horizons. The old farm, the old candy store, the factory job, did not look so good anymore. Not only had individuals' aspirations grown, but the need for technicians, engineers, managers, and scientists had expanded as well. America had become the "leader of the Western world," and with that new role came great demands for knowledge, technological skill, and political acumen.

To meet the multiple challenges, a whole new generation of educated people was needed. Prior to World War II a college education was the mark of the upper class. A tiny percentage of the population had a college degree. The small elite of educated people would no longer be able to meet the personnel needs of a world power embarked on a serious competition with another world power.

The World War II GI Bill, which provided generous comprehensive education and training to the returning veterans, changed the face of the nation. It has been well documented that the GI educational benefits transformed American higher education and raised the educational level of that generation and generations to come. With many provisions for assistance in upgrading their educational attainments, veterans pulled ahead of nonveterans in earning capacity. In the long run it was the nonveterans who had fewer opportunities.

Besides the GI Bill, a comprehensive compensation and pension system was created for disabled and older veterans who became needy. "Veterans' programs constitute a major part of the total welfare system, providing millions with income support, medical care, education and training, and means for aquiring housing and life insurance programs."[2]

Veterans' benefits budgets have ballooned; there has been skepticism voiced about the justification for treating veterans so generously who were not wounded or maimed by war. While compensation is seen and accepted almost universally as an "unassailable duty to the victims of war," there is far more controversy over whether a pension is justified. It has been suggested— and most of the veterans' organizations agree—that pensions represent delayed compensation for services rendered to the nation. There is another school of thought, however, that regards pension as a gratuity.

> To supporters, the pension program is a variant of social insurance, wartime military service constituting the premium payment. To skeptics, veterans pension is a dignified but indefensible separate assistance program.[3]

The differences in treatment of the veterans and nonveterans have been striking to students of the welfare system. Since veterans' incomes have been higher than those of nonveterans, they need less help. There is the contention that Social Security and veterans' pensions have eliminated poverty among old and disabled veterans of World War II. (This is not the case for World War I veterans, who are older and dying off quickly. A pension system has never been legislated for them, although there has been legislation pending for years.) Since indigent older veterans do not have to submit to a means test, they are generally given more humane consideration by the VA. Advocates of welfare reform and the social support system for the aged and the poor suggest the VA system might become a model for a welfare system for the whole population.

The VA hospital system also provides medical care for veterans with non-service-connected disabilities and illnesses, on a space-available basis or as outpatients. There has been a continuing debate on this issue because there is some doubt as to whether this was the intent of those who designed the VA hospital system. Doctors and administrators within VA have maintained that non-service-connected cases are needed to maintain a high quality medical care for veterans within the VA's hospital system.

Periodically, the VA hospital system comes under attack from the private sector. Criticism of the VA's treatment of non-service-connected illnesses often is the major point of the attack. Warning about the threat of an all-out attack on the VA hospital system, Dr. Donald Curtis, the VA's chief medical director, told a Senate hearing last year:

> Should that ever happen, it would so disturb our patient mix that our ability to continue to provide a teaching base for health manpower would be gone, and with it our ability to attract quality health professionals into the system would be gone. It would be the beginning of a reversion to an old soldiers' and sailors' home system so well remembered from the 1930's. . . .
>
> And beware of the specious argument that somehow the non-service-connected veteran, the needy, medically needy non-service-connected veteran somehow is not entitled to care

in the system. *The system cannot exist caring only for the service-connected.*[4]

During the 1950s, a Presidential Commission under the chairmanship of General Omar Bradley was created to examine and reappraise the entire veterans' benefits system. The Commission's recommendations aroused great controversy because it questioned the rationale for many of the benefits, particularly for those who had not been wounded or maimed in battle. It concluded that the justification for non-service-connected benefits was quite weak, and that society had other methods at its disposal to meet the needs of veterans who were not wounded in war.

The Commission did not realize how difficult it would be to end a social program with a vast constituency. It tried to lay the groundwork for new policy formulations for veterans, but its work has remained a matter for historical research. Very few of the commission's recommendations were actually carried out.

Several years ago the American Medical Association House of Delegates passed a resolution recommending that the VA hospital system be phased out. While this trial balloon did not go very far, veterans' organizations and veterans were alerted to possible future attacks on the system.

In 1977 the National Academy of Sciences did a thorough review and study of the VA hospital system in which it proposed sweeping and fundamental changes in the entire VA health care system. The VA concurred with many of the recommendations of the NAS study, but took exception to some of its major suggestions, particularly with regard to reallocation of resources. The VA further rejected an NAS suggestion that the VA develop a relationship to a national health policy that does not yet exist. Extensive hearings were held by the Senate Veterans' Affairs Committee on both the NAS study and the VA's response.[5]

More recently, a task force appointed by the President and headed by J. Peter Grace looked at the VA and reportedly gave serious consideration to eliminating the VA and distributing its functions to other agencies. Another task force looking at the VA hospital system is reportedly considering suggesting that the VA's hospitals be consolidated with the Department of Defense hospitals. If that is not possible, the report goes on, it may recommend that the VA hospitals be turned over to communities to run (*Washington Post,* March 24, 1982).

* * *

Survivors also are included in the VA pension system. Since 96 percent of the veterans are men, survivors are usually women. There have been some survivors' benefits (for widows of officers) since 1780, but compensations for widows of Revolutionary War casualties were not awarded until 1836. After 1957 Dependency and Indemnity Compensation was paid to dependent survivors. Widows and dependent children were not limited by any income or social benefits they might have had, although surviving parents were. The pensions for survivors, however, were less than for the non-service-connected veterans. If a widow remarried, she was no longer eligible for a survivor's pension. Furthermore, if a widow received both a pension and Social Security benefits, she was usually disqualified from other public assistance. Thus, this group of women was penalized by such provisions and was likely to be needier than the veterans.

Differences in Benefits for Women Veterans

Theoretically, men and women veterans are equally entitled to benefit programs administered by the VA and by other agencies. However, women have not always been entitled to, or been able to obtain, the same benefits as men. One difference in treatment is derived from the ambiguous status of two of the women's services of World War II: the WAAC and the WASP. The WAAC was not part of the Army, although it was attached to it. The WASP was supposed to be militarized during the war, but never actually was, and was disbanded before the end of the war. Women who served in either unit were not considered veterans for the purpose of receiving benefits administered by the VA, even though they thought they were part of the military forces. Veterans' status came much later for them.

The WAAC

From the start the WAAC's legal position was ambiguous and frustrating for all connected with it. As an auxiliary to the Army, the WAAC, for legal purposes, was considered not a military body but a civilian unit. Congress had rejected letting the WAAC become a military body. One of the fears was that a WAAC's husband would get a government allotment whether he needed it or not, since the law provided this for a soldier's wife whether she needed it or not. Originally, the War Department had set up the plans for the WAAC as though indeed military status was assured despite the fact it was decreed an auxiliary.

The big issue was whether the women's corps of the Army was to be militarized or whether it was to continue as part of the civil service. To assuage another fear that had stood in the way of the legislation's passage, the Army assured Congress that WAACs would not displace civil service employees since they would be called upon only when civilians were not available.

Because it was not clear just what status the WAAC would have, planners at the War Department came up with two sets of plans—one for a military unit and one for a civilian unit. The debate in Congress was an acrimonious one. There was opposition to putting women directly in the Army because this would mean they would receive the same disability benefits and pensions as men. Also, the bugaboo was raised that women generals would be giving orders to male personnel. There was apprehension that the women not only would belong in the corps but in the rest of the Army as well.

The going was rough despite the strong supporting statements of the War Department and General Marshall of the need for the women's corps. By the time the War Department realized the problems a civilian auxiliary corps would cause both legally and logistically, the legislation was already on its way to passage in that form. Amendments were introduced to give the corps equal status in the Army but they were resisted strenuously. It took almost a year to get the legislation enacted. Finally, on May 14, 1942, Edith Nourse Rogers's bill, HR 4906, became Public Law 77–554.

Be it enacted, the Senate and House of Representatives of the USA in Congress assembled, that the President is hereby authorized to establish and organize in such units as he may from time to time determine to be necessary, a Women's Army Auxiliary Corps for non-combatant service with the Army of the United States for the purpose of making available to the national defense when needed the knowledge, skill, and special training of women of this Nation. The total number of women enrolled or appointed in the Women's Army Auxiliary Corps shall not exceed the number authorized from time to time by the President, and in no event shall exceed one hundred fifty thousand.

The text of the law contains the ambiguity that was to haunt the WAAC during its short lifetime and to cause problems for the women who served in that body for years to come. Section 12 states clearly that "the corps shall not be a part of the Army, but it shall be the only women's organization authorized to serve with the Army exclusive of the Army Nurse Corps." On the other hand, another section of the law stipulates that members of the Corps are subject to the Articles of War, and that the women would be under the Army's disciplinary regulations. Section 19 provides that "persons in the military service include Army, Navy, Marine Corps, the Coast Guard, WAAC, all officers of the Public Health Service detailed by proper authority for duty either with the Army or the Navy," which implies that the WAACs are in the military service.

The WAACs thought they were in the Army of the United States; so did the men soldiers and the American public. They were certainly disciplined and discharged the way members of the Army were.

36.a. An enrolled member of the WAAC may be discharged for the convenience of the Government by the Secretary of War, when, in the discretion of the Director, retention in the Corps would *not* be for the best interest of the Government, and a member so discharged may be given an honorable discharge (white certificate), a discharge (white certificate), or a summary discharge (blue certificate).[6]

WAAC officers were instructed to convene an administrative board for purposes of disciplinary action or discharges according to Army regulations.

The War Department added to the confusion by grouping the

WAACs together with women in the other services, who were regular members of those services. For example:

> V. Hospitalization by VA facilities: defines "veteran." Veteran will be potentially entitled to hospitalization as a beneficiary of the VA, provided such person is not dishonorably discharged. Eligibility under the conditions stated above will also be attained by members of the WAAC, Women's Reserve of the Navy and Marine Corps and the Women's Reserve of the Coast Guard.[7]

Contradictions abound as to where the WAACs were with regard to the Army. The *Officers' Guide* of 1942 welcomes the WAACs but clearly places them outside the Army:

> The Army bids welcome to the Women's Army Auxiliary Corps—the WAACs. With the Army Nurse Corps, it constitutes the second organization of women who volunteer to serve and work with the armed forces. The Corps was established by an Act of Congress (Public Law 554–77th Congress) and approved at the White House on May 11, 1942. The Corps *is not part of the Army* [emphasis added], but it is the only women's organization authorized to serve with the Army, exclusive of the Army Nurse Corps.[8]

In that same *Officers' Guide* the benefits for WAACs are spelled out:

> Medical and dental services, hospitalization, and medical and hospital supplies are provided as nearly as practicable to similar services rendered to the personnel of the Army.

The possibility of WAACs becoming sick or injured was recognized:

> Provisions are included in the Act for the payment of compensation to those members of the Corps who become physically injured or otherwise incapacitated under broad limitations while in the line of duty.

Section IX of the WAAC Regulations 1.93 spells out the medical and dental benefits:

118. Medical and dental attention—a. Members of the WAAC on active duty or in actual training will receive medical and dental services through the Medical Department of the Army. b. Medical care will not include any care incident or resulting from pregnancy or any member except necessary care prior to discharge. c. Medical reports and records will be those prescribed in Army Regulations.[9]

On the other hand, the WAACs who were injured or who had died while on active duty were to be treated like civilian employees. The WAAC or her beneficiary were to be

entitled to all the benefits prescribed by law for *civilian employees* [emphasis added] of the United States who are physically injured while in the pertormance of duty or who die as a result thereof, and the United States Employees' Compensation Commission shall have jurisdiction in such cases and shall perform the same duties with reference thereto as in the cases of other civilian employees of the United States so injured or otherwise incapacitated.

Even though an injured WAAC would be treated as a civilian employee, she would be discharged as though she was in the Army.

b. Members who become incapacitated for further service will be discharged upon completion of such treatment as is authorized.[10]

Furthermore, provisions for disability are referred to the U.S. Employees' Compensation Commission. At the same time, the benefits of the Soldiers and Sailors Civil Relief Act of 1940 were extended to members of the WAAC.

Members of the WAAC were subject to Army regulations. Officers were entitled to all leave privileges afforded to officers of the Army of the United States by AR 605–115. Nonofficers were called "enrolled" women rather than "enlisted" women, but they were entitled to the same privileges as enlisted men. Regarding military courtesies, WAAC officers and enrolled women had to salute all officers of the services as well as officers of allied or friendly nations.

The "enrollment" of women was circumscribed by the regulations. No woman could be enrolled if she had anyone dependent upon her for financial help. Also, if she had one or more children under fourteen years of age, she was disqualified.

The Army was concerned that the women working with it in the WAAC were duly accommodated and that steps be taken for their well-being.

(1) Commanders will apply the principle that procedure for the utilization of members of the WAAC, both in their living and working conditions, will vary from that for male Army personnel in such ways as are necessary because members of the Women's Army Auxiliary Corps are women, and in order to assure their health, morale, and general well-being. This principle will be applied in respect to the following fields, among others: hours of employment; numbers of women needed to perform heavy tasks; provisions for safety and security; disciplinary measures and administration; and insurance of suitable recreational, educational, and morale provisions.[11]

One of the reasons the War Department supported the establishment of a women's corps was that field commanders were asking for women to take over clerical and administrative duties. The WAAC legislation did not permit women to serve overseas; they would be going abroad without any of the protections or benefits of military status. They could not receive extra overseas pay; they were not eligible for government life insurance; and they would not be entitled to veterans' hospitalization. If they were killed, their parents could not collect death gratuities; if captured by the enemy, the WAACs would not have any protections a prisoner of war would have, since they were considered nonmilitary personnel. Furthermore, the WAAC's life insurance policies would probably be invalidated because of the dangers of being overseas.

Even more damaging to the WAACs' status was that they were not entitled to lifetime pensions and hospitalization that soldiers and sailors and also the WAVES were entitled to if they suffered disabling injuries or illnesses. The WAACs were under the Federal Employees Compensation Act and as such they would receive only a tiny compensation if they were hurt or disabled. The Army could give a WAAC hospitalization only until her disability was pronounced permanent, at which time she had to be discharged and leave the military compound. Thereafter, she had no right to a veteran's pension or hospitalization. Under these circumstances the Army felt it was difficult, if not impossible, to send the WAACs overseas.

The confusion over the status of the WAAC in the Army increased as time went on. No one knew exactly which Army regulations applied to the WAAC and which didn't. An example of a simple thing that became a complicated issue was in deciding if the WAACs had the use of the franking privilege. In 1943, when a pay raise was given to military personnel, the WAACs were not included because they were not strictly "military."

In the matter of state bonuses for military persons, it was left up to the state to decide what to do with the WAACs. The quartermaster general ruled that WAACs were not eligible for burial with a flag, military honors, or an escort to accompany the remains home. Furthermore, WAACs could not be awarded good conduct medals or sleeve patches, and they could not be appointed warrant officers. Both the judge advocate and comptroller general agreed that allotments could not be made under the Serviceman's Dependents Allowance Act, not even if the WAACs had the allotments taken from their own pay.

Another example of the arbitrary decision making concerning the rights and obligations of members of the WAAC was the congressional decision that WAACs who left civil service jobs had soldiers' rights to reinstatement, but those who had left other jobs did not have similar reemployment rights. Again, in some instances WAACs were treated like regular members of the Army, while in others they were not. Often authorities took opposing positions as to what military rules or benefits applied to WAACs. The shaky legal status of the WAAC so perplexed government officials that they often could not decide what to do.

Since the WAACs were not military personnel according to interpretations by Congress, they were not subject to the court-martial system or to military justice. How then were the WAACs to be disciplined? If they were "in the field," then the Articles of War could be applied and WAACs would be subject to the court-martial system. The judge advocate general in one case ruled that, if a commanding officer wanted to try a WAAC, first he had to get a decision as to whether the post was currently "subject to attack." The judge advocate general also ruled that there was probably no legal foundation to the WAAC's disciplinary system, and any punishment given by the WAAC's company commanders might be unconstitutional. The Army discovered that it had only a little more control over the WAACs than it did over civilian employees. It became obvious that the ambiguous status of the corps prevented it from becoming the useful arm that the Army had hoped for.

The War Department decided officially to back legislation that would militarize the WAAC and put it solidly in the Army. Mrs. Rogers introduced a bill on January 14, 1943, that would take the *auxiliary* out of the WAAC and make it WAC (Women's Army Corps). General Marshall testified in favor of the legislation, which he said was needed for the effective functioning of the women's organization. It took six months for Congress to approve the legislation, which was signed into law on July 5, 1943.

The Army was given ninety days to dissolve the WAAC and inaugurate the WAC into the regular Army. Like everything that had been occurring with the WAAC, this turned out to be a bureaucratic nightmare. Questions persisted about the legal status of the WAAC. Information about the conversion either did not reach the proper officers or was held up so that those who needed it didn't get it.[12] Later, separation centers did not know how to credit WAAC service or what benefits the new WACs were eligible for.

Even though the newly created WAC clearly belonged to the military, the situation with regard to the benefits for the new WACs was still a muddy one. There continued to be a series of rulings by either the Comptroller General or the Adjutant General as to what the entitlements of the new WACs were. The Comptroller General decided that the WAACs were not entitled to reemployment rights even if they enlisted in the WACs because they did not go straight from their civilian jobs into the Army. This ruling was corrected in 1946 when legislation was passed to reestablish the WACs' eligibility for reemployment rights.

The Comptroller General ruled that Congress intended for the WACs to collect dependent allowances. Earlier he had ruled that the WAVES and the nurses, who belonged in the military order, could not get dependency allowances. Another question was whether WAAC service would be counted for credit in the future in determining the grade for those who entered the WAC. Legislation had to be passed to assure WACs of NSLI insurance, hospitalization, and domiciliary care and burial benefits. It took until 1959 for legislation to be passed that gave credit for service in the WAAC. Except for the right of promotion, the law credited that active service in the WAAC to other service.

Only in 1980 were WAACs who chose not to become WACs awarded veterans' benefits, after the passage of Public Law 95–202 (the same legislation that gave WASPs veteran status) on November 23, 1977. Later the Department of Defense also gave recognition to the women who served in the WAAC but who did not enlist in the WAC (this constituted one-fourth of the original WAACs).

In April 1980 a press release from the VA stated that women who served in the WAAC who wished to establish their eligibility for VA benefits must first apply to the Army for an honorable discharge. However, all veterans' programs before 1977, when the legislation was passed, were excluded. This means that former WAACs who gained veterans' status thirty years after their service cannot get any of the World War II educational benefits. They are eligible for medical, hospitalization, and burial benefits.

The WASP

The Women's Air Force Service Pilots (WASP) represented the merger of two groups of women flyers under the Army Air Force at the beginning of World War II. One was the elite group of highly experienced women pilots, the WAFS (Women's Auxiliary Flying Squadron), which under Nancy Love's direction was activated in September 1942. The other group was Jacqueline Cochran's Women's Flying Training Detachment (the WFTD), which trained women to fly in domestic aviation missions so that male pilots could go overseas. These two groups were merged on June 28, 1943, into the WASP.

The story of the WASPs became well known in recent years from several congressional hearings and considerable media attention. In 1942 the War Department authorized the training of hundreds of women at Avenger Field in Sweetwater, Texas, in the delivery of planes from factories to air bases, in test flying new aircrafts, and in target towing. The WASPs flew everything including big bombers, B–20s, and B–17s, but they were not permitted to fly them across the Atlantic. Some of the aircraft the women flew were considered too dangerous by male pilots. There were 38 casualties among the 1,047 women graduates of Avenger Field.

When the War Department initiated the WAF and the WFTD on an experimental basis, it had in mind to militarize them if they worked out. Since they were successful, it was taken for granted that militarization of the WASP would occur.

Jacqueline Cochran, in her final report to the commanding general of the Army Air Force, pointed out that the women were flying the same planes as the men but were not subject to the same rules. The women were living on the same bases but they were governed by a different set of regulations. Furthermore, there was no progressive schedule of advancement or pay, nor was there government life insurance. It was difficult to get hospitalization rights for the women in case of sickness or accident.

When the War Department finally went to Congress to ask for the militarization and expansion of the WASPs, it found that its own earlier policies were not helping its cause. It had underplayed the WASPs' contributions so that there was little publicity given them. Worried about public reaction it kept a low profile about the entire program. This lack of public awareness hurt the chances of the WASPs' militarization. When the War Department went before Congress to ask for a change of status for the WASPs they found a hostile committee that was annoyed at them for not having sought specific authorization for the WASP program. In fact, no Army budget had ever mentioned the WASPs.[13]

In 1944, there was an influx of out-of-work civilian male flying instructors since the Army cut back its flying training program. At the same time the Secretary of War was proposing commissioning women in the Army Air Force as pilots. The male pilots launched an active campaign against the commissioning of women pilots. They attacked the WASPs as "glamor girls" and fed the same negative publicity to legislators, who were already annoyed at being bypassed by the War Department. Also, during the committee hearings, the legislators were even more annoyed to find that fifty million dollars had been spent to train five hundred graduates at Avenger Field.

The legislators did not see the point in training inexperienced female personnel when there was a supply of trained male personnel.[14] The air fighting in the war was slackening off. The intense correspondence campaign from the male pilots influenced the committee. The committee came to the conclusion that at this stage of the war such a proposal on behalf of women pilots was not justified.

The committee pointed out that the women were recruited as civilians under the civil service, that they enjoyed the democratic freedom of civilians, and "that no question of rank can arise to mar the present amicable relationship." Even though General Arnold presented testimony in favor of the bill, the War Department did not want to fight with Congress. This combination led to the defeat of the bill. Cochran felt that if the WASP was not militarized, it should be disbanded.

The WASP was retired on December 20, 1944. Surprisingly, the final report from the Army Air Force on the WASP was negative. Cochran wrote one last report refuting this. After the disbandment, the women had limited options—join the Red Cross, fly private planes, join the WAC, or return to civilian life.

The women who wanted to fly did not have an easy time finding berths. They were barred from commercial cockpits except as Linker Trainer Operators (which both WACs and WAVES were doing). Some found commercial ferrying work; some were able to attach themselves to small private airports. But most of the women remain grounded. However, arrangements were made so that their flying experience in the WASP was recognized by the Civil Aeronautics Administration in issuing commercial pilots' licenses and in horsepower rating.

It wasn't until 1948 that the Air Force offered all former WASPs who met certain criteria commissions in the Air Force and its Reserve, in a nonflying status. It gave some credit for the WASP experience as well. However, women who joined the Reserve had to resign if they subsequently had children. Those who did enlist in 1948 and thereafter were not given credit for the time they served in the WASP when they retired. This was an important benefit to lose.

In 1972 a bill was introduced to get some veterans' benefits for the WASPs, but this bill died. It wasn't until September 1977 when hearings were held by a select committee of the House Veterans Committee. That legislation, finally enacted as Public Law 95–202, gave veterans' status to the WASPs.

The VA and some veterans' organizations had opposed veterans' status for the WASPs for years. During the 1977 hearings the VA made the argument that there were a great number of civilians who had worked for the Army on hazardous duties, including those who were in the Merchant Marine as CAA flying instructors. Congress was petitioned by them and legislation was introduced on behalf of those civilian groups who had not been militarized during the war. They also sought veterans' status. Passage of PL 95–202 meant that the WASPs, the WAACs and the Signal Corps Operators of World War II were also given veterans' status.

However, the WASPs did not get all the benefits that World War II veterans did. They did not receive GI educational benefits, National Service Life Insurance, or farm and home loan provisions. There is still ambiguity about retirement credit for those WASPs who went into the Army Air Force after 1948 and made the military their career. During a 1981 oversight hearing on the legislation, this issue was given prominence.

When the WASPs sought to use their benefits, they found other roadblocks. Some of these were revealed during the 1981 oversight hearings. One former WASP reported to the committee that she had been denied veterans' preference, an important veterans' benefit. The reason given her was that "WASPs were not included within the scope of veterans' preference under the Veterans' Preference Act."[15]

Former WASPs pointed out that the intent of Congress was clear from a letter written by the author of the WASP bill, Senator Barry Goldwater. He stated that Public Law 95–202 not only meant that WASPs would be considered in active duty for purposes of the laws administered by the VA, but that Congress intended that all other laws referring to veterans would apply. To date, clarification still has not been made concerning the WASPs' eligibility for these important benefits.

B. Health Care and Other Benefits

The Veterans Administration's slogan, "To care for him who shall have borne the battle," is carried out in its provision of health and medical care for the veteran population. Administered by the Department of Medicine and Surgery, the VA runs 172 in-patient and outpatient facilities and a group of nursing homes and domiciliaries for the benefit of the veteran population.

Perhaps no other veterans benefit is so important as the comprehensive and long-term care delivered by the VA hospital system. While the hospital system's purpose was to take care of war's wounded and disabled, its mission has developed considerably, and its concerns are broader. Those who were hurt or disabled, whether it was a war injury, an accident, or an illness while in service, are called "service-connected." An ailment or an illness occurring after military service and which has nothing to do with the period of military service is called a "non-service-connected" illness. VA officials consistently state that the hospital system is meant for all veterans who need medical care, non-service- as well as service-connected.

Over the years, the VA became an outstanding health care delivery system. One reason was that, in order to give the highest quality care, the VA developed strong clinical research and teaching programs that attracted outstanding medical and biochemical research personnel. For many years physicians sought residencies and teaching positions affiliated with VA hospitals. The VA medical system played a large role in the post–World War II training of physicians. Its medical research has been outstanding and has led to Nobel prizes in medicine and chemistry.

The Department of Medicine and Surgery maintains that, in order to provide the best medical care to the war injured, it must have the patient mix of the non-service-connected and the service-connected. Only in that way can it attract top doctors and scientists to participate in the system. Since the war wounded are a minority of the veteran population, the VA hospital system has become more and more the health care supplier for the general veteran population—that is, the non-service-connected. In 1980 almost 90 percent of the VA's inpatients received medical care for non-service-related illnesses.

The Department of Medicine and Surgery is made up of a staff of 195,000 employees with a budget of 7.3 billion to operate the facilities around the country. Funding for the VA's medical programs has been steadily rising. Between 1960 and 1972 the costs of medical care more than doubled. While much of this rise is accounted for by the rising costs of all aspects of medical care, the increases in the VA have proportionately been far lower than in the private sector. On the other hand, the VA has expanded its services to reach out to a larger segment of the veteran population and has sought to increase its clinical and basic research, and teaching programs to maintain high-quality care.

One sector of the VA's health care system that continues to grow is in the care of the aging-veteran population. In 1980, 30 percent of the VA's hospital resources were devoted to the acute and nonacute care of veterans who are 65 or over.[1] The veteran population is an aging one: The median age for male veterans in 1981 was 50.3 years, and is rising every year. It is estimated that by 1990 more than half of U.S. males over 65 years will be veterans, and that by 1995 veterans will represent 60 percent of all males over 65.[2] In 1980 there were 24.5 million individuals in the U.S. over 65 years, with a projection of 30.6 million by the year 2000. Furthermore, the proportion of this of veterans over 65 will rise from 26 to 59 percent by 2000, or from 2.6 million to 7.1 million during the same period.[3]

Faced with this staggering aging population, the VA has been refurbishing its facilities to accommodate the expected increased strain. It is planning to expand six extended-care programs in order to accommodate the growing elderly veteran population. These are nursing homes, community nursing-home care, hospital-based home care, domiciliary care, residential-care homes, and state home-programs.[4]

To develop research and training for the health care of this older population, the VA has also moved ahead to provide fellowships and other support for the career development of geriatric personnel. Under a mandate from Congress, the VA established the GRECC program (Geriatric Research, Education, and Clinical Centers), and from 1974 to 1979 established eight GRECC centers. More are being planned for when Congress allocates the funds. Each GRECC center emphasizes one area of research in aging. The GRECC program and other initiatives in the geriatric field funnel both information and trained personnel into health care services in the private sector. This kind of leadership is in the highest tradition of VA medicine.

*   *   *

In no other area have women veterans been so overlooked as in health care. Until the 1980s women were never included in any study or projections concerning health care. The National Academy of Science 1977 study of the VA hospital system, the VA's response to the NAS Study, and a work entitled *Report on the Aging Veteran* (January 5, 1978), never mentioned women veterans.

Because they were less than 2 percent of the veteran population from the 1940s through the 1960s, the medical needs of women veterans have not been particularly addressed. Either it was assumed that women veterans would not seek medical care from the hospitals, or that, if they did, the hospital system would accommodate them as best it could; it therefore rarely provides accommodations or bath and toilet facilities specifically for women.

When women veterans become patients at VA hospitals, there are often makeshift, ad hoc room arrangements and inconvenient and sometimes embarrassing toilet and bath facilities. Women veterans could not feel that the system was responsive to their medical needs. As a result, not many women availed themselves of medical care or hospitalization through the VA system. A commentator writing about the VA medical system noted that "very few women and no children" were treated at VA hospitals.[5]

Since no studies included women veterans, and little data was kept on the utilization of the VA hospital system, it was almost as though women didn't seem to exist as far as the VA hospital system was concerned. It wasn't until August 1982 that the VA did any study of the hospital system as it related to women veterans. The report, entitled "Women Veterans Usage of VA Hospitalization," came out one month before the Government Accounting Office's report on women veterans. The VA report concluded:

> The available data on women veterans usage of VA hospitalization benefits show that the number of women beneficiaries of VA hospitalization benefits is growing. This trend is ex-

pected to continue. The immediate demand for hospitalization occurs among young women veterans, but, in the long run, demand for medical services will be increased among older women veterans as well. However, the lack of data on women veterans precludes any attempt to clarify specific future requirements in terms of services and suggests the need for an examination of patterns of use in the population which is to be served. Such information cannot be obtained from those sources currently available within the VA.[6]

This report noted that "the historical data indicates that there are relatively few VA hospital discharges accounted for by women veterans." The data that the VA did gather during the 1970s indicated that younger women used the system at a higher rate than men, and older men more than older women. Since, demographically, younger women are becoming veterans at a proportionately higher rate than men, and the women veteran population is getting younger, these facts are not surprising.

Indeed, the demographic picture reveals important facts about the women veteran population. Because of the expansion of the number of women in the military during the sixties and the establishment of the All-Volunteer Force in the seventies, there has been an unparalleled growth in the number of women serving in the military. As a result, many more women became veterans, increasing women's representation in the veteran population to 3.8 percent. It is these younger women leaving the service after one or two tours of duty that account for the increase, and it is they who are availing themselves of the VA medical care system more than women veterans from World War II.

In a demographic profile on women released by the VA last year, the significant rise of the women veteran population has important implications for future use of the VA's hospital system.

The significant upturn in the number of female veterans over the last few years has brought with it a concommitant reduction in the median age of these women. The vast bulk of new entrants to the female veteran population are quite young, and this has led to a decline in the median age from 50.5 years as of September 30, 1977 to 46.2 years at the end of FY 1981. This stands as a marked contrast to the advance in age observed in the male veteran population for which the median age has grown steadily from 45.1 years on June 30, 1970 to 50.3 years on September 30, 1981. Since the size of the male veteran population has recently begun to decline, the aging process should gain momentum in the coming years.[7]

Most critical for the future of the VA hospital system in relation to women is that this trend is expected to continue and to increase women's representation in the veteran population.

While the count of active duty males may rise slightly during the next few years in the wake of our nation's anticipated military buildup, the number of women in the armed forces will very likely continue to grow by significant numbers. Should this trend persist, the female veteran population will maintain a course of steady growth since the possibility of eligible entrants will be increasing. As the estimated count of female veterans rises in the years to come, an increasingly vital aspect of the VA's mission will be the special consideration given to the problems of this group of former military personnel with respect to the administration of various types of veteran programs, such as medical care, counseling, loan guaranty and education.[8]

Not only will the VA have a larger younger women's population to deal with; it will have a group whose expectations are considerably different from those of the World War II generation of women veterans, who considered themselves volunteers and were unconcerned about the benefits coming to them. The present generation of women who enlist do so to large measure for economic and career purposes. Veterans' benefits are part of the package of rewards and remuneration that they expect. Therefore, it is likely they will take advantage of their veterans' benefits more than their predecessors. Furthermore, when they become an aging population, their readiness to use the VA health care system will also be greater. These demographic changes pose important challenges to future VA policies and planning.

The greatest deficiencies for women veterans have been the lack of facilities and treatment for gender-specific illnesses and ailments. The VA has only seven fulltime gynecologists on staff.

It has claimed that, up to now, it has not seen a need to keep specialists in women's health at the majority of the facilities because the demand has been so small. When a VA hospital is unable to provide a gynecologist or a gender-related specialist, it can provide the service on a contract or fee basis, in which the VA is billed for the service by an accepted doctor or hospital. This is due to a specific entitlement in the U.S. Code which provides for a woman veteran to seek care in a private hospital if she cannot get proper care in a VA hospital, or if she lives too far from a VA hospital.[9] In 1981 and 1982, there were 1,190 admissions to private hospitals on either a contract or fee basis for women, although only 9.3 percent were gender-related ailments.[10]

This provision in the U.S. Code, however, is only for a service-connected ailment or disability. Women who do not have an emergency or have a non-service-connected, gender-related illness or ailment are not eligible. Therefore, if a VA facility does not have a gynecologist on staff, which is true for over 95 percent of the facilities, a woman is out of luck if she needs treatment for such an ailment.

In the last Congress Senator Alan Cranston sought to remedy this by introducing an amendment to the omnibus bill, Health Care Programs Improvement and Extension Act of 1982, which would provide fee-basis outpatient care for gender-related illnesses for female veterans, regardless of whether it was service-connected or not.

> This provision should insure that in those cases in which a woman veteran is otherwise eligible for basic VA ambulatory care but cannot receive the care because the VA is unable to treat her gender-specific condition, the VA will be able to furnish care through a contract or fee arrangement with another provider. . . . This new authority is likely to facilitate provision of care to female veterans where VA medical facilities do not have attendants or consultants with specialties in female medical problems.[11]

The above provision was struck out of the final compromise version because it was feared that if this were enacted the VA would not refurbish up its facilities to provide in-house gender-specific care for outpatient treatment that women veterans would need in the future. This concern, that if the VA were given authority for the fee services for outpatient non-service-connected patients, it would never spend the resources on in-house care for women veterans who have been omitted from treatment up to now, has been expressed time and time again. However, the point was made by Senator Cranston and concurring veterans organizations that until the time the in-house capability is reached for all 172 facilities, women veterans were not going to get adequate treatment. It might take years for the VA to get to this stage.

One particular case was cited in a letter addressed to Senator Cranston which highlighted the problem. A woman from northern California who thought she had a gynecological disorder sought treatment at a VA facility and found that there were no gynecologists in any of the VA facilities in northern California. One, the Palo Alto facility, had a gynecologist as consultant, but it would be months before she could get an appointment. Advised to go to a private doctor at her own expense, the woman veteran, who was a retiree, went to an Army hospital where they discovered she had cancer. Fortunately, the surgeons were able to remove most of it. The veterans' service officer writing to Senator Cranston asked,

> What about the thousands of women in Northern California who may have gynecological problems but do not have the advantage of being retired from the service? These women who served their country when needed may now need their country. The women residents of the California Veterans Home, who are being told to wait for the VAMC to get a GYN or go to a doctor at their own expense when they barely can afford the essentials.[12]

Senator Cranston reintroduced the fee-basis authority for non-service-connected ailments for women veterans on an outpatient basis in his bill, S.11, which he introduced on January 26, 1983.[13] Hearings for this bill were held on March 9 and 10, 1983.

It was the General Accounting Office report issued on September 24, 1982, entitled "Action Needed to Secure That Female Veterans Have Equal Access to VA Benefits," that focused attention on the deficiencies of the VA health care system with regard to female veterans. The report was in response to a request by Senator Daniel Inouye to investigate the VA on this issue. It focused on the health care system because of complaints received by the senator and others on precisely the lack of proper medical care for women in VA hospitals.

Surveying a number of VA medical facilities, the GAO investigating team found that, because of the lack of privacy in older VA facilities, women veterans could not benefit from some specialized care. Furthermore, they were not admitted to ten of the sixteen domiciliaries they visited. The GAO confirmed the lack of GYN/OB care. Only one of the seven medical centers they visited had monitored physical examinations to insure that female patients had both pelvic and breast examinations. Also, pap smears were not given routinely.

One of the most startling inequities for women veterans was the lack of outpatient services. Eighty-nine percent of outpatient services in 1980 were given for non-service-connected disabilities, and women accounted for very few of those outpatients. Almost all outpatient medical needs of non-service-connected male veterans are taken care of, whereas only a small percentage of women veterans with non-service-connected ailments have been able to use the outpatient services. In one California facility, ten women were denied outpatient care for non-service-connected gynecological problems while the medical needs of men with non-service-connected problems were routinely met.

The GAO study cited a number of instances in which women were turned away from specialized programs because the VA did not have either enough staff to supervise a sexually-mixed psychiatric group or could not ensure adequate privacy for its women patients. The GAO called upon the VA to increase physicians and other VA staffers in the hospital system and to be more aware and sensitive to the needs of its female patients.

Among the GAO report's suggestions for the VA Administrator were that women have equal access to all VA treatment programs; that a woman veteran receive a complete physical examination that includes breast and pelvic exams; that gynecological care be provided. Furthermore, the GAO urged the VA to start planning and providing for the increased number of women veterans that are expected to place demands upon the system in the coming decades. The GAO report pointed out that no outreach efforts had been made to women veterans to inform them of their benefits, and that such efforts were needed to inform women of the kinds of programs they were entitled to as veterans.

The GAO report concluded that the VA system was not being responsive to women veterans' medical needs.

> VA facilities have generally been sized and staffed to accommodate both service-connected and non-service-connected veterans. Thus male veterans can generally obtain needed care from a VA facility regardless of service connection. The same is not true for female veterans because of problems in insuring privacy in older facilities and variations in the availability of gynecological care.[14]

An important aspect of women veterans' dissatisfaction with VA hospital treatment, as reported by many women veterans, are the attitudes of patients and staff toward them. There have been instances not only of rudeness and arrogance but of absolute disregard for the women veterans' feelings. Since physicians and staff have not had much experience with female patients, there is a tendency to treat them brusquely or indifferently. Women patients have not felt that they belonged in such facilities:

> As far as a hospital bed in VA hospitals, there are channels . . . disabled veterans, service connected, and finally non-service connected and only if beds are available. As a result medical services for female veterans is not the greatest. . . .[15]

On the other hand, some women have reported excellent treatment, and prompt and efficient care. At other times the care has been most unsatisfactory:

> Rooms are often cold. The boiler does not always seem to work at that big expensive hospital in Washington, D.C. And that situation is not good for heart patients. Sergeant G was once ordered to the hospital. In fact they sent an ambulance for her. But after she arrived, it took hours to get her into a room and it was cold. Daily physical therapy, if required, is not possible for women. There is no self-help ward. Often women patients are sent home to care for themselves if they

live alone, but there is more room for men patients, even if they are ambulatory. G was told to go home and stay in bed except for trips to the refrigerator. She lives alone.[16]

One woman veteran before the House Veterans Subcommittee on Hospitals reported excellent and prompt care when she needed an emergency tonsillectomy at one hospital in New York City. Ten years later, in an emergency situation, she was not only treated brusquely at a Brooklyn VA hospital, but was misdiagnosed. She tried another VA hospital in New York and was mailed an appointment letter to see the visiting gynecologist four months later—the earliest appointment available. In pain, and feeling anxious, this woman veteran resorted to the private sector and found out she needed a partial hysterectomy to correct her condition. If she had not had to wait or had been diagnosed correctly, the surgery might not have been necessary.[17]

Long waits to get appointments with specialists, particularly gynecologists, are one of the most frequent complaints of women veterans who have sought to use the VA medical system.

Another witness testified at the hearing that she had received reports of women receiving incorrect examinations, of doctors using gynecological instruments improperly, and of a lack of privacy during these kinds of procedures. She reported that physicians who were not qualified gynecologists were giving gynecological exams. Also, during such examinations women were subjected to having the exams administered in full view of men passing through the exam area.[18]

These reports corroborate the reports that many veterans' organizations had been getting concerning lack of privacy and responsiveness and the inability to get gynecological exams. One veterans' organization magazine, that had invited responses from women veterans to the GAO report's evaluation of the VA hospital care program, reported,

> By far there were more negative than positive comments in this issue of DAV magazine mail. Most letters, though, reflected mixed feelings about VA care among women veterans. . . . Most of the respondents felt the care they received from VA medical professionals was good. On the other hand, most complained about inadequate or nonexistent gynecolog-

ical care and lack of privacy for women patients at the VA facilities they use.[19]

One recent dissertation pointed out that the VA had done three nationwide surveys of patient satisfaction, in 1974, 1976, and 1978. However, the survey did not factor out women veterans' responses but rather treated them as part of the total study population. This study highlighted the way in which male bias has generally entered into research as well as into treatment throughout the VA system, at least until the 1980s. Since the VA system was designed by men for men, male-biased attitudes persist throughout the system about the physical and mental health of women.[20]

This study of women veterans treated at VA hospitals found that they preferred being with other veterans and identified strongly as veterans. A more positive attitude toward VA's treatment of women was reported here. Three quarters expressed dissatisfaction with the patient-physician relationship. However, this finding would probably not be different from the evaluation of male patients. Ninety percent of the women queried wanted preventative care related to female health problems and wanted yearly gynecological exams, including the PAP test. In the hospital setting the majority wanted more recreational facilities and the opportunity to get together with other women to discuss mutual concerns. The women "found a paucity of treatment programs geared to the specific needs of women." They pointed out that women need two physicians: a general health care physician and a special OB/GYN doctor.

Another study done at a psychiatric hospital in California investigated treatment barriers for female veterans at VA facilities. For women veterans seeking health care in a VA facility or program, the fact that the treatment is offered in a predominantly male environment is in itself a barrier. Women veterans are apt to be put off by that situation; attention must be paid to the attitudinal environment of the hospital. Female veterans who have been patients in a VA facility have reported difficulties with the staffs who often consider women patients "management problems" or refer to them as "overly demanding" or "overly emotional." Furthermore, staffs are often resistant to changing ward environments to accommodate the female patients.

This particular study, which focused on the female patients in one facility, found that the patients expressed comparatively greater dissatisfaction with regard to gender-specific health care than with general health services that affect both genders equally. The investigator found that decisions to shunt women to treatment programs were made on the basis of security and convenience factors rather than in terms of what was suitable for the patients. Lack of privacy bothered about half the patients surveyed. On the other hand, about the same number found the presence of men therapeutic. About one-third of the patients wanted a stricter separation of women from the men, and another 37 percent preferred an all-women's ward.

With regard to personal security, one-third of the women patients surveyed indicated that they did not feel safe either in their own wards or on the hospital grounds. They complained about harassment, and more than a third of them indicated they had either been threatened or actually had violence done to them. Despite these negative indicators, overall satisfaction with the treatment was high. There was also a very strong desire expressed for a women's support group.

> . . . in addition to monitoring the services which are provided
> to female veterans now at VA facilities, research will need to
> be conducted around the important areas of overcoming per-
> ceived and actual treatment barriers to female veterans, and
> techniques for implementing effective outreach efforts.[21]

No discussion about women veterans' medical treatment can omit the special needs of the Vietnam-era women veterans. The women who served during that era indeed shared the hostility that male Vietnam veterans experienced when they returned home to "the world." It took almost a decade for the VA to appreciate the psychic damage and emotional turmoil of the Post-Traumatic Stress Disorder (PTSD) for the men veterans and to finally agree that it needed treatment. PTSD is defined as an anxiety disorder caused by prolonged severe and externally induced stress. While a major research study was carried out over the period of years on the impact of the Vietnam War on the men who served, women were not included in this study.[22] It is one more tragedy of that war that the tribulations of those who served did not end when their service did. As the woman veteran put it so aptly above, a population sick of the war and angry that it had been so deeply embroiled in it, carried the hostility over to the young men and women who were in the war. Even after the public and Congress finally recognized the toll of that war upon the shattered lives of the veterans, women were not included among the group considered to need help.

In testimony before a House Subcommittee, a woman veteran who served as a nurse in Vietnam attested to the mental health problems of the women who served during the Vietnam era, particularly those who actually went to Vietnam, mostly nurses.[23] While attention began to be paid to the symptoms of the PTSD that manifested themselves in the male veterans, little heed was given to the women who also served and also had the constellation of negative societal attitudes to deal with as well as their own depression as a result of what they experienced in Vietnam. The women, being fewer in number, were more isolated than the men, and suppressed their feelings and anxieties. Generally, the VA psychiatric facilities did not address the PTSD and of the few that did, only one woman has been admitted.[24]

A recently completed master's thesis at the University of Maryland, "Women Vietnam Veterans and Their Mental Health Adjustments: A Study of Their Experiences and Post-Traumatic Stress," confirmed the theory that women also are suffering from PTSD. The study pointed out that previous research efforts had not included the approximately eight to ten thousand women who served in Vietnam, mostly as medical personnel. The research done for the study "provided preliminary evidence that Post-Traumatic Stress Disorder may be applicable to the experience of women Vietnam veterans.[25] Also, the investigator found that there was evidence of mental distress among the women sampled. Among the problems identified by a significant minority of the women veterans queried were suicidal thoughts, inability to be close to someone they cared for, and repeated feelings of depression. Despite the negative aspects of the war experience, the women tended to emphasize the positive growth aspects of their service experience both in their personal and professional lives.

With the new interest in the population of women veterans there is hope that the Veterans Administration will address the mental health care needs of the Vietnam-era veterans. The Readjustment Counseling Service, which was mandated by law to address the needs of the Vietnam-era veterans, is facilitating the veterans' abilities to talk and reflect on their war experiences. The University of Maryland study, along with others, pointed out that there is still a great amount of comprehensive research that needs to be done concerning the problems—mental, emotional, physical—of women veterans of the Vietnam era.[26]

Other Inequalities

Women veterans have not always had equal access to all veterans' benefits because of legal or regulatory provisions differentiating them on the basis of sex. One glaring example was the fact that both the World War II and the Korean GI Bills did not pay the same educational benefits to married female veterans as to married male veterans. If the woman veteran was married, she was generally not paid an additional allowance based on having a dependent husband, while a male veteran was given an allowance for his dependent wife. This inequity was finally corrected in the 92nd Congress in 1972, with Public Law 93–540, which equalized the treatment for dependents of female veterans. Congresswoman Heckler, who introduced the amendment, commented that 537,000 women veterans would benefit from this law, which would allow them to receive additional GI payments for their husbands.[27] The law also made all VA benefits for dependents and widowers the same as if they were dependents of male veterans. The VA fact sheet, "Federal Benefits for Veterans' Dependents" up to the time of the change of law maintained that the dependents and survivors of female veterans had eligibility requirements different from those of male veterans.

For purposes of receiving death compensation benefits, the widower of a female veteran would be eligible if he was incapable of self-maintenance and at the time of the wife's death, permanently incapable of self-support due to a physical or mental disability. On the other hand, the widow of a male veteran would be ineligible only if the widow remarried or lived openly with another man and held herself out openly to the public as his wife. Nothing was said about the widow having to be incapable of self-maintenance or having a physical or mental disability to be eligible for the death compensation benefit.

The fact sheet during those years also left out female veterans' survivors eligibility for GI Loans for homes, farms and businesses. The fact sheet stated that "Unremarried widows of men who served in either World War II, the Korean Conflict, or the post-Korean Conflict, and who died in service or after separation as a result of service-connected disabilities are also eligible for GI Loans." No provision was made for the widowers of female veterans.

After the 1972 change in the law, the VA carefully made clear that no statement or VA publication should be made "in a manner that seems to preclude benefits for female veterans, dependents or beneficiaries." The clarification in the regulations emphasized that unless otherwise indicated "words importing the masculine gender include the feminine as well." Furthermore, the VA regulation urged that more precise terminology should be used, such as *his or her* or *the veteran* "to avoid giving grounds for the misconception which may arise from the use of the term 'his,' when in fact both sexes are eligible for the benefits under discussion."[28]

Another pattern of discrimination operated against married women veterans until 1968. Up until that time, if a married woman veteran applied for a loan, her income was not considered among the criteria used to determine whether the couple was a sound credit risk, despite her veteran's status (and even if her husband was not a veteran). In this instance she was seen as a working wife. Until 1968 a working wife's income was not considered when a veteran applied for a home loan, since her income was seen as supplemental and unstable.

However, in 1968 the VA recognized that times had changed and that many wives worked outside the home.

> The incidence of employment of wives has continued to increase in recent years and has become more and more a part of the family life. From a review of loan files which are sent

to Central Office by field stations for various reasons, we have concluded that there is some misunderstanding on the part of some stations as to VA policy in respect to the consideration which may be given to a wife's income in connection with a guaranteed, insured, or direct loan application. This, of course, can result in approval of loans which do not qualify and in rejection of others which do.[29]

To clarify what should be the policy, that same VA document stated that the income of the wife may be considered in determining the ability of the veteran to meet the estimated shelter expenses, provided that the wife's employment is stable and that it is reasonable to conclude that her employment will continue in the foreseeable future.

If a single woman veteran applied for a VA loan, she had to meet the same credit loan criteria as a male veteran to be given the loan.

Despite the 1968 statement from the central office, apparently there was further need of clarification to the regional offices. In 1973 the Department of Veterans' Benefits felt compelled to put out an information bulletin indicating how "wives' income" was to be considered when veterans apply for a house mortgage loan.[30] The guidelines put out by the central office allow the regional offices considerable discretion in determining whether the wife's income may be considered toward the proper repayment of the loan.

In a case where a married veteran's income is not sufficient to qualify him for a loan, consideration may be given to his wife's income. There is no hard-and-fast rule in this respect. The respect to which a wife's income is taken into account depends upon the reliability of such income. In a case where it is not reasonable to conclude that the wife's income will continue throughout the term of the loan, VA may, nonetheless, consider her income as an offset against short term family obligations.[30]

A proper conclusion that the wife's income may be considered toward the repayment of the loan obligation requires a determination as to whether her employment is a definite characteristic of the family life; i.e., a condition which normally may be expected to continue.[31]

In July of that year the Department of Veterans' Benefits sent through a DVB manual change that spelled out how the income of the borrower's wife was to be considered in the evaluation of his credit. The new procedures made clear that the wife's income was to be carefully considered in the evaluation of the applicant for the loan as a good credit risk.

While this difference in benefit up to 1973 actually affected more nonveteran women than women veterans, it reveals the different perception that an institution like the VA has of working women. The practice of the VA (whether it was universal or not) of not taking a gainfully employed wife's income as a serious effort and an important contribution to the family income perhaps is indicative of the perceptions of the larger society in not appreciating the value and importance of work by women. Since wives who worked outside the home became a commonplace phenomenon during World War II and continued to be an accepted pattern in our society, it is difficult to understand how and why the VA allowed such discrimination to persist until 1973.

·PART IV·

WHERE THEY
ARE TODAY

·7·

Women Veterans
in Organizations

The war's end meant going home for the women veterans. Back to sweethearts, lovers, husbands, and the family hearth. For some it meant starting a new life in a new town with a new set of perspectives.

The women who served during the Second World War—in the WAC, the WAVES, the Marines, the WASP, the Coast Guard—were now veterans, women veterans. The demobilization was rapid and chaotic with little time or energy for briefings or counseling about what veterans were entitled to. The men—the GIs—had the same experience, but as they were the overwhelming majority, more attention was paid to their benefits, and they had more opportunity to get the basic information about them. Besides, policy makers were worried about the tremendous number of men who were about to be released into the civilian work force. They weren't as worried about the women because they were relatively few in number and weren't necessarily going back into the work force and so there was a lag in getting the information to them. The problems that the director and women officers encountered in looking out for the well-being of their women continued to the end.

Lack of knowledge about veteran benefits was pervasive among the World War II women veterans. A typical comment about them:

> When I got out, I had the understanding that the GI Bill was only for those who did not have college degrees. . . . I went

to college for teaching credits, which I paid for myself, because I did not know that I could go under the GI Bill. If I knew then what I know now.[1]

Women's sense of themselves as veterans seemed to be different from that of men. While they had enormous pride in having served and taken part in the action, they didn't seem to place their contributions on an equal level with the men's. It was not just that they knew the men were in combat or had the potential of being in combat, it was that they saw their roles as supportive and helpful. The defense of the country was not resting on their shoulders. They had wanted to do their bit, but they had certainly not been hailed as "heroines."

> I was proud of my service in the Coast Guard Women's Reserve, and was appreciative of the benefits. I remember feeling vaguely apologetic about it—at some point there is a distinct impression that our service was not considered really "military" because there was no front line activity—never mind that some of us did go overseas (Alaska), and that there were millions of men who performed vital services behind the lines also. Like our sister Rosie the Riveter—and I was that too— there was a distinct message that we should now let the men take over the real world and we should silently return to the kitchens.[2]

Particularly if the woman veteran married a veteran, she was not likely to compete with her husband with her "war stories." Young women coming home also may have had a father who had been in a combat situation, with whom she may or may not have shared her war experiences. While women veterans who married veterans had an additional bond of both having been in the military service, which some judge to be a contributing factor to a stable marriage, her military service was not likely to be seen in the same light as his. While there was often pride in her accomplishments, there was also ambivalence about its importance.

Women had a tendency to think of themselves the way society thought of them. While the World War II women veterans did return with a stronger sense of self, and an awareness of what they could do, this did not mean that they shed the traditional image they had grown up with. If anything, they may have been in conflict about their newfound strength and the traditional expectations of those around them, including veteran husbands, who saw them as homemakers and nurturers.

Different women dealt in various ways with these sometimes divergent perceptions. No doubt many found it easier to shed the "veteran" image and blend into a preservice mode of thinking, similar to the other women around them. This was a natural way of handling a potentially divisive situation, one that avoided pressures upon the family structure as well as upon themselves. The women's military service came to be seen as a great adventure, a temporary episode, a one-time foray into a forbidding male world.

Not helpful to their veterans' identity was the slander campaign against women in the services that persisted throughout the war years. Despite the fact that there was no basis in reality for the aspersions on their morals—the rumors were publicly refuted time and time again by military and civilian leaders—the innuendos and snickering dogged the women who served, long after the war ended. To this day military women have had to put up with a tainted image that has enraged them and their supporters. Only a few years ago a well-known general made a public though off-the-record statement, that women who joined the services were either "whores" or "lesbians." Disavowing the quote that appeared in a prominent military newspaper did not undo the damage.

It is understandable that women veterans would not proclaim their veteran status to the world that, at best, had a confused or ambiguous vision of their characters. Just as women have had difficulty in dealing with sexual harassment and discriminatory practices of all sorts that mitigated against their well-being, so women have been helpless or ineffective in countering slanders of this sort. Only when it becomes official policy to refute allegations and condemn actions, with accompanying sanctions can this kind of campaign be muted.

With the addition of *sex* to *race* in the mission to insure equal opportunity during the seventies, women have begun to have recourse within the military establishment. Still, the record is not great, and women have continued to suffer from all kinds of disturbing and even threatening situations. The difference today is these practices are not condoned, and official policy is to eradicate them. However, myths die hard and cultural attitudes are not easily displaced. Still, thanks to the civil and equal rights movements, society has taken a giant step to confront discriminatory practices against women although there is still a long way to go.

The ambivalence that women felt about their veterans' status probably explains why many did not seek out information about veterans' benefits or else let it pass them by. This may also account for the fact that many women never considered joining an existing veterans' organization. However, this was not unique for the women. Despite the large memberships of the established veterans' organizations, the majority of male veterans are unaffiliated with any veterans' organizations.

However, there were a number of women veterans who had a strong veterans' identity and did try to join the veterans' organizations in their community or hometown. In the years before the reawakening of the women's movement, which had a widespread impact upon societal attitudes, the established veterans' organizations were not very hospitable to the women veterans who said, "I am a veteran, and I want to join." In fact, while many veterans' organizations finaily accepted them into full membership, it is only in the decade of the eighties that they began to take notice of female veterans. In many instances the women were shunted off into the auxiliary, which consisted of female relatives of the male members. Women veterans did not take kindly to this lack of respect for their veterans' status. Some withdrew completely from the veterans' organizational world; others worked in the auxiliaries and bided their time until they could find more sympathetic male veterans or until more women veterans demanded to be let in and recognized for their service.

> In K. we were invited to Veterans of Foreign Wars membership, and in a very short time also "invited out"—it was for males only. Wish now I had kept my membership card, as in younger days I delighted in insisting I once belonged to that exclusive group. I seem to remember that women are now welcome, but for me separate but equal was not what I wanted—and the Ladies' Auxiliary was not for me.[3]

The American Legion, in recent testimony on women veterans' legislation, stated that women were members since its founding in 1919.[4] The Legion claims one hundred all-female posts and thousands of women among its members. There are active posts in Washington, D.C., and New York City and on Long Island. At the time of this writing there is a woman serving as a vice-commander, and other women have served in a variety of national, state, and local offices; however, the testimony was given by one of the male officers during the hearing that dealt exclusively with women veterans. The Legion stated that there are several women serving as claims representatives and department service officers and accredited representatives in state and county veteran services.

The Disabled American Veterans, who testified at the same hearing, indicated that they have many women among their members who have been welcome since its formation in 1922.[5] There are three service-connected disabled women veterans employed as national service officers, and women serve as commanders in three states. Recent issues of the DAV magazine have featured articles on issues of interest to women veterans. One issue queried its women as to what their experiences had been with the VA medical system and reported on those responses.

The Veterans of Foreign Wars for many years excluded women from their ranks, until under threat of a lawsuit from a woman veteran several years ago, the VFW opened its doors. However, women have not been very visible in that organization.

The leader among veterans' organizations to recognize the achievements of women veterans and call attention to their neglect has been the American Veterans Committee (AVC). Founded during World War II by a group of idealistic servicemen and women, who were seeking a voice different from that of the established veterans' organizations, the AVC has been a champion of civil and equal rights. Women played important roles in the founding of the organization and have continued in positions of national and local leadership. It was the AVC in the mid-seventies that initiated a study of government response to women veterans, paving the way for the belated acknowledgement of women's contributions to the armed forces and their subsequent neglect.

The organizations that sprang up during and after the Vietnam

War for Vietnam veterans—the Vietnam Veterans Against the War, the National Association of Concerned Veterans, and the Vietnam Veterans of America—have had sizable numbers of women among their membership. These younger women veterans have taken active roles and have been at the forefront of the organizations' formation and activities. The Vietnam Veterans of America has a women's director and has become a strong advocate for the rights of women veterans. Many of the women veterans who served and made the military their career joined the military associations and the retiree organizations. Some have taken leadership positions but not often or in great numbers.

The Veterans Administration lists only one woman veterans' association—the WAC Veterans Association. This organization is the only one of the women's services that has a formal structure and meets regularly since it was founded in 1947. The WAC Veterans Association grew out of another organization, the WAC Mothers Association. A group of mothers and ex-WACs met together in 1946 to discuss the possibilities of creating a new organization of former WACs. On May 14, 1951, the anniversary of the founding of the WAAC, the WAC Veterans Association was incorporated in the District of Columbia. Both former WAACs and WACs are eligible for membership in the organization.

WAC Vets, as they call themselves, have taken the emblem of the WAC, the goddess Pallas Athene, as the emblem of their organization. Pallas Athene is seen by the WAC Vets not only as the goddess of victory but also the goddess of the city, protector of the home and guardian of the peace. In her dual role Pallas Athene symbolizes the true spirit of both organizations—the active military and the active veteran.

The WAC Veterans Association is a nonprofit, nonpartisan membership organization: "No woman who is eligible for membership is barred because of race, creed, color, or political belief, unless such belief is contrary to the principles of the Constitution and the government of the United States of America."[6] With a membership of several thousands, the WAC Vets have chapters and members at large all over the country. The major mission of the WAC Vets is to be of service to all veterans and to emphasize organizational work in VA hospitals and in community programs.

The Association puts out a monthly newsletter, *The Channel*, which is distributed to all its members. Although the Association does not have its own separate national headquarters, it is run effectively from the home of its national president. Every year, the Association puts out the formal minutes of its annual convention. Strictly governed by its constitution and bylaws, the WAC Vets' Association follows parliamentary procedures in its governance.

Many of the WAC Vets chapters put out their own newsletters, such as the Great Lakes Chapter No. 15 which publishes a lively little paper called *We WACs* under the editorship of Mrs. Esther Lukos. One of the California chapters, No. 43, puts out a newsletter edited by a former national chairperson, Lucille Tauscher, and there are many more. The WAC Vets are active in all kinds of community activities: visiting patients in VA hospitals, running fund-raisers for hospital and charity events, and holding social activities of various kinds for their members and families.

WAC Vets Association had its first convention in Chicago in 1947; since then it has been meeting annually. The thirty-sixth convention took place in Columbus, Ohio, in August 1982, and celebrated the fortieth anniversary of the founding of the WAC. The convention revealed that the *esprit de corps* is still there, the verve and the camaraderie of years past is still very much alive.

The WAC Foundation was inaugurated in 1969 to promote the contributions of women in the Army through the WAC Museum at Fort McClellan, Alabama, where WAC officers were trained until the WAC was integrated into the regular Army in 1978. The purpose of the Foundation is to raise funds to store, maintain, protect, and preserve momentos, uniforms, documents, pictures, and related items concerning the WAAC, the WAC, and women in the Army today. The Foundation puts out a semiannual newsletter, and there is a biennial reunion in May on even years. The Foundation does not have a membership, but donors are called "friends of the WAC Foundation" and receive the newsletter and are eligible to attend the reunions. The Foundation is managed by a board of directors which meets once a year.

The WAVES never established a central national organization such as the WACs did with their WAC Vets Association. Rather, the women who served in the WAVES chose to associate themselves in local geographical units, and organize themselves as they saw fit. In 1982 a reunion took place in Seattle, Washington, and was hosted by the Pacific Northwest WAVES. Reunions are held every two years in different cities around the country and are hosted by the local WAVES organization in the area. There is considerable rivalry among the WAVES groups to host such a reunion.

The national WAVES reunion celebrated the fortieth anniversary of the WAVES in Seattle, July 20–August 1, 1982. It was in July 1942 that President Franklin Roosevelt signed the legislation that authorized women to enlist in the U.S. Naval Reserve. Unlike the WAAC, whose military status was never clear, the WAVES were unquestionably a part of the U.S. Naval Reserve. It would not be until July 1948 that women would become part of the regular Navy.

To commemorate the anniversary Secretary of the Navy James Forrestal wrote each WAVE:

> You have served in the greatest Navy in the world. No other Navy at any time has been so great. For your part in these achievements, you deserve to be proud as long as you live. The Nation which you served in a time of crisis will remember you with gratitude.

Unlike the WACs, the WAVES remained in a loose confederation with organized reunions every two years. The attendance was always tremendous and indicated that there were still strong bonds pulling the ex-Navy women together. In recent years several different groups have sought to pull together a cohesive national organization, formally structured and governed. At the 1982 reunion there was a lengthy and heated debate whether such an organization should be formed. The decision was put off, and a committee was appointed to investigate the possibility and report back to the next reunion. Delegates voiced concern that they need to get the younger women veterans to come into the organization. They suggested that the formation of a national organization would further this objective. Furthermore, such an organization could promote the well-being of women today in the Navy and the Naval Reserve and also would be better able to help former WAVES who were in need.

Founded in 1960, the Women Marines Association has over sixty chapters, all over the country, and numbers about 2,500 women. The organization encompasses women who were in the Marines in World War I and II and women who have served in the modern-day Marine Corps. The WMA holds a convention every two years.

The major purposes of the WMA are charitable and educational and among the many activities of this nature that the association carries out, both on a national and chapter level, are the funding of scholarships for promising students to go to college. Also, the Association is active with VA hospital programs, nursing homes, children's hospitals, and other worthy community projects. Among the more recent activities of theirs was raising money for a contribution to the Vietnam Veterans' Memorial. The members share a spirit of having been in the Marine Corps, and maintain their interest in the Corps programs and activities. In February 1983 the Women Marines Association celebrated the fortieth anniversary of the establishment of the Women Marines during World War II.

The Air Force, the youngest of the military services, was the last service to bring women into its ranks. Some of the WASPs were recruited along with Army officers and a very few Navy women after World War II. It was Korea that brought a large group of women officers into the Women's Air Force. Women who had served during World War II and remained in the Reserves were asked to sign up in the Korean Conflict. "These were the real trailblazers of the Air Force—although few of us thought of ourselves in that light at the time."[7]

One organization of Air Force women arouse after a group of retired women officers wanted to continue their friendship on a regular and organized basis. The WAF Officers Associated for Retirement was founded in 1975 "by a group of retired women line officers in San Antonio, Texas, who recalled with pleasure their many friendships while on active duty and regretted losing touch in retirement."[8] Now more than seven hundred women are members of the WAF Officers Associated. Besides their periodic reunions, the organization has promoted interest in preserving the history of women in the Air Force. They were pleased that the Air Force Historical Society placed a woman officer on its board, and they hailed the assignment of a woman Air Force officer to write a complete history of the WAF (through 1973).

For some reason, San Antonio, Texas, and Washington, D.C., have the largest concentration of retired WAF officers. The Association puts out rosters of individuals and seeks to establish connections with the women officers who shared the same or similar experiences while they served in the Air Force. Reunions take place biennially with an average attendance of about 150. Most of the members of the WAF Associated have moved on to second careers, or marriage, or both. According to the current president, they still have the deep friendships that developed during those active duty years when they shared a oneness of purpose in their military careers—always overwhelmingly outnumbered, no matter where they were, and for the most part loving it.

The emphasis of the organization is primarily social in character. All the work of the organization is done by volunteers who give generously of their time. Their purposes according to the bylaws are

> To promote and sponsor periodic reunions for members and their guests at various times and places for the purpose of renewing acquaintances, and friendships, meeting spouses and making new friends; and choosing a time and place and sponsoring group for the next such reunion.[9]

The women of the Coast Guard, the SPARs, celebrate their anniversary periodically. In 1982, September 30 to October 3, they commemorated the fortieth anniversary of their founding at a 3-day meeting in Boston. Almost 900 SPARs and their families and friends attended the joyous occasion at the anniversary banquet. While the SPARs have not formed a structured organization, they get together for important anniversaries. Individuals volunteer to keep lists and to send out mailings to the SPARs who are all over the country. In this way, a network of SPARs is kept active.

At the fortieth anniversary, the first Director of the SPARs, Captain Dorothy Stratton, addressed the former SPARs:

We are here because we can never forget those three years behind the mast. It is because as John Mason Brown wrote at Christmas 1943 to All Hands: We are happy that we are included within the parenthesis of our own times. In our hearts we know that we could not have expected to share in the future unless we had shared in this unmerry and appalling present . . . I mean the simple satisfaction we will always have, so long as we have life, of having been included emotionally and experientially in the major challenge of our time.[10]

* * *

The Navy Nurses also have no formal organization. However, they have maintained a network around the country so that whenever a Navy nurse visits another part of the country, she is sure of being able to find a fellow Navy nurse to stay with. The Navy nurses used to celebrate their birthdate, May 13th, with a luncheon on duty stations. However, in recent years, they were not permitted their own celebrations but had to join with other medical corps specialties in joint parties.

This year, 1983, was the seventy-fifth anniversary of the formation of the Nurse Corps, U.S. Navy—May 13, 1908. A committee planned a gala celebration just for Navy nurses at this event. Navy nurses from all over the country and overseas who had served in the Corps back to World War I gathered together for a spectacular reunion at the Bethesda Marriott the weekend of May 14–16. Close to a thousand Navy nurses, retirees and active duty, took part in the festivities. Volunteers who had kept up the lists did the mailings, maintained contact with the Nurses, and made the anniversary the largest of its kind.

* * *

Army Nurses have their own association. Known as the Retired Army Nurse Corps Association, it was founded in October 1976 by a group of 36 retired Army Nurse Corps officers at a meeting in San Antonio, Texas. The primary purpose of the RANCA is "to provide educational and social opportunities" for its members.

As the Association grew, other purposes developed, among them "to cooperate fully with the Chief, Army Nurse Corps in the dissemination of information to the public" and "to support the Army Nurse Corps Foundation by preserving the history of the United States Army Nurse Corps and promoting literary, educational and artistic endeavors."

The Association publishes a quarterly newsletter, "The Connection." Conventions are held every two years on the even years. The first two conventions were held in San Antonio, Texas, but other locations are being sought for future conventions. The 1980 convention had an attendance of over 700 members; it honored the Army Nurse Corps Veterans of World War I.

One of the first projects of the new organization was to participate in the dedication of the new Colonel Florence Blanchfield Army Community Hospital at Fort Campbell, Kentucky. Members of the Association contributed funds to provide a sculptured bust and portrait of Colonel Blanchfield. This is the only Army hospital named for an Army nurse.

One organization that has taken women from all the military services is the Women's Overseas Service League (WOSL). Solely a women's organization, the WOSL was founded in 1921 by and for women who had served overseas during wartime. This included the women who had served in uniform—the Yeomanettes of the Navy and Coast Guard—and the women who served in the U.S. Marine Corps. It also included the many women not in the military service who served with the Army overseas, some in very dangerous positions near the front lines. Those in the Signal and Quartermasters Corps among others suffered dangers and deprivations while making invaluable contributions to the war effort. There were fifty-two American agencies and forty-six foreign agencies under whose sponsorship these women were— including the American Red Cross, the American Friends Service, the American Relief Administration, the American University Union, American Transport Service, Knights of Columbus, the Women's Auxiliary Aid, the Overseas Theater League, and the YWCA. "It seemed to matter not which uniform was being worn, the goal and purpose were the same."

Incredible as it may seem, 90,000 women served with the U.S. forces overseas. Of the 19,877 Red Cross nurses who served during World War I, 11,000 were with the Navy and the Army Nurse Corps. Other women were with the Treasury Department and Secret Service. These women were in most of the countries of

Europe that were touched by war. Three hundred forty-eight American women lost their lives during their overseas tours, most from diseases contracted after months of strenuous service.

The purpose of the WOSL, as set forth in the Articles of Incorporation, is:

> To keep alive and develop the spirit that prompted overseas service; to maintain the ties of comradeship born of that service and to assist and further any patriotic work; to inculcate a sense of individual obligation to the community, state and nation; to work for the welfare of the armed services, to assist, in any way in our power, the men and women who served and were wounded or incapacitated in the service of their country; to foster and promote friendship and understanding between the United States and all the other nations of the world.[11]

The WOSL opened its membership to women who 'served in World War II, Korea, and Vietnam, and cold war confrontations such as in Berlin, where the armed forces were engaged. Today the membership is divided among women who served officially in the armed forces and those who served as civilians.

One of the first organizations to be recognized as an official observer at the UN, WOSL continues to be represented there. In 1933 an international group of veterans, the FIDAC (Fédération Interalliée des Anciens Combattants) invited them to become an auxiliary, but the organization refused, feeling it was not a "proper step for women who had been in active service overseas to become an auxiliary to any organization."

During World War II the League actively supported the formation of the WAAC. One of its members in Congress, Mrs. Edith Nourse Rogers, introduced the legislation creating the WAAC. The League's Legislative Committee worked hard to support equal rights and benefits for the WAAC and urged passage of amendments that would

1) Equalize the pay schedules of the WAAC with the Army.
2) Make provision for dependents of WAAC personnel similar to those provided Army personnel.
3) Provide Government Life Insurance to the WAAC.

4) Incorporate the WAAC into the Army to give the personnel the protections they would get as members of the Army.[12]

The WOSL also sought to have women doctors in the Army on a par with men, and equivalent pay for Army and Navy nurses with men of the same rank. The League continues to press for equal rights for women in the military services and to be concerned about the welfare of veterans, particularly women.

Since the civilian women who had served in World War I and in subsequent wars were not entitled to any kinds of benefits or compensation from the government, even if their health was impaired, WOSL lobbied the government to open up two sanatoriums for Army and Navy nurses. Nothing was done for the civilian women by the government. Not even the civilian organizations that had sent these women abroad made any provision for them, healthwise, or helped them if they were in financial distress. The League has not only aided many civilian women during the difficult period of readjustment but continues to provide financial aid for illness and other critical needs.

"Members have demonstrated not only that the same spirit that motivated the patriotic service of women overseas in wartime can inspire equally devoted service on the home front in peacetime, but that it can take on new and broader social significance and express itself in many forms of constructive effort for the common good."[13]

One major general who served overseas commented:

Many women who served overseas are entitled to the same honors as are our soldiers.[14]

Another accolade:

These women brought into the desolate territories of war a new spirit, a new courage, a new constancy; they wrought greatly to bring the final victory; they are worthy of much honor.[15]

·8·

Current Situation and
New Policy Initiatives

A combination of circumstances and developments in the private and public sectors have led to a new interest in women veterans. The American Veterans Committee investigation of the VA and other agencies' response to the women veterans in the late seventies which revealed the lack of data keeping, the GAO report of 1981 which pinpointed numerous deficiencies in the VA's health care system for women veterans, and the VA's own reports in the eighties, have all contributed to an awareness that the women veteran population had been largely forgotten or ignored during the past four decades. Furthermore, the increasing percentage of women in the veteran population and the anticipated increase in numbers due to the rising number of women in the armed forces have also created a momentum for recognizing the existence of women veterans. The women's movement itself, with its push for social, economic, and political equality in all areas of national life, also contributed to the increasing awareness.

Advisory Committee on Women Veterans
One of the important initiatives to bring equity to women veterans was the American Veterans Committee suggestion early in 1979 to set up an Advisory Panel on Women Veterans at the VA, to parallel the Defense Advisory Committee in the Armed Services (DACOWITS) which provides information and advice to the secretary of defense on military women.

Advisory committees abound throughout the federal government. They provide a valuable link to the private sector permitting input from interested citizens and organizations. The independence of advisory committees, being outside official government agency channels, gives credibility to its suggestions to the agency. The VA itself has over a dozen advisory committees, some of which have been appointed recently, including the Advisory Committee on Former Prisoners of War, created after the Prisoners of War Health Care Benefits Act was passed in 1981, and the Advisory Committee on Health Related Effects of Herbicides.

AVC suggested that an Advisory Committee on Women Veterans would give advice to the administrator concerning women veterans and "review policies and programs relating to women veterans and make recommendations to the VA administrator concerning such policies and programs."[1] Other organizations endorsed the AVC proposal and urged the VA to take steps to initiate such an Advisory Panel.

During the period when Max Cleland was administrator, the AVC had a continuing dialogue with him concerning the merits and mechanics of such an advisory committee. After correspondence and a series of meetings, Mr. Cleland decided to allow the new administration to make the decision.[2] The AVC renewed the dialogue with Robert Nimmo, President Reagan's first appointee at the VA who also conceded its merits but didn't take action.[3]

With the appointment of Harry Walters as administrator late in 1982, the suggestion for an advisory committee fell on a receptive policymaker. In a meeting with AVC officials early in January 1983, Mr. Walters announced his intention to create an Advisory Committee on Women Veterans.[4] An important milestone had been reached.

Congressional Hearings

A new breakthrough in achieving the Advisory Committee on Women Veterans was reached on March 3, 1983, when Congressman Bob Edgar of Pennsylvania, the new chairman of the Subcommittee on Hospitals and Health Care of the House Committee on Veterans Affairs, held hearings on HR 1137, a bill to establish an Advisory Committee on Women Veterans in the Veterans Administration. Senator Alan Cranston had already introduced a bill (S. 11) which would set up such an Advisory

Committee, but the House Subcommittee held the first hearing. Congressman Don Edwards of California was a cosponsor of the bill. Plans for introducing this legislation were already in motion by the time Administrator Walters made known his intention to set up an advisory committee.

This was the first time that the interests and problems of women veterans specifically were addressed by any Committee of Congress. There had been references in omnibus health bills before (1982 Omnibus health bill) which had addressed a narrow issue concerning certain specific health care needs of women veterans, but this was the first time that a hearing had been devoted exclusively to women veterans.

In a moving opening statement, Congressman Edgar pointed out that women made major contributions to the defense of the country and are likely to do more, and in greater numbers.

> During this decade, a shrinking pool of eighteen and nineteen year old males available for military service will present an ever larger need for women to volunteer for the armed services. . . .
>
> We intend to see that equality of military service is matched by equal rights and benefits provided through the Veterans Administration, regardless of sex, age or race.

Congressman Edgar pledged a resolve to deal with this issue before his Subcommittee and the assembled witnesses. He also told the hearing that

> We are still attempting to grapple with the problems and needs of women veterans without the adequate statistical evidence and analytical tools to address these needs.
>
> As just one example, with growing evidence of unique readjustment disabilities, or potential health problems, among female Vietnam veterans, unbelievably no one right now even knows how many women actually served in Vietnam.[5]

A major point of contention between the VA and the Subcommittee was the VA's assertion that it was moving ahead with an advisory committee on its own, and therefore this legislation (HR 1137) was not necessary. The VA's statement of intent corroborated the statement made to the delegation of AVC officers on January 14, 1983, by the new Administrator Harry Walters that he indeed was moving ahead to create such a committee.

Despite this statement of intent, the VA witness, Dr. Donald Custis, director of the VA's Department of Medicine and Surgery, was adamant in opposing enactment of legislation that would set up an Advisory Committee on Women Veterans.

> A measure such as HR 1137, which mandates the establishment, mission, general composition, duration, reporting requirements and mode of operation of an advisory committee, deprives this Agency of the discretion and flexibility so important to sound program and administration. Instead of a flexible tool to respond to Agency needs, the advisory committee to be established by HR 1137 represents a mechanism which, in its rigidity, could actually prove a greater burden than a benefit.[6]

The VA witness told the subcommittee that it was addressing many of the criticisms that the GAO report had presented. The VA has issued a circular (1–83014, January 28, 1983) that addresses these reported deficiencies. However, the VA denied that because it has taken remedial actions as a result of the GAO report, that it "be taken to imply a broad-based need for remedial action."

Dr. Custis stated that the VA, based on its own survey of women patients, found that over "80% of the facilities providing bed services for women had no problems with providing privacy for women." The VA's testimony was directed toward countering the impression they felt was in the GAO report that the VA was not meeting its medical care obligations to its women veterans.

> It is important, in my judgment, to note that the majority of our facilities presently have the means to meet the medical care needs of female patients. . . .
>
> For example, in 1973 VA nursing homes were first required to accept eligible females, and at present, 86% of all nursing homes report that they can adequately provide for female patients. I believe our recent efforts will help us broaden our service capability and assure that female veterans have equal

access to care. We will certainly strive to continue to make needed improvements in a timely manner.[7]

A panel of women veterans presented strong evidence with individual citations of incidents in which women veterans did not get health care or else got inadequate services from the VA health system. Lynda Van Devanter of the Vietnam Veterans of America, who served as a nurse in Vietnam, Sarah McClendon, who served with the WAC during World War II, Ruth Young, who was in the WAC during the beginning of the Vietnam War, and Norma Griffiths-Boris, who had also been a nurse in Vietnam, testified eloquently about the deficiencies of treatment and of callous attitudes on the part of hospital staffs. Their statements gave credence to the allegations of the GAO report that the VA's health care system was not serving the needs of women veterans.

> Because of the fact that women veterans have in the past not been represented in the VA, there are instances in which conditions of female veterans have not been declared service-connected when corresponding conditions of male veterans have been declared so connected. For example, a male veteran who loses a testicle whether by disease or battle injury, is service-connected and compensated for the loss of reproductive capacity. In one case, a woman veteran of fifteen years in the military had an ovary removed as a result of a tumor while in the service. When she applied for service connection and compensation, she was denied such connection and compensation despite her corresponding loss of reproductive capacity.[8]

* * *

> When you look at the jobs women perform today, you can see we are going to get more patients. They serve as jet engine mechanics, tank turret repair technicians, they refuel aircraft in the air, refuel tankers, fly helicopters and C–141 planes, ferry passengers and cargo to naval air carriers at sea, jump as paratroopers, serve on destroyer and submarine tenders, operate with air evacuation teams. They serve in most of the jobs offered in the military, with few exceptions. . . .
>
> I am asking that the VA alert contractors in future to make sure that hospital facilities include necessary accommodations

for women. In the past, these contractors have taken the tax-payers' money—and the VA inspectors have let them get by with it—without thought for women. They did not provide a shingle to be hung on doors to restrict showers temporarily. . . .

Daily physical therapy, if required, is not possible for women. There is no self-help ward. Often women patients are sent home to care for themselves if they live alone, but there is more room for men patients, even if they are ambulatory. . . . Sergeant Gouvela was told to go home and stay in bed except for trips to the refrigerator. She lived alone. What about hot meals?[9]

* * *

While I hold no malice in my heart for what I consider to be a lack of sensitivity and callous treatment in the medical problems of females that I experienced at the two VA hospital facilities, I would hope that this testimony would help to prevent future situations of this nature from happening to other female veterans who request care and medical treatment, especially emergency medical services, at VA medical facilities.[10]

* * *

Any receiver in the mental health care system certainly and perhaps rightfully, has criticism of its delivery of that care. To be improperly diagnosed and then treated for ten years for that diagnosis is a source of anger for me today. Definition of a problem is a necessary step in treating any psychological disability. The practice of accepting a narrow range of symptoms as the normal or common ways of women to cope puts off the attempt to define the problem.[11]

The American Veterans Committee emphasized its long struggle to achieve the creation of the VA Advisory Committee during the hearings. It also reported the stated intent of the new VA Administrator Harry Walters to establish such a committee, and commended him for that statement. AVC supported enactment of the legislation.

However, we believe that the role of the VA Advisory Committee on Women will be enhanced by having Congress also endorse the committee by enacting this legislation. Congressional commitment to the importance of such an independent advisory group that will concern itself solely with the problems and needs of women veterans will be reassuring to women veterans.[12]

The AVC brought out the demographic challenges facing the VA in the years to come. Citing the recently published statistical brief on the female veteran population, which indicated that the female median age is getting younger, AVC suggested that the VA will have to provide health care for an increasingly large and young female veteran population, whose medical needs will often be gender-related.

On the other side of the coin, AVC suggested that the World War II population, which is by far the largest part of the veteran population, is getting older. It has been estimated that close to 11 million veterans, male and female, will reach the age of sixty-five within the next several years. Women are among this group, and as they get older, they, like the male veterans, will require more medical services, as do all older persons. Furthermore, with the increasing awareness of their rights to use the VA system, and with the decreasing financial resources that older persons, particularly women, face, it is more likely that older women veterans will turn to the VA hospital system for their health care needs.

The very fact that these hearings are being held, the fact that the administrator has indicated an Advisory Committee on Women is very likely to come into being, will without a doubt increase women veterans' awareness of their benefits and their rights.

What has happened to the women with non-service connected illnesses or injuries? They theoretically should have the same access to treatment, as an inpatient and outpatient basis, that men do. This has not been the case for several reasons. One is based on the institutional inability to provide gender-related care and treatment. The VA has only seven full-time gynecologists on staff for 170 facilities. Those kinds of health-care services, if service-connected, can be contracted out or provided for on a fee basis.

But for those with non-service connected gender-specific health problems, there is no provision for non-VA care on a contract or fee basis. There have been horror stories of women veterans

with acute conditions being told to come back six months to
a year later. Legislation to provide fee-basis care in such circumstances should be seriously considered.[13]

Other veterans' organizations also testified. The American Legion stated its support of "the establishment of an Advisory Committee on Women Veterans within the Veterans Administration."
The Legion stated that "an Advisory Committee on Women
Veterans would provide equally important data on which to
determine the needs of female veterans, and whether or not these
needs are being totally addressed by the Veterans Administration."

> It is obvious that women have some unique medical needs
> which must be addressed. It is the belief of the American
> Legion that every VA medical care facility should have the
> capability of conducting pelvic examinations, to include PAP
> smears and other tests, and breast examinations in the course
> of providing total physical examinations to determine the sta-
> tus of the female veterans' health. Likewise, we feel it im-
> perative that inpatient and outpatient gynecologic services be
> readily available for both service-connected and nonservice-
> connected conditions.[14]

The Disabled American Veterans (DAV), one of the largest
of the veterans' organizations, also supported enactment of HR
1137. In its comments, the DAV suggested that the chairman of
the Advisory Committee should be a woman and that the recognized authorities who would be appointed to the Committee,
whenever possible, be women.

> Mr. Chairman, there is no doubt in our minds that female
> veterans—simply because of the fact that they are female—
> do not have access to VA health care as do their male coun-
> terparts. . . . The DAV finds itself in basic agreement with
> the actions recommended in the GAO report. Specifically,
> efforts are necessary to insure that (1) Men and women have
> equal access to VA treatment programs and medical facilities;
> (2) Women treated in VA facilities receive complete physical
> examinations; (3) Sufficient plans are made for the anticipated

increase in the female veteran population; (4) Female veterans are adequately informed on their benefit entitlement.[15]

While the AMVETS, which also testified before the committee, supported the legislation generally, "it closely parallels present studies underway, within the VA, it will to a degree insure the recognition of the unique problems which are faced by the female veteran and, as such will act to a degree as an oversight committee."[16]

However, the AMVET witness reported that the organization had canvassed its National Service Officers to determine any deficiencies in medical care for female veterans. It reported that without exception they were advised that "the medical needs of the female veterans were being adequately met by the Veterans Administration based on its current indicated needs."

AMVETS claimed that many female veterans did not know they were eligible for the medical care at VA hospitals and urged the VA to engage in a public relations effort to encourage females' usage of the hospital services available to them as veterans.

The conclusions of Jenny Schnaier's master's thesis "to assess the nature and extent of mental health problems, specifically PTSD (posttraumatic stress disorder) affecting female Vietnam veterans" were also presented at the March 3 hearing. The study found that PTSD may be applicable to the experiences of women Vietnam veterans. Further, this research, according to Schnaier, found that there is evidence of mental health distress among the women sampled.

The General Accounting Office, which is the oversight arm of the Congress, and which had written the report on the VA's Health Care System as it relates to female veterans, also testified during the March 3 hearings. The GAO, as a government-financed agency, did not take any position regarding the Advisory Committee but its testimony reviewed some of the problems which it had elaborated on in the 1982 report *Actions Needed to Insure That Female Veterans Have Equal Access to VA Benefits.*

Because of the lack of privacy at older VA facilities, women, including those with service-connected disabilities, could not obtain some specialized medical care. Although staff and pa-

tients were sometimes inconvenienced, medical-surgical facilities were generally able to handle the current number of
female patients. However, psychiatric facilities and domiciliaries were not.

Problems in insuring privacy at older medical centers created concerns for female patients and inconvenienced the staff.
Wards in older facilities have many eight to sixteen-bed rooms
and frequently have communal shower and toilet facilities. . . . Because there often are not enough female patients
to fill large rooms, females had to compete with isolation
patients for the hospitals' limited number of private rooms. . . .

Women could not participate in some treatment programs
at two of the six psychiatric facilities we contacted. . . .

Neither service-connected nor nonservice-connected female
veterans were admitted to ten of the VA's sixteen domiciliaries
because of a lack of privacy in sleeping and toilet facilities. . . .

Women require gynecological and obstetrical care. However, women with nonservice-connected disabilities could not
always get gynecological care, and women with normal pregnancies could not obtain obstetrical care.[17]

In its summary, the GAO stated:

Although progress has been made in insuring that medical
care is available to female veterans, action is needed to insure
that:
   —men and women have equal access to VA treatment pro-
     grams and medical facilities.
   —women treated in VA facilities receive complete physical
     exams.
   —needed gynecological care is provided, and
   —sufficient plans are made for the anticipated increase in
     female veterans.
   Actions the VA has taken to implement our report recommendations should, if effectively implemented, signifi-
cantly improve female veterans' access to health care.[18]

The Advisory Committee on Women Veterans received another boost when provision for such a committee was included in
an omnibus "Veterans' Programs Improvement Act of 1983,"
S.11, introduced by Senator Cranston. Cosponsors of the bill were

Senators Jennings Randolph, Matsunaga, Dennis DeConcini, and Mitchell. Hearings on S.11 and other related legislation were held March 9 and 10 by the Senate Veterans Affairs Committee, under the chairmanship of Senator Alan Simpson.

Besides authorizing the Advisory Committee on Women Veterans, S.11 also included a fee-basis authority for the VA to provide nonservice-connected female veterans with gender-related care. In a statement in the *Congressional Record* (January 26, 1983) Senator Cranston outlined his argument for this provision:

> This report (GAO) has convinced me that there is a real need for a fee-basis authority for the foreseeable future while the VA takes the steps necessary to evaluate the likely demand from women veterans for gender-related care and to acquire the staff necessary to meet the demand. Without such fee-basis authority, it is likely that the situation found by the GAO will not improve for a long time, particularly in light of the 18 months the VA has indicated it will need just to collect data on the current situation. Once the VA can demonstrate very clearly that this situation no longer prevails, I would be willing to reconsider the necessity for continuing such an extraordinary fee-basis authority. But until such time, such authority is needed if the VA is to offer the same range of services to male and female veterans.[19]

June A. Willenz of the American Veterans Committee and Lynda Van Devanter of the Vietnam Veterans of America presented testimony in favor of the Advisory Committee on Women and the fee-basis authority for the VA so that nonservice-connected women veterans could receive contract services for gender-related ailments, until the VA was able to bring its services for women veterans up to a par with male veterans. Dr. Nora Kinzer, Special Assistant to VA Administrator Harry Walters, also testified, reiterating the VA position that Congress does not need to legislate an Advisory Committee because the Administrator was proceeding to create one administratively.

Response of VA to GAO Report

The Veterans Administration had responded favorably to some of the recommendations in the GAO report that came out in

September 1982. Then Administrator Robert Nimmo, in his response to the report, agreed to develop guidelines to assist all VA health care facilities in improving female veterans' access to outpatient gynecological and other care not available at VA facilities. The Administrator also agreed that new health care facility construction will provide the special facilities needed for the treatment of female veterans when the VA's health care programs require those facilities. He did suggest that, because of existing physical constraints and limited resources, interim solutions would often be necessary. He indicated that a forum would be developed whereby successful solutions to individual problems for female patient care and privacy would be developed on a local level. He also concurred in the GAO's recommendations that projections needed to be developed on the number of service-connected and nonservice-connected female veterans who used VA facilities, for future planning of new VA facilities and renovations.

Not all of the GAO recommendations were favorably received by Mr. Nimmo. He refused to consider an evaluation of female veterans' awareness of benefits, insisting that female veterans were veterans and that as such they had full access to benefits information and assistance available to all veterans. Neither did he agree to establish procedures to insure that female veterans would be notified of major changes in veterans' benefits that affect them.[20]

Regarding outreach efforts, Administrator Nimmo did promise that veterans' organizations with predominantly female memberships would be included in future outreach efforts.

From the testimonies given in the Subcommittee on Health and Hospitals of the House Veterans Affairs Committee and the Senate Veterans Affairs Committee on Health and Hospitals, there was concern that the VA was not going to meet the criticisms of the GAO report. The GAO itself expressed satisfaction that, if the VA carried out what it said it was going to do, it would meet the health care needs of the women veterans.

In other actions to carry out its stated commitment to women veterans, the VA's Department of Medicine and Surgery put out a circular on January 28, 1983, directing its medical centers to come up with a written plan for the care of female veterans by

June 1, 1983. That plan had to address at a minimum the following:

1. The definition of a complete physical examination for a female as including breast examination and pelvic examination (when no pelvic examination is done, the reason for this must be clearly documented in the medical record).

2. Provision of inpatient gynecologic services for hospitalized female veterans as well as those in VA nursing homes and domiciliaries.

3. Provision of outpatient gynecologic services so that eligible (NSC and SC) female veterans are able to receive care for gender-related conditions on a par with the care male veterans receive for their gender-related ailments. Fee-basis care alone is not sufficient for this purpose. (Outpatient gynecology can be provided through the use of staff, attending or consultant gynecologists, referral to another VA medical center, and/or sharing agreements with affiliated hospitals or DoD installations.)

4. Referral procedures so that female veterans can receive necessary services currently unavailable at the medical center because of privacy considerations.[21]

Besides the written plan, the medical center was ordered to review current methods of giving outpatient gynecological services and upgrading them when needed. In-house capability was indicated as preferable; however, when not available, a number of alternative methods were suggested. The medical centers were also advised that they were expected to correct privacy limitations so that women veterans were not excluded from any medical programs. The centers were asked to provide plans for correction of barriers that could be incorporated in the five-year facility plans. The medical centers were required to submit progress reports to the Department of Medicine and Surgery (DM&S) by June 30, 1983.

Besides the above circular, with its comprehensive instructions to the local VA medical facilities to accommodate women, the DM&S appointed one of its staff, Dr. Susan Mather, to serve as the liaison and point of contact for women veterans. If written plans or reporting is not up to expectations, the DM&S will call the local facility to account for the shortcomings and to meet the requirements set forth. The VA also is preparing to conduct an in-depth survey of women veterans to develop the missing statistics and profiles on women veterans that have so embarrassed the VA.

With these initiatives, the VA has responded to the criticisms of the GAO report, the findings of the AVC preliminary investigation, and the testimonies of women veterans and veterans' organizations. Only results will indicate whether the VA has indeed fulfilled its pledge to meet the needs of its female veterans, putting them on an equal basis with its male veterans. The women veterans themselves—the consumers—will be the best judge as to whether the VA is indeed meeting its commitment to women veterans as it said it wants to during the congressional hearings this March.

The Advisory Committee on Women Veterans, with a reporting requirement to the Congress, will help to monitor the VA's actions. Both committees are confident that the legislation requiring the setting up of the Advisory Committee on Women Veterans will pass. Even at the unlikely possibility that this does not happen, Administrator Walters is on record to set up such a committee administratively. Checking into VA's progress in gearing up its facilities, and in making up the deficiencies in staff and equipment to provide women veterans with the health and hospital care they need, will be one of the Advisory Committee's functions.

With the congressional hearings and the attendant publicity, the women veterans themselves are finding out more about their benefits. Furthermore, with increasing use of the VA hospital system by women veterans, the demand will forestall any pulling back on the plans now in motion to upgrade the services for women veterans. As more women veterans have good experiences using the VA medical centers, the word will spread and other women veterans will be encouraged to come forward and use them also. Indeed, as a result of the developments of the last couple of years, women veterans are becoming a "visible population." They themselves are beginning to think of themselves as veterans and are not likely to allow themselves to be sidestepped or overlooked in future veteran policy decision making. The demographic evidence is there, the congressional interest is abundant, the media have begun to take notice of women, and female veterans themselves are developing a stronger sense of their identity as veterans and vocalizing their needs and concerns.

Vietnam Women Veterans

Mention must be made of the special situation of the Vietnam women veterans. Although the Department of Defense has not released the exact figures for the number of military women who actually served in Vietnam, it has been estimated that at least seven thousand women served there, mostly as nurses. Until recently the problems of readjustment and the emotional toll that their war experiences had on their mental health were not considered. The long haul to get proper attention and treatment for the mental health problems of the male Vietnam veterans led to the legislation that created the Vietnam Vet Center Readjustment Counseling Program within the VA in 1979. However, this program, which offered counseling and treatment sessions to Vietnam veterans, did not focus on the problems of the women. Being a small number and, in characteristic fashion, not stepping forward with their problems and illnesses, the women veterans were largely ignored, although many had symptoms of delayed stress and anxiety for years.

The nurses who served in Vietnam had unusually traumatic experiences in assisting the war injured because many seriously injured troops were saved by quick helicopter evacuations. It has been suggested that, as a result, the nurses took care of wounds and injuries that nurses of other wars probably did not, simply because men like these would have died before they reached medical assistance. Because of the nature of the guerilla warfare and our own retaliation with napalm and other extreme measures, the nurses also saw and treated gruesomely wounded civilians. Because of their professional positions, they were expected to deal with all they saw and experienced without demonstrating any of the emotion or anxiety they felt. As a result, many bottled up their own pain and other feelings for years because they were expected to take everything in their stride. Besides this bottled-up stress, the nurses and other women who served in Vietnam also suffered the same isolation and rejection in society that the male veterans experienced when they returned home.

All the public and private outreach efforts toward the Vietnam and Vietnam-era veterans were directed toward men. It wasn't until the Vietnam Veterans Readjustment Counseling Program was under way for two years that it became aware of the situation with regards to women veterans who served in Vietnam. The GAO report, the growing number of complaints from women veterans, the beginning of women veterans' self-help groups, and the gradual education of the media and the veterans' organizations of the problems of women veterans finally had an impact.

In September 1982 the VA's Veterans Readjustment Counseling Program set up a "Working Group on Women Vietnam Veterans" to address the issues raised by the women Vietnam-era veterans and to try to relate their needs to the services provided by Vet Centers which were operated around the country by the Readjustment Counseling Program. This "Working Group" has been meeting under the office of the director of the Vet Center Program and has begun to effect changes that will benefit the women veterans.

As the result of the new commitment by Dr. Arthur Blank, the Director of the Veterans' Readjustment Counseling Program, to assist the women who served during Vietnam, sixty-three out of the one hundred and thirty-six Veterans Centers around the country now have at least one female staff person who does counseling. Five women are team leaders at the centers and twenty-eight counselors are women. The other women staffers do some counseling along with clerical and office duties.

To carry out its commitment to women veterans, the director's office is providing training to the staffs of all the Vet Centers so that they will be sensitized and equipped to deal with the emotional and other problems of the women veterans who come to the centers. While there was initial indifference to the needs of women and real resistance to the training to help them relate to the women veterans, the center staffs are now accepting the new orientation. The program leadership feels they are just beginning to make progress to provide women veterans with the counseling and support services they need. Because the women's component got such a late start, the Readjustment Counseling Program is seeking an extension of time from the Congress to continue its delivery of services to them and to other Vietnam veterans. Furthermore, twenty-eight centers were first formed in 1982 and have not really had a chance to service the veterans in their areas yet.

An extension of one year for the Veterans' Readjustment Counseling Program is contained in the omnibus Senate bill S.11. Most of the witnesses actively supported that extension although the program itself would like to have an extension of three years because in many areas, including the women's one, they are just beginning to become effective.

In its report to the director of the Veterans Readjustment Counseling Program, the "Working Group" urged that more women be placed in staff positions in the Vet Centers, and the centers themselves try to make an effort to create a more inviting environment for the female veteran. At present the centers, with their posters, literature, and other decorative features, are too male-oriented. Also, the report pointed out that the locations of many centers are such that women are fearful to go into those neighborhoods and that the practice of placing female veterans in other groups such as wives, mothers or girlfriends are not salutory for female veterans whose problems are quite different. Also, the report suggested that it is not judicious to place the female veterans into all-male groups unless there is careful therapeutic preparation of female veterans and male members.

"If the group members are not sensitized to the issues of being a female veteran, the group experience can be less than therapeutic at best, and devastating at worst," the report suggested, also citing the need for considerable outreach to women veterans and the need to develop publicity materials in order to reach those who have not been aware of the Vet Centers' interest in women veterans. Outreach materials for women veterans are lacking and should be distributed to the centers and throughout the VA system, the report recommends.

The working group is continuing its task of monitoring the Vet Centers as their recommendations for needed services to Vietnam-era women veterans are implemented.

Agent Orange

Another vital issue that has been of great concern to Vietnam veterans is the Agent Orange controversy. There have been sixty-six studies of the effects of Agent Orange and other dioxins on Vietnam veterans, none of which have included women. These studies were either done or funded by different government agencies in response to the growing evidence that exposure to Agent Orange produced devastating effects upon the veterans and their offspring. The presumption was that, because there were so few women veterans in Vietnam, the chances of their exposure was negligible. However, these women veterans are as concerned about the long-term consequences of Agent Orange as the men.

The VA, ordered to do an epidemological study of Vietnam Veterans by Congress (PL 96–151) in 1979, never got off the ground to actually do the study. While a protocol had been written by U.C.L.A. for the VA, that was all that was done. Congress was irate. Hearings held in 1982 took the VA to task for its failure to comply with the congressional mandate to perform an in-depth study. Congressman Sonny Montgomery, Chairman of the House Veterans Committee, bypassed the VA and negotiated with the Secretary of Health and Human Services to have the Centers for Disease Control of the Public Health Service perform the study. The Centers for Disease Control (CDC) in Atlanta, Georgia, is the most prestigious body for the investigation of diseases.

As a result of the Montgomery initiative, a Memorandum of Agreement was worked out between the Veterans Administration and the Department of Health and Human Services for the CDC to undertake the study for the VA, which is providing the funding. The CDC was given three years to do the study and report back to the VA, which in return will report its findings to the Congress. This is the key study that Vietnam veterans have been looking toward for years to affirm their experiences as victims of a higher mortality rate and the higher incidence of birth defects in their offspring as a result of exposure to Agent Orange. To date, it is not known whether women will be included in this epidemiological study.

The VA has been under fire for years now for not treating those veterans exposed to Agent Orange who have developed all kinds of ailments, including cancer, and whose children have had birth defects. The epidemiological study now under way by the CDC is to give scientifically sound answers to the many questions concerning the long-term effects of the dioxins on the human body and its genetic structure. The VA created an Advisory Committee on Health-Related Effects of Herbicides in 1979 to provide guidance to the VA in dealing with the increasing number of cases of veterans who had been exposed to Agent Orange seeking treatment from the VA. Since passage of the Veterans Health Care, Training and Small Business Loan Act of 1981, VA facilities are authorized to provide certain health care services to any Vietnam-era veterans who, while serving in Vietnam, might have been exposed to dioxin or other defoliants. However, the guidelines are vague so that neither the veterans nor the VA staff are clear what health services are available, and for what ailments.

Another initiative of the VA that may shed light on the Agent Orange controversy is a VA mortality study that is due by the end of 1984. Furthermore, the VA has announced that four monographs on environmental and occupation factors that may have had an impact upon the health of military personnel who served in Vietnam are in preparation.

Court Case

A recent court case has great significance for younger women veterans. A woman veteran challenged the VA's contention that pregnancy is a physiological condition, not a disability, and therefore not entitled to hospital care. While the statute does not spell out this bar, the VA stands by a regulation it enacted in 1926 which states: "Women veterans will not be entitled to hospital care for pregnancy and parturition unless it is complicated by a pathological condition."[22]

With an increasingly younger women veteran population, this bar is a significant disadvantage to women veterans using the VA hospital system. With a larger proportion of the women veteran population of child-bearing age, the existence of this regulation means that important and expensive services are denied women veterans.

A young woman who was honorably discharged from the Navy

questioned the VA practice. In a lawsuit requesting "declaratory and injunctive relief" Evelyn E. Kirkhuff challenged the validity of the VA regulation barring otherwise eligible women veterans from eligibility for hospital care benefits for "uncomplicated childbirth." The case, *Kirkhuff* v. *Cleland* was heard in the U.S. District Court, District of Columbia, May 8, 1981, and was decided in favor of the plaintiff. The District Court held that

> (1) review of statutory or constitutional validity of regulation was not barred by statutory ban on judicial review of veteran's claim, and (2) regulation was in excess of defendant's (VA) authority and also was not sustainable under any rational basis.[23]

The reasoning of the District Court in upholding Kirkhuff's claim is interesting. The court pointed out that as far back as 1926 (the same time the regulation was promulgated) Congress passed the World War Veterans Act Amendments of 1926. The director of the then Veterans Bureau, General Hines, noted that

> The first change is in section 10 . . . which provides general hospitalization for all ex-servicemen of all wars and all disabilities where facilities are available and the veteran is in need of hospitalization. The change contemplated provides that where the facilities of the government will not take care of women veterans entitled to hospitalization under this provision, that we be authorized to place them in contract (private) hospitals.[24]

The District Court was convinced that Congress had intended that women veterans would have equal access to veterans' benefits. The court was also convinced that Congress was aware that VA facilities for women veterans were limited and not equipped to deal with the disabilities unique to women. Furthermore, the court thought that the Congress was consistent in continuing to maintain the provision for hospital care for women veterans as a distinct group, even since Section 601(4)(c)(iv), cited earlier, was enacted in 1926. Although there had been many amendments and changes in the statute over the years, Congress kept that provision in.

An important piece of veterans' health legislation was enacted into law in 1976 to respond to the influx of Vietnam veterans into the veteran population and to provide sufficient facilities and programs to meet their needs.

The Senate report to the 1976 health legislation pointed out that the new language would

> Limit the authorization of fee-basis service for service-connected or nonservice-connected disabilities—to those situations when regular VA hospitals or clinics (or other federal facilities) *are* genuinely unable to provide the needed services themselves.[25]

Even that act retained the provision that women veterans were eligible for the contract services. Furthermore, the District Court was impressed that the omnibus act of 1976 also included provisions that eliminated all gender-specific language throughout Title 38 of the U.S. Code. The court took issue that Congress was aware of the VA policy on pregnancy.

> There is also little reason to infer Congressional awareness of—or acquiescence to—this particular VA policy affecting women veterans also. It is reasonable to presume that the traditionally small numbers of women veterans has led to their limited voice in veterans lobbying organizations, organizations which have often been responsible for legislative change.[26]

The court suggested that Congress intended at least since 1976 "a broad nondiscriminatory reading of that term [disability] to be applied by the administrator in determining eligibility for hospital care benefits." Conversely, the court suggested that there was "no Congressional intent to exclude uncomplicated parturition specifically from the statutory definition of 'disability.' "

> The legislative history of pertinent veterans benefits statutes reveals absolutely no support for the contention that Congress intended hospital care benefits to be authorized only in the instances of "ordinary" disabilities.[27]

The VA had based its decision not to reimburse for childbirth care costs on a medical opinion in 1929 that perceived only "ordinary disabilities to which the ex-service person is liable" could be treated through hospitalization. The court took issue with the VA's argument that an uncomplicated pregnancy must be excluded as an eligible disability since it does not fall within the category of "ordinary" disabilities to which veterans are prone. The court also threw out the VA's contention that uncomplicated pregnancy is a physiological condition "not susceptible to cure or decided improvement through hospitalization." The court was receptive to the medical opinion offered by Kirkhuff that "normal childbirth imperils the health of the mother, and thus requires hospitalization." This medical opinion testified that "any distinction between 'physiological' and 'pathological' is meaningless in determinations of the need for, and efficacy of, hospital care." The court took the VA to task for not seeking out any medical opinion more recent than the 1944 one cited by the VA.

The VA appealed the case, and on July 20, 1982, the U.S. Court of Appeals for the District of Columbia overturned the lower court's decision. That Appeals Court ruled that the regulation was sufficiently reasonable and disallowed Kirkhuff's claim against the VA. The court stated

> Cost considerations attendant to the provision of natal and prenatal care, the difference between pregnancy and other "disabilities," and the limited nature of VA medical facilities suffice to provide a rational link between the regulation and the VA's primary purpose to provide medical care to veterans with service-connected disabilities, and its secondary purpose to provide care to other needy veterans, consistent with efficient usage of its resources.[28]

The court ruled that the regulation challenged in the case survived "statutory and constitutional muster."

The question of judicial review of VA decisions was dealt with. (VA decisions are final and not subject to court scrutiny, according to U.S. Code, 38 U.S.C. 211 (a).) The court admitted that previous court decisions have recognized various exceptions to the statutory limitation on judicial review. However, the court sidestepped the question of judicial review and overturned the lower court's ruling.

The extent to which Veterans Administration decisions are exempt from review [judicial] raises serious questions. Nevertheless, because we hold that the judgment of the District Court must be reversed, even assuming that we may review the decision of the Administrator in this case, we may not reach this difficult question.[29]

The court chose to rule only whether the government's regulation, which had been challenged by Kirkhuff, furthered some government end. Rejecting the notion that pregnancy was a disability because it required hospitalization, the court insisted that Congress had clearly indicated that "disability" only includes three types of conditions: injury, disease, and defect. Citing legislative history, the court rejected the notion that the VA hospitals were intended to provide services for childbirth. The court concluded that the VA does not discriminate on the basis of gender when it denies coverage for nonpathological pregnancy and childbirth.

With the ruling of the U.S. Court of Appeals for the District of Columbia Circuit in favor of the VA's claim that its regulation denying VA hospital benefits for normal childbirth, the hopes of young women veterans that their pregnancies could be taken care of by the VA hospital system ended. To date, Kirkhuff has not appealed the Court of Appeals decision. At this time it is not known if she plans to take her case to a higher court.

Other Developments
The actions of the VA in 1982 and the congressional initiatives in early 1983 have raised the level of interest in the situation of women veterans around the nation. Not only have the veterans' magazines and newspapers begun to have articles and items of interest to women veterans, but the daily newspapers are also recognizing the forgotten population of women veterans.

The newspaper *Stars and Stripes* (the veterans' edition) has carried a column for over two years on women's issues, written by this author. The *Army Times*, in recent months, has also begun to take notice of women veterans. While "Straight Talk" in New York and "Panorama" in Washington, D.C., have been TV programs that in past years had talk shows on women veterans, the TV medium has mostly paid little attention to the subject, even when programs have been held on Vietnam veterans. In Washington, D.C., at the end of 1982 and the beginning of 1983, at least two talk shows covered the subject of women veterans.

The VA, recognizing this new awareness and the rising consciousness of women veterans themselves, in the first part of 1983, had a Women Veterans exhibit built that can be set up at conventions or in hospitals and is available on loan. This is the first time that the VA has given women veterans prominent publicity of this nature. It will be used for the first time by the midwestern WAC Vets at their 1983 conference in St. Louis.

POW Nurses Honored

Paying tribute to the American nurses captured by the Japanese during World War II after the fall of Bataan and Corregidor, the VA, along with the Department of Defense, flew thirty of those nurses into Washington, D.C., April 7–9, 1983. They were special guests of the VA in ceremonies marking POW-MIA Day, April 9. The nurses who had survived three and a half years of captivity in the Philippines were honored and feted for three days. The President of the United States received them at the White House, members of Congress paid tribute to their courage, and the Secretary of Defense participated in a special reception honoring them at the Pentagon.

The nurses, who were in the Army and the Navy in the Philippines when Pearl Harbor was bombed on December 7, 1941, had moved with the American forces as they were slowly driven out of the Philippine Islands. They attended the wounded and worked day and night under incredible hardships and constant bombardment and, with the American doctors, tried to save lives and give aid to the injured. Their heroism and devotion during those dark days of battle, which finally culminated in the surrender of General Wainwright on Corregidor, were recognized when they first returned to the United States after their release in 1945.

In all the years since the nurses had heard nothing from their government about their achievements and sacrifices, nor did they expect any rewards. Finally, when an Advisory Committee on Prisoners of War was created, one of the POW nurses, Col. Madeline M. Ullom, was asked to serve on that committee.

Until 1981 many of the ailments the nurses had developed as a result of their imprisonment and starvation diet and the unsanitary conditions under which they lived were not recognized as service-connected and therefore were not treatable by the VA. The women prisoners of war, like the men, were finally able to turn to the VA for medical care after the prisoners of war legislation was enacted in 1981.

One of the problems they and the other POWs had was that there were no records of their imprisonment, which meant the VA had nothing to go on for an evaluation of their conditions. Their dental problems had not been treated even though they were directly derived from their wartime captivity. With the passage of the War Health Care Benefits Act of 1981, the VA agreed to treat former prisoners of war conditions and ailments that could be reasonably judged to have resulted from their captivity.

Of the 81 women taken prisoner—67 Army nurses, 11 Navy nurses, two dietitians and a physical therapist—all survived. The women were separated from the doctors and American forces and sent to Santo Tomas prison camp which held over 4,000 civilian prisoners. They were liberated by the American troops in February 1945. While they were in Santo Tomas, the nurses and other women provided nursing care to the members of the camp who were ill and malnourished; many in the camp died.

Not only did the nurses maintain their dignity and *esprit de corps* during their long ordeal, but they played crucial roles in the survival of the other prisoners. They did themselves and their country honor by their courage and devotion to duty. It took forty years for the government to finally acknowledge their extraordinary feat, but it did—on April 9, POW-MIA Day, 1983.

During the reception the Secretary of Defense held for the POW nurses, Secretary Caspar Weinberger announced that a permanent corridor is being established in the Pentagon honoring military women. It would, he said, "highlight the history of women in the military and . . . incorporate authentic artifacts and memorabilia dating from the Revolutionary War to current achievements." The idea of a corridor in the Pentagon honoring military women was originally suggested by the DACOWITS in the late 1970s.

International Developments

For the first time in its history, the World Veterans Federation, the only international veterans' organization in the free world, founded in 1950, held its first session on women at its seventeenth General Assembly in Nice, France, October 26–29, 1982. The Special Session on Women, attended by over four hundred delegates from forty-five countries, discussed "The Role of Women in War and Their Contribution to Establishing Peace."

The Special Session on Women covered the many roles that women play in war: as soldiers, as resistance fighters, as nurses, as victims, as widows, as survivors, as wives, as prisoners of war. This author was one of the panelists in the Special Session, representing the American Veterans Committee, whose chairman, Gus Tyler, currently chairs the United States Council for the World Veterans Federation.

Ms. Willenz stressed the many roles of women during wartime and the widespread impact of war upon women. She pointed out that the full impact of war upon women has not been fully realized or investigated. Therefore, it is impossible for nations to adequately address the needs and problems of their female populations as a result of war.

Other panelists were: Andrée Weitzel, a member of the International Committee of the Red Cross; Una P. Boyce, head of the War Widows Association in Australia; and Kartini Rajas, Vice-Chairman of the veterans' delegation of the Republic of Indonesia. Bodil Seehusen, a member of the Danish Resistance during World War II, chaired the session.

As a result of the wide interest in the Special Session on Women, the World Veterans Federation is planning to initiate a continuing group within the WVF to focus on the special roles of women as a result of war. Fuller participation of women within the World Veterans Federation is another goal that evolved out of the Seventeenth General Assembly's Special Session on Women.

The Future

With increasing national and international awareness of the roles of women in modern wars, women veterans are emerging out of long isolation and neglect. In this country they are becoming visible in the media and are finally being heard by the government agencies that are supposed to service them. Women veterans are achieving legitimacy as veterans. No longer can excuses be made that they are a small minority and therefore cannot hope to have the same benefits or facilities as the male veterans. They have written pages in American history that don't appear in the school textbooks at this time. However, the developments of the last few years and the increased momentum for changes in their status in the first months of 1983 portend a new period of recognition and response to the women veterans of America—forgotten heroines.

However, optimism must be balanced with awareness that a trend of interest can come to nothing substantive unless it is translated into public policy. While the Veterans Administration's new stated commitment to provide the needed medical services for women veterans is heartening, unless the medical centers and hospitals actually implement the directives sent out from the central office of VA, these services will not materialize. Most of the VA hospitals are old and not designed to provide bathroom facilities and privacy for women. It is much easier to redesign future construction or make changes in facilities now being renovated. Commitment has to be translated into dollars and cents. The VA furthermore has to allocate financial resources to upgrade and change the medical facilities to accommodate its women veterans. Otherwise, ten years from now, women veterans will be in the same position they are in today—with a minimum of medical services available to them.

Besides the actual physical changes needed in the medical facilities, additional staffing, training, and equipment are required, particularly for gender-specific ailments or diseases. These take money and must be budgeted. A full-scale training program to sensitize VA medical staff throughout the country of their obligations to serve women veterans must not be overlooked. Basic attitudes must be changed; deep prejudices need to be overcome. Otherwise the VA's medical circulars will have little import for the women veterans who turn to the VA for health care.

The demographic and other studies that the VA has promised to do on women veterans are other steps toward fulfilling the VA's thesis that it serves *all* veterans. But because of the long neglect and lack of information that women veterans have experienced, it is necessary to initiate a widescale outreach program. Otherwise the new services that will be available to women veterans will not reach the prospective clients. Women veterans have to be reached and educated as to their rights and benefits. Many of those benefits have long since expired for a large part of the population of women veterans; they are lost forever. But the others, particularly the health services, are still applicable. Outreach and information are essential corollaries to the VA's campaign to provide equal services to the women veterans of America.

An Advisory Committee on Women Veterans at the Veterans Administration can provide the overview to insure that the VA will indeed fulfill its national commitment to do justice by the women who served in the uniform of the United States. Just as the DACOWITS in the Department of Defense continually reviews the position and problems of military women, an Advisory Committee can maintain constant vigil with regard to the hitherto forgotten population of women veterans.

Epilogue

Just as this book was being typeset, the Administrator of Veterans Affairs announced the formation of an Advisory Committee on Women Veterans. A press release issued August 3, 1983, by the Veterans Administration announced that Administrator Harry N. Walters had appointed an eighteen-member Advisory Committee "to counsel him in planning for special needs of women veterans." The Committee is to consult with the Administrator on "the needs of women veterans with respect to health care, rehabilitation, benefits, compensation, outreach programs and other programs of the Veterans Administration." The Committee, to be chaired by Colonel Lorraine Rossi, U.S. Army (Ret.), will hold its first meeting in September 1983. The author has been named a member of the Advisory Committee and, subsequently, its Executive Committee.

Notes

Chapter 2

1. U.S. Code, Title 38, Section 101 (2).
2. Ibid., Subchapter I, 601 (4) (3) makes provision for private health care for women veterans with a service-connected disability when the VA cannot provide treatment.
3. Mattie E. Treadwell, *The Women's Army Corps* (Washington, D.C.: Office of the Chief of Military History, Department of the Army, 1954), p. 4. Much of the material on the history of the WAAC and the WAC comes from this definitive volume.
4. Mary Beth Norton, *Liberty's Daughters* (Boston: Little, Brown & Co., 1980), p. 212.
5. Linda Kerber, *Women of the Republic* (Chapel Hill, N.C.: University of North Carolina Press, 1980), chap. 2.
6. Ibid.
7. Linda Grant De Pauw, "Women in Combat: The Revolutionary War Experience," *Armed Forces and Society* 7, no. 2 (Winter 1981), pp. 209–226.
8. Kerber, p. 58.
9. Ibid., p. 33.
10. Quote from the Introduction by Alexander Medlicott to Lucy Brewer, *The Female Marine* (New York: Da Capo Press, 1966), p. xv.
11. Elizabeth A. Shields, ed., *Highlights in the History of the Army Nurse Corps* (Washington, D.C.: U.S. Army Center of Military History, 1981), p. 8.
12. Ibid.
13. Ibid., Surgeon General's Report of 1899.
14. Philip A. Kalisch and Margaret Scobey, "Female Nurses in American Wars," *Armed Forces and Society* 9, no. 2 (Winter 1983), pp. 215–44.
15. *Highlights . . . of the Army Nurse Corps*, p. 12.
16. Kalisch and Scobey, p. 220.
17. Ibid.
18. *Highlights . . . of the Army Nurse Corps*, p. 28.
19. Capt. Linda L. Hewitt, USMCR, *Women Marines in World War I* (Washington, D.C.: History and Museums Division, Headquarters, U.S. Marine Corps, 1974), p. 4.
20. Ibid.
21. Treadwell, p. 11.
22. Ibid., p. 24.
23. Ibid., p. 66.
24. Ibid., p. 24.
25. "Women in the Navy," *Shipmate* (U.S. Naval Academy Alumni Association) 45, no. 2 (March 1982), p. 14.
26. Susan H. Goodson, "The Waves in World War II," *Proceedings of the U.S. Naval Institute* 1071, no. 12 (december 1981), p. 46.

27. Barbara Selby, "The Fifinellas," *Flying Magazine* 33 (July 1943), pp. 76-78, 166-67.

28. Sally Von Wagenen Keil, *Those Wonderful Women in Their Flying Machines* (New York: Rawson Wade, 1979), chap. 4.

29. Natalie Jeanne Stewart-Smith, "The Women's Air Force Service Pilots (WASPS) of World War II: Perspectives on the Work of America's First Military Aviators (master's thesis, University of Washington, 1981), p. 41.

30. Ibid.

31. Lt. Col. Pat Meid, USMCR, *Marine Corps Women's Reserve in World War II* (Washington, D.C.: Historical Branch, C-3 Division, Headquarters, U.S. Marine Corps, 1968).

32. Capt. M. E. Bachand, "Women in the Coast Guard and the Coast Guard Reserve" (Washington, D.C.: USCGR Historian's Office, U.S. Coast Guard), p. 1.

33. Treadwell, p. 752.

34. Report of the Commission on Organization of the Executive Branch of the Government, November 19, 1948, quoted by Treadwell, p. 763.

35. Maj. Gen. Jeanne Holm, USAF (Ret.), *Women in the Military: An Unfinished Revolution* (Novato, Calif.: Presidio Press, 1982), p. 113. Material on women in the Air Force comes from General Holm's account.

36. In Britain this is not the case. Women doing the same job as men in the military service are paid on a lower scale.

37. Holm, p. 127.

38. *Women in the Armed Forces* (Washington, D.C.: Office of Information for the Armed Forces, Assistant Secretary of Defense [Public Affairs], Department of Defense).

39. Linda Grant Martin, "Angels of Vietnam," *Today's Health* 45 (August 1967), pp. 17-22, 60-62.

40. Kalisch and Scobey, p. 235.

Chapter 5

1. Helen Rogan, *Mixed Company* (New York: G. P. Putnam, 1981), chap. 6.

2. Ibid., chap. 7.

3. Lt. Col. Pat Meid, USMCR, *Marine Corps Women's Reserve in World War II* (Washington, D.C.: Historical Branch, G-3 Division, Headquarters U.S. Marine Corps, 1968), p. 1.

4. A World War II woman veteran from Easton, Maryland.

5. A World War II woman veteran from upstate New York who served as a WAAC at Selfridge Field Air Base Hospital.

6. A World War II woman veteran, a WAAC, who reenlisted in the WAC, from Springfield Gardens, New York.

7. A member of the Coast Guard Reserve in World War II, now connected with the State University of New York at Buffalo.

8. "Health Care for American Veterans," National Academy of Sciences, 1977.

9. The VA prepared a 600-page report in response to the National Academy of Science study, "Veterans Administration's Response to the Study of Health Care for American Veterans," published by the Senate Veterans Committee as Senate Committee Print No.7. During the extensive hearings on the Report and the VA Response, the AVC was the only organization to mention women veterans.

10. A woman veteran from Syracuse, New York.

11. A woman veteran from Madison, Wisconsin.

12. Gene W. Rothman and Isabel Moriarty, "From Action-Research to Institutional Change: Service Delivery to Institutionalized Female Mental Patients in a Predominantly Male Environment (unpublished paper, 1981).

13. The American Veterans Committee in 1979–80, with the support of the Ford Foundation, conducted an exploratory investigation of what kinds of data government agencies were collecting and had collected historically on women veterans.

14. Veterans Administration, *Vanguard* 28, no. 4 (January 1982).

15. Produced by the Office of the Assistant Secretary of Defense (Manpower, Reserve Affairs, and Logistics), October 1981. The current policy study done by the Army was released late in 1981 and is now being validated.

16. A disabled Vietnam-era woman veteran from Alhambra, California.

17. The study was mandated by Public Law 95–202, Section 304(b), November 23, 1977.

Chapter 6

A. Historical Background

1. Sar A. Levitan and Karen A. Cleary, *Old Wars Remain Unfinished* (Baltimore: Johns Hopkins University Press, 1973), chap. 1.

2. Ibid., p. 27.

3. Gilbert Steiner, *State of Welfare* (Washington, D.C.: The Brookings Institution, 1971), p. 237.

4. Remarks of Dr. Donald Custis before the Senate Veterans Affairs Committee Hearing, 97th Congress, Second Session, VA Health Care Programs Improvement and Extension Act of 1982, p. 276.

5. A report, "VA Response to the Study of Health Care for American Veterans," September 22, 1977.

6. WAAC Circular (No. 2, War Department) Washington, D.C., June 6, 1942.

7. WAAC Circular (No. 37, War Department) Washington, D.C., February 1, 1943.

8. War Department Circular (No. 103) Washington, D.C. April 15, 1943.

9. WAAC Regulations (War Department, 1.93) Washington, D.C., June 1943.

10. Ibid., p. 94.

11. WAAC Regulations, section on "Health, Morality and Well-being."

12. Treadwell, p. 222.

13. Committee of the Civil Service, House, 78th Congress, Second Session.

14. House Report No. 1600, pursuant to H. Res. 16, 78th Congress, Second Session.

15. Statement of Ealine D. Harmon, September 29, 1982, House Veterans Affairs Committee, Subcommittee on Oversight and Investigation.

B. Health Care and Other Benefits

1. Dr. Paul A. L. Haber, "Geriatrics and Extended Health Care in the VA," *The Aging Veteran Population: Interorganizational Relations*, Seventh National Association of Social Workers Professional Symposium, November 21, 1981, Philadelphia, PA., p. 10.

2. "A Report on the Aging Veteran," Senate Committee Print, No. 12, January 5, 1978, p. 17.

3. Ibid.

4. Haber, pp. 9–10.

5. Levitan, p. 70

6. "Women Veterans, Usage of VA Hospitalization," VA Report, Office of Reports and Statistics, August 1982.

7. "The Female Veteran Population: An Overview of its Growth in the Last Decade," statistical brief, March 1982, Office of Reports and Statistics (VA).

8. Ibid.

9. U.S. Code 601c

10. Interview with Dr. Susan Mather, the VA's Dept. of Medicine and Surgery by the author at Central Office, VA, January 1983.

11. Hearing, Senate Veterans Affairs Committee, on VA Health Care Programs Improvement and Extension Act of 1982, April 21, 1982, p. 204.

12. Ibid. p. 274.

13. S. 11 Sec. 202.

14. GAO report HRD-82-98, p. 15.

15. Letter to author from World War II woman veteran in New Hampshire, September 17, 1979.

16. Sarah McClendon testimony, March 3, 1983.

17. Ruth Young testimony, March 3, 1983.

18. Lynda Van Devanter testimony, March 3, 1983.

19. DAV Magazine, January 1983.

20. Maxine Hammer, "Perceptions of Female Veterans: Their Health-Care Needs in VA Hospitals" (dissertation, University of Southern California, 1979).

21. Gene Rothman, "They Also Served: Forgotten Female Veterans" (unpublished article).

22. "Legacies of Vietnam, Comparative Adjustment of Veterans and Their Peers," a study prepared for the VA, pursuant to PL 95-202, March 9, 1981.

23. Lynda Van Devanter testimony.

24. Ibid.

25. Jenny Ann Schnaier, "Women Vietnam Veterans and Their Mental Health Adjustment: A Study of Their Experiences and Post-Traumatic Stress" (masters thesis, University of Maryland, 1982).

26. Ibid.

27. *Congressional Record*, February 20, 1973, pp. 877-78 (remarks of Congresswoman Margaret Heckler).

28. VA Regulations, Trans. Sheet 166, November 19, 1982, "Words and Statements Denoting Gender."

29. VA Department of Veterans Benefits, Interim Issue 26-68-3, Section 2, April 9, 1968.

30. VA, DVB, Information Bulletin, DVB IB 26-73-1, February 2, 1973.

31. Ibid.

Chapter 7

1. A World War II woman veteran from New Hampshire.

2. A woman who served in the Coast Guard Women's Reserve during World War II, now living in Buffalo, New York.

3. Ibid.

4. Statement of the American Legion before the Subcommittee on Hospitals and Health Care, House Veterans Affairs Committee, March 3, 1983.

5. Statement of Disabled American Veterans, same hearing, March 3, 1983.

6. Women's Army Corps Veterans Association brochure.

7. Letter from Lt. Col. Norma V. Breedlove, USAF (Ret.) to author, February 1, 1983.

8. Membership brochure, WAF Officers Associated.

9. Ibid.

10. SPAR 40th Anniversary Newsletter, Souvenir Edition (Boston, September 3-October 3, 1982), p. 7.

11. "Lest We Forget: A History of the Women's Overseas Service League," Helene M. Sillia, historian (July 1978), frontispiece.

12. Ibid., pp.15-16.

13. Ibid., p. 2.

14. Ibid., p. iii, Maj. Gen. Clarence R. Edwards, Commander 26th Div.
15. Ibid., p. iv, Alvin Owsley, National Commander, American Legion, 1923, Chicago Convention.

Chapter 8

1. Letter to VA Administrator Max Cleland from AVC National Chairman Gus Tyler, February 21, 1980.
2. An exchange of letters took place between Max Cleland and the AVC from early 1980 to 1981, with Mr. Cleland reversing himself several times before he decided not to make the decision. See AVC/Cleland letters, AVC files.
3. Mr. Nimmo also changed his mind about the Advisory Committee. Shortly before he resigned, Mr. Nimmo told AVC (in a letter of August 24, 1982) that he would give full attention to the matter.
4. The AVC presented the following memorandum to Administrator Walters, January 17, 1982, suggesting the rationale and composition of an advisory committee:

AMERICAN VETERANS COMMITTEE PROPOSAL
for a
VA ADVISORY PANEL ON WOMEN (VAPOW)

We suggest that the VA set up an advisory committee on women veterans under the terms set forth by 5 U.S. Code Appendix Section 1 (Federal Advisory Committee Act of 1972). This committee should be at the Administrator's level.

Such a committee is necessary at this time for the following reasons:
1. The increasing number of women veterans identified by the VA, with an upward trend of younger women veterans in the years ahead.
2. GAO Report identified problem areas in the VA hospital system for women veterans. Also, the GAO did not review the other programs. VA reports also have shown problem areas within the VA medical programs.
3. Historically, the VA has little data on women veterans. It is important to gather as much current data as possible. This committee would facilitate such data gathering.
4. There have been no information programs or outreach efforts targeted to women veterans.
5. There has been no survey or evaluation of what benefits women veterans have found useful, or what they might find useful. Also, there have been no studies on whether women veterans are knowledgeable about their benefits and rights.
6. An advisory committee could serve as a useful independent channel through which women veterans could make known their concerns and recommendations.

We suggest that there be approximately 30 individuals on the Committee. They would be appointed by the Administrator who will call upon women veterans groups and veterans organizations for their suggestions.

Two-thirds of the Committee should consist of women veterans and from veterans organizations with a strong interest in women veterans. The other third should be experts in fields relevant to women veterans concerns: medicine, social work, employment, education, business, etc. Representatives of all the VA departments would be members ex-officio. Provision for representatives of other concerned government agencies such as Department of Labor, HHS, or OPM, or DoD to join in the meetings will be made.

The Committee should meet at least four times a year and will prepare an annual report for the Administrator.

There should be appropriate staff support to assist the committee in the carrying out of its functions.

5. Statement of Congressman Bob Edgar, March 3, 1983, Subcommittee on Hospitals and Health Care, House Veterans Affairs Committee.

6. Statement of Dr. Donald Custis at March 3, 1983 hearing.

7. Ibid.

8. Lynda Van Devanter testimony, March 3, 1983 hearing.

9. Sarah McClendon testimony, March 3, 1983 hearing.

10. Ruth Young Testimony, March 3, 1983 hearing.

11. Norma Griffiths-Boris testimony, March 3, 1983 hearing.

12. Statement of June Willenz for the AVC, March 3, 1983 hearing.

13. Ibid.

14. Statement of American Legion, March 3, 1983 hearing.

15. Statement of Disabled American Veterans, March 3, 1983 hearing.

16. Statement of AMVETS, March 3, 1983 hearing.

17. Statement of U.S. General Accounting Office (GAO), March 3, 1983 hearing.

18. Ibid.

19. Senator Alan Cranston's remarks, *Congressional Record*, January 26, 1983, pp. S.180–S.183.

20. GAO Report, Enclosure III.

21. VA Department of Medicine and Surgery Circular 10-83-14, January 28, 1983.

22. U.S. Code, Title 38, C.F.R. § 17.48 (e).

23. *Kirkhuff* v. *Cleland*, Federal Supplement, vol. 516, p. 363.

24. Ibid.

25. Senate Report No. 94-1206, 94th Congress, Second Session, 1976, cited in *Kirkhuff* v. *Cleland*.

26. *Kirkhuff* v. *Cleland*, p. 365.

27. Ibid., p. 368.

28. U.S. Court of Appeals for the District of Columbia Circuit, No. 81-1770, *Evelyn Elizabeth Kirkhuff*, Appellee, v. *Robert P. Nimmo, Administrator Veterans Affairs*, Appellant; decided July 20, 1982.

29. Ibid.

Recommended Reading

Berkin, Carol Ruth, and Norton, Mary Beth. *Women of America*. Boston: Houghton Mifflin, 1979.

Binkin, Martin, and Bach, Shirly J. *Women and the Military*. Washington, D.C.: The Brookings Institution, 1977.

Chafe, William. *The American Woman*. New York: Oxford University Press, 1972.

Degler, Carl N. *At Odds*. New York: Oxford University Press, 1980.

DePauw, Linda Grant. *Seafaring Women*. Boston: Houghton Mifflin, 1982.

Dessez, Eunice C. *The First Enlisted Women 1917–18*. Philadelphia: Dorrance & Co., 1955.

Douie, Vera. *Daughters of Britain*. Oxford: The Author, 12 Charlbury Road, 1949.

General Accounting Office (GAO). *Actions Needed to Insure That Female Veterans Have Equal Access to VA Benefits* (GAO/Hrd-82-98). Washington, D.C.: GAO, 1982.

Greenwald, Maureen. *Women, War and Work*. Westport, Conn.: Greenwood Press, 1980.

Hancock, Joy Bright. *Lady in the Navy*. Annapolis, Md.: Naval Institute Press, 1972.

Hewit, Linda L., Capt., USMCR. *Women Marines in World War I*. Washington, D.C.: History and Museums Division, Headquarters U.S. Marine Corps, 1974.

Holm, Jeanne, Maj. Gen., USAF (Ret.). *Women in the Military*. Navato, Calif.: Presidio Press, 1982.

Keil, Sally Van Wagenen. *Those Wonderful Women With Their Flying Machines*. New York: Rawson Wade Publishers, 1979.

Kerber, Linda. *Women of the Republic*. Chapel Hill, N.C.: University of North Carolina Press, 1980.

Levitan, Sar A., and Cleary, Karen. *Old Wars Remain Unfinished*. Baltimore and London: Johns Hopkins University Press, 1973.

Meid, Pat, Lt. Col., USMCR. *Marine Corps Women's Reserve in World War*

II. Washington, D.C.: Historical Branch, C-3 Division, Headquarters, U.S. Marine Corps, 1968.

Murphy, Irene L. *Public Policy and the Status of Women*. Lexington, Mass.: Lexington Books, D.C. Heath & Co., 1973.

Norton, Mary Beth. *Liberty's Daughters*. Boston-Toronto: Little, Brown & Co., 1980.

Rogan, Helen. *Mixed Company*. New York: G.P. Putnam's Sons, 1981.

Steiner, Gilbert. *State of Welfare*. Washington, D.C.: The Brookings Institution, 1971.

Treadwell, Mattie E. *The Women's Army Corps*. Washington, D.C.: Office of the Chief of Military History, Department of the Army, 1954.

Index

249